ENCYCLOPAEDIA OF INDIAN GOVERNMENT: PROGRAMMES AND POLICIES

ENCYCLOPAEDIA
OF
INDIAN GOVERNMENT:
PROGRAMMES AND POLICIES

Vol. 7

Tourism: Development & Planning

Edited by

Satish Tiwari

ANMOL PUBLICATIONS PVT. LTD.

NEW DELHI - 110 002 (INDIA)

ANMOL PUBLICATIONS PVT. LTD.
4374/4B, Ansari Road, Daryaganj
New Delhi - 110 002

Encyclopaedia of Indian Government: Programmes and Policies

First Edition, 2000
ISBN 81-261-0515-1 (Set)

PRINTED IN INDIA

Published by J.L. Kumar for Anmol Publications Pvt. Ltd., New Delhi - 110 002 and Printed at Mehra Offset Press, Delhi.

Contents

Preface

Encyclopaedia of Indian Government: Programmes and Policies contains authoritative information on about fifty departmental policies and their future developmental programmes.

Organised to be completed in 40 volumes, this gigantic work covers Agriculture; Atomic Energy; Chemicals and Fertilizers; Coal; Commerce; Communication; Culture; Defence; Education; Environment and Forests; External Affairs; Finance; Food & Consumer Affairs; Food Processing Industries; Health and Family Welfare; Home Affairs and Internal Security; Human Resources; Industry; Information and Broadcasting; Labour; Law, Justice and Company Affairs; Non-conventional Energy Sources; Ocean Development; Parliamentary Affairs; Personnel, Public Grievances and Pensions; Petroleum and Natural Gas; Planning and Programme Implementation; Planning and Statistics; Posts and Telegraphs; Power; Rural Development; Science and Technology; Social Justice and Empowerment; Space; States Affairs; Steel; Steel and Mines; Sugar and Edible Oils; Surface Transport; Textiles; Tourism; Urban Development; Water Resources; Women and Child development etc.

Based on the information derived from authoritative sources, this work contains authentic facts and figures. I am deeply beholden to all the scholars whose writings are cited or substantially made use of in the present work. I am also thankful to Anmol Publications Pvt. Ltd. for undertaking publication of this encyclopaedia. I am solely responsible for shortcomings in presentation of matter.

Encyclopaedic in nature, this will prove a dependable reference work for scholars and academics besides those appearing for different competitive examinations.

—Satish Tiwari

1

Tourism Development in India

Tourism has come into its own in India. The Asia-Pacific region has been forecast by the international agencies as the centrepiece of tomorrow's tourism and India is part of it. Tourism as a general economic service and social phenomenon is a post-Independence development. It is a trend that is evident worldwide as tourism has become the largest export industry. It is recognised so by the World Tourism Organisation. India has been striving to get a major slice of tis industry though for various reasons it has had to be content with a marginal share of 0.4 per cent of the global traffic. But, the efforts will continue and the prospects of India becoming a favourite destination are ever stronger than before. Last year, close to 2.12 million visitors from abroad arrived in India which, of course, has a massive domestic movement of people of over a hundred million.

Tourism has been recognised as the largest single source of foreign exchange with very little outgo. Because of its multiplier effect it generates faster and at lesser cost more jobs than any other industry, which is a national priority. The economic reforms which have given rise to foreign investment opportunities, coupled with the development of tourist facilities including operations by international air carriers, are facilitating factors. Still, the extent of expansion of the tourism sector could be assessed from the fact that until 1947 it was not an organised activity with government support. Some foreigners were coming on holiday or to see the Taj. There wee no packages, no big league hotels or a domestic air network that could take the visitor to the vaction spot. The travellers of those days were either on official business or scholarly pursuits going to some university. Domestic travel was essentially for pilgrimage or for family reasons. The concept of holiday outing had not struck roots nor were there any facilities.

During the colonial rule the administration used to move to the hill stations in summer time in almost all the then provences. Even then the movement was essentially compulsive to these areas for obvious reasons for the bulk of the staff. Even in respect of big hotels only the metro cities had some such properties mostly for the use of visiting Englishmen, or, during wartime, Allied army officers. Conditions changed overnight soon after Independence, helped by the vision of Jawaharlal Nehru with his commitment to international understanding. His oft quoted observation "welcome a visitor and send back a friend" underpinned this commitment. It was in 1949 that a tourism cell was first created in the Department of transport. This was the beginning of a process that climaxed in the formation of aseparate Ministry of Tourism under the charge of afull cabinet minister in the 60s. The first Cabinet Minister was Dr. Karan Singh. It was the time when tourism had developed into an organised industry in the principal originating markets of Europe ad north America and Air India had begun its operations. The potential of the tourism sector was foreseen by some far sighted persons like Somnath Chib, Romesh Thapar and M.S. Oberio. As the contours of national economic development came to be outlined, tourism came to be recognised as a potential tool.

Obviously, it could not get priority in the face of other national imperatives like agriculture, health and education. Even so, private entrepreneurs established travel related services heightening the need for tourism infrastructure.

Thus was born the Indian Tourism Development Corporation (ITDC) in the role of a catalytic agent to develop tourism. And, India's first hotel of international standards, the Ashok, came up, again at the behest of Jawaharlal Nehru who took personal interest in all its stages from concept to commissioning. As already mentioned there were hotels which were western oriented but Ashok was the first hotel of its class to have a complete Indian orientation not only in its architecture and decor but also in its cuisine, culture and entertainment and other facilities.

By that time tourism had acquired several dimensions, one of which was convention tourism. It was noticed that international conferences and even conventions of corporate and commercial bodies attract a sizeable number of delegates who outside their business hours would engage themselves in leisure time pursuits. They patronise hotels, souvenir shops and tourist destinations. In fact, it was primarily for the UNSCO which was meeting for the first time outside Paris that the Vigyan Bhawan and Ashok Hotel were built. Both have since proved as great national assets and monuments to the vision of Jawaharlal Nehru on tourism's potential. Ashok Hotel was a pace setter. Not only it introduced Indianness in its ambience, it also turned a vehicle for India's cultural renaissance. Most of the celebrities in the world of art today had their debut in the convention hall of Ashok Hotel where the guests could experience the richness of India's performing and fine arts. Once Ashok provided the lead others were quick to follow. The Ashok's success also triggered the emergence of such classy hotels in not only metro cities but elsewhere too.

In a parallel development, the government sponsored India Tourism Development Corporation went to areas which the private sector was shying away from for want of a ready market. In almost all the tourism destinations, ITDC put up hotels, motels and resorts. Simultaneously it created a separate division to produce promotional literature of world class which had been lacking. It may sound strange today when we recall that until Independence any information on even the Taj Mahal and other great monuments and temples was in books written and published abroad or by occasional scholar writers on their infrequent visits. Now, for the first time a would-be visitor could be provided with all the relevant data including history and available facilities on the destination.

Meanwhile, global tourism had been taking strides and this had necessarily had its impact on the Indian scene. New enterprises engaged in ticketing, accommodation and other facilitations were launched. Travel agencies primarily engaged in this task and tour operators who were exclusively servicing overseas visitors opened shop. Some of them started their offices overseas for promoting India and worked in collaboration with Air India and also the overseas offices of the Tourism Department which had come into being. These offices were located in the originating markets like the USA, UK, Europe and Japan and later on the West Asia.

Spain hosts 50 million tourists annually, double that of its population. Tiny Hong Kong received 9.5 million visitors and even communist China, opened its doors to 23 million tourists in 1995. That year, as many as 567 million tourists crossed international boundaries. And what was India's share of the cake? As little as 0.4 per cent.

Does this reflect a lack of potential/ With a physical, historical and cultural variety that few can match, this would hardly seem so. Inadequate and unfocused marketing of product India is quoted as a major reason for lack of interest in the country. Further, India's image management requires a serious overhaul. An incident occurring in one corner is all that it takes to initiate a travel advisory against visiting the whole country.

The greater problem lies at home. There has been a clear failure of public relations in tourism. Allocations to tourism over various plan periods has never exceeded 0.5 per cent of the total. Though tourism ranks as the third largest foreign exchange earner (and the second largest net foreign exchange earner) the annual allocation stands at just one per cent of the total income. Tourism was not mentioned in the budget of 1996097, nor in the economic survey. In a list of 52 priorities once drawn up by the Planning Commission, tourism occupied the 51st place, the 52nd being occupied by lighthouses!

In a strategy paper suggesting an investment of over Rs. 30,000 crore to put to tourism on the rapid growth path, former secretary of tourism, Mr G. Sundaram lamented the "persistent lack of awareness about the real benefits of tourism, on the part of the Planning Commission and finance ministry."

"It's really a question of mindset," says former director-general of tourism, Mr Ashok Pahwa. "Tourism has come to be associated with elitism, with a five-star culture." "Small wonder," says tourism expert, Mr Rabindra Seth, "that a country of 900 million people has only 58,000 rooms in its hotels, while Las Vegas alone has close to 100,000. Even Bangkok city has as many rooms if not more than the whole of India."

"Tourism has not been projected in a proper manner," says Mr Subhash Goyal, president of the Indian Association of Tour Operators. "We keep talking of economic liberalisation, but this is not necessarily going to increase employment, in fact it could be the reverse. Tourism is the one exception—it is labour-intensive industry. One out of every nine workers in the world is employed in this industry which both the World Bank and the IMF have recognised as the world's largest.

"One of India's problems is the migration from rural areas to cities. If tourist destinations and circuits are developed away from cities—as has been done at Bekal in Kerala and Shivpuri in Madhya Pradesh—the economy of such places changes. It really can be a catalyst for growth," he says.

At 1985-86 prices, the labour-capital ratio for a million rupees investment in the hotel and restaurant sector is 89 jobs against 44.7 in agriculture and 12.6 in manufacturing industries.

This is definitely an industry to be encouraged. Yet at all the major conventions of the travel trade, the minister for tourism is absent. Why has tourism been relegated to the periphery? Why do decision-makers brush it aside?

A major responsibility for this lies with the travel trade and its failure to present a strong case for tourism. There have been some efforts, by Assocham's expert committee on tourism and Pacific Area Travel Association (PATA) which helped create a better understanding, but by and large, these have been isolated. That apart, the industry fails to present itself as a cohesive body. The different segments, hoteliers, travel agents, transporters, etc are more keen on pushing their own case and resolving their individual problems than ironing out their differences and presenting themselves as aunified body to the government. Several years ago, a bureaucrat remarked, "First, let them get their act together, then talk about resolving the problems of the industry."

And there are a number of issues that concern them all—rationalisation of taxes, institutional changes in laws, single-window clearances for projects. Recently, there was some move towards an apex body—the National Tourism Council, which would be the industry's single voice, but that, predictably has yet to get off the ground. If tourism is to get its due, the industry will have to get their act together.

The 1997 travel scenario is depressing. In over two decades of analysing the Indian travel scene we have never seen anything more dismal than the outlook today. In the last 12 months rail accidents have occurred with hurtful regularity. An IGIA terminal was burst down, an aircraft collided in midair, a number of near-collisions were reported, but, again, no one has done anything discernible about them. Political survival, apparently, is more important than pinning responsibility.

Air-India is, seemingly, so broke that it did not print calendars this year and the minister painted a morbid picture of the financial state of our airlines. But he also refused to allow the superbly efficient Singapore International Airlines to enter into a collaboration with the Tatas to upgrade our civil aviation standards. The control of patronage and power, apparently, is more important than efficiency.

Our roads, particularly the important tourist highways out of Delhi, are disgraceful stretches of vehicle-destroying potholes; and they're getting worse. Moreover, the power situation is dark and getting darker; pollution chokes our cities; shaky governments opt for prohibition making the dishonest richer and the visitor poorer. People after all don't come to India to drink, but then people don't come to India to travel in cars, so must we ban motor vehicles just because of traffic accidents?

The oil-pool deficit has touched a whopping Rs. 15,500 crore, 1 so a hike in petrochemical prices is inevitable, the cost of travel will soar. Business traffic and foreign investments are falling, while inflation is rising. The criminalisation of the bureaucratic-political nexus has reached such hideous dimensions that influential criminals are trying to put themselves above the law; this also seems to be one reason for the setting up of the central board for bank frauds.

In other words, the foundations of travel, the basic life-support systems of the economy, have been weakened by neglect. All this happens because, in an age when national economies are going global to survive, many of our legislators haven't the education, background or the vision to rise above their regional concerns. Consequently, since tourism is, essentially a global business it was ignored in the budget. And if the industry doesn't make its presence felt now, it will continue to be ignored.

For years politicians and bureaucrats ignored the opinion of defence experts, skulking behind the veil of the Official Secrets Act. Then the retiring chief of naval staff, Admiral V P Shekhawat, spoke out blaming the bureaucrats and the politicians for the deplorable state of our defence planning. The result? There has been a sudden flurry of activity with the purchase of sophisticated aircraft and talk of buying and aircraft carrier; and many brave statements from our hitherto arrogant *netas* about how our defence needs will never be compromised.

The industry must do for travel and tourism what Mr. Shekhawat did for defence. It must concentrate on a single-point programme. It must make the people of India aware of the fact that tourism is the only industry, that can give them jobs, food, houses and a better quality of life within the next 10 years. It worked this economic miracle for Austria after the Second World War, it can do it for India today.

To create this awareness we must set up a Confederation of Indian Travel Industries (CITI). Every Indian organisation which earns more than 51 per cent of its income from the movement of people should be eligible to enroll its CEO as a member of CITI. In other words, CITI will be the national equivalent of the extremely powerful 7—member World Travel and Tourism Council (WTTC).

According to the WTTC, tourism creates more than 10 per cent of the global economic output and one in nine jobs today; is expected to grow at real rate of 5.5 per year through 2005; will add one new job every 2.5 seconds, stimulate US $ three billion of capital investment every day and drive US $ 3.4 trillion of output every year. Consequently, the mission of CITI should be "... to make travel and tourism a strategic economic development and employment priority, to promote competitive environmentally sustainable markets and to eliminate barriers to growth; in the process creating wealth, jobs, trade and investments in India". We cannot afford to let on ill-informed government drift away from opportunities any more.

Tourism is now recognised as an industry

generating a number of social and economic benefits. It promotes national integration and international understanding, creates employment opportunities and augments foreign exchange earnings. Tourism also gives support to local handicrats and cultural activities.

International tourism in India has grown substantially over the last three decades. Foreign tourist arrivals including the nationals of Pakistan and Bangladesh during 1994 were 18,86,433 as compared to 17,64,830 during 1993, registering an increase of 6.9 per cent. India's share in the world tourist market at the beginning of the Seventh Plan was 0.39 per cent, and it remained almost the same by the end of the Plan. Foreign exchange earnings from tourism during 1993-94 were provisionally estimated at Rs. 6,509 crore and for 1994-95 at Rs. 7,449 crore. Thus, tourism has become one of the largest foreign exchange earner of the country. With the increase in income levels and emergence of powerful middle class, the potential for domestic tourism has grown substantially during the last few years.

In order to further accelerate the development of tourism in the country, the thrust during the Eighth Five Year Plan on various activities are enumerated as under: (a) development of selected tourist places/areas; (b) diversification from culture-oriented tourism to holiday and leisure tourism; (c) development of trekking, winter sports, wildlife and beach resort tourism; (d) exploring new source markets in regions and countries having cultural affinity; (e) restoration of national heritage projects; (f) launching of national image building and marketing plans in key markets; (g) providing inexpensive accommodation in different tourist centres; (h) improving service efficiency in public sector corporations; and (i) streamlining of facilitation procedures at airports.

The organisations involved in the development of tourism at the Centre are Department of Tourism, Indian Institute of Tourism and Travel Management, National Council for Hotel Management and Catering Technology and Indian Tourism Development Corporation Limited.

The Department of Tourism under the Ministry of Civil Aviation and Tourism is responsible for the formulation and implementation of policies and programmes for the development of tourism within the country and for attracting foreign tourists to India by way of developing tourist infrastructure, publicity and promotion overseas, dissemination of information on tourist places, coordination and supervision of activities of various segments of industry and travel trade such as hotels, trave agencies, tour operators, etc.

There are 20 tourist offices in India, which include four regional offices located at New Delhi, Bombay, Calcutta and Madras. These offices supervise the functioning of other offices at Aurangabad, Goa, Khajuraho, Jaipur, Varanasi, Agra, Patna, Bhubeneswar, Bangalore, Hyderabad, Cochin and Port Blair. there is also a sub-regional tourist office in the north eastern region at Guawahati which supervises the work of tourist offices at Shillong, Imphal and Itanagar. Tourist offices in India and abroad handle tourist equiries, diseeminate tourist information, undertake promotion by means of advertising and publicity, maintain liasion with trade and press. Tourist offices abroad also counter the adverse publicity by the foreign media in respect of various events taking place in India. The feed-back which is received from tourist offices abroad helps in determining the overseas marketing policy of the Government. With the objective of achieving optimum impact, the Department of Tourism and Air India under the operational scheme are engaged in joint promotional efforts in Europe, UK, America, East Asia, West Asia and Australia through 18 tourist offices located in various parts of the world.

The India Tourism Development Corporation (ITDC), a public sector undertaking, was established in October 1966. The activities of the Corporation include: (a) construction, management and marketing of hotels, restaurants, travellers lodges for tourist at various places in the country; (b) provision of tourist transport facilities; (c) production, distribution and sale of tourist publicity materials; (d) provision of entertainment facilities such as light and sound shows, music concerts, etc; (e) provision of shopping facilities including duty free shops; and (f) provision of consultancy-cum-managerial service in India and aborad.

The Indian Institute of Tourism and Travel Management is an autonomous body set up to impart post-graduate level education in Tourism and Travel Management to meet the demands of professionally trained personnel in the tourism industry. It also organises executive development programmes, seminars and workships relating to tourism and travel management. The Institute has also assisted several universities for running courses at the post-graduate level. The Department of Tourism has accorded high priority to the development of manpower to meet the growing needs of hotels, restaurants and other tourism industries. For this purpose, the Department has set up 31 intitutes of hotel management and catering technology and food crafts in the country. These institutes conduct diploma courses in the fields of hotel management, catering technology and applied nutrition and craft courses in food and beverage services. Food craft institutes conduct craft courses for a duration ranging from six months to one year for operational staff.

In order to encourage adventure tourism, the Department of Tourism has set up a National Institute of Water Spots at Goa and the IISM at Gulmarg. The Indain Institutes of Skiing and Mountaineering conducted five courses at Auli, Patnitop, Gulmarg and Kulu and trained 330 persons during 1994-95. The National Institute of Water Sports conducted 15 courses for 166 participants in various activities, sailing, scuba diving, water skiing, etc. The institutes act as a nodal institute for adventure and sports oriented tourism activities in the country. These assist the state governments in building up tourism infrastructure in water sports and winter sports activities.

Strengthening of Tourism Infrastructure

Development of tourism is primarily the responsibility of the state governments. However, the Central Department of Tourism extends financial assistance for the augmentation of tourism infrastructural facilities like yatri niwas, tourist lodges, wayside facilities, restaurants, cafeterias, tourist bungalows, etc. In addition, financial assistance is extended for adventure sports activities, tourist transport, tented accommodation, etc. To consolidate the development of tourism infrastructure, 17 circuits/areas have been identified for intensive development. It has been decided to take up five focus centres as 'special tourism areas' for integrated development.

The hotel sector from one of the most important segments of the tourism industry with high potential for employment generation and foreign exchange earnings. To give impetus to this sector, the Government provides tax benefits and other incentives to encourage the hotel industry. The Industrial Policy has now placed the hotels and tourism related activities as a priority industry. Foreign investmet and collaborations are now facilitated under the new economic policy. Upto 51 per cent foreign equity is now granted automatically. Non-resident Indians are allowed cent per cent investment.

India also started taking part in international tourism events like annual meetings of Pacific Asia Travel Association, the American Society of Travel Agents, the International Tourism Exchange in Berlin and trade marts. Besides, Indian delegations participating in international conferences on a wide range of disciplines invited these bodies to hold their future meetings in India thereby giving an exposure to the manifold facets of the Indian tourism product.

Until the 70s the accent had been on cultural tourism. It still remains a major draw. At the same time, the need was felt to respond to global trends in tourism preferences by diversifing the roduct. The preferences varied according to age groups, origin of the market and the economic opportunites available at different places. Thus new attractions like beach holidays, wild life viewing, adventure travel and special interest tours were developed. Northern Europe shivering in winter sees a great exodus of holiday makers in search of sun and sand. Most of them used to go to the Mediterranean coast or islands off northern Africa or the Caribbean. For the first time, the Indian beaches at Kovalam, Goa, Mammalapuram, and Puri were marketed. These places used to receive only an occasional visitor from abroad until new facilitations were introduced and publicised. A measure of the progress of beach tourism is that charter flights by the dozen are operating every week to Goa and Kovalam (Kerala). New beaches have also been developed at Bekal, also in Kerala, Diu and Ahmed Mandvi on the Gujarat coast and quite a few resorts in Orissa in the Konark-Puri area.

For the more adventurous, trekking in the mountains as well as river rafting, kayaking and canoeing, skiing and hang gliding are being popularised and these find ever increasing stream of annual visitors. So much so, a section of the travel trade today finds it a profitable business to concentrate on this segment only. In promoting mountains and beaches a new accent is being laid on preservation of environment. And tourists are encouraged only to the limits of carrying capacity of these places. Still, happily the country is so extensively endowed with natural assets that it could welcome many more thousands of nature lovers is another thrust area fast being promoted in hills, islands and other remote areas.

In the wake of economic reforms yet another market segment has been enlarged. This is corporate travel. Investment and other business opportunities presented by the opening up of the Indian economy have set thousands of travellers in industrialised countries on their journey to India. A visible evidence of the spurt in business travel is the high occupancy rate in the classy hotels of metro cities—Delhi, Mumbai, Calcutta, Chennai and Bangalore. There has been an acute shortage of rooms in these places where in the last fifty years since Independence the accommodation sector has grown five hundred times. The position today is that the country is short of 65,000 rooms to reach a goal of 125,000 rooms just four years away when the number of international arrivals is targeted to reach a still modest figure of five million—a far cry from the officially listed 17,000 at the time of Independence.

Arrivals are going up gradually while there is phenomenal expansion in domestic travel. With increase in numbers of people having disposable income, change in life style, holiday outing is becoming a part of life. Destinations for the domestic visitor are no longer limited to pilgrim centres and hill stations. They go to other vacation spots with their families as far away as the Andamans and the Lakshadweep. The introduction of leave travel allowance for millions of employees of the Central and State governments as well as public sector undertakings and also holiday schemes in the private sector have added incentives for leisure time journeys.

To meet the demands of this vast movement of people a series of steps have been taken by the Union Ministry of Tourism as well as State governments. Incidentally, tourism remains a State subject. To encourage investment by entrepreneurs at least 22 States have declared tourism an industry entitling promoters to various tax concessions and other incentives. These are Andra Pradesh, Assam, Bihar, Haryana, Himachal Pradesh, Jammu & Kashmir, Kerala, Madhya Pradesh, Tamil Nadu, Tripura, Karnataka, Uttar Pradesh, Pondicherry, Maharashtra, Mizoram, Arunachal Pradesh, Andaman & Nicobar Islands, Rajasthan, Lakshadweep, Orissa, Chandigarh and West Bengal. The other states too are offering a range of incentives. New destinations are being developed as in Himachal to take the pressure off from places like Shimla and Manali. New products are also being developed like house boats in Kerala backwaters which have become an instant hit with both domestic and foreign tourists.

A National Action Plan for tourism was unfolded in 1992 to cover the development of infra-structure projects as well as promotion. In a follow up, a strategy paper has also been formulated calling for investment in different segments of infrastructure from approach roads to airport development. The private sector will be the major player in this exercise involving an estimated outlay of Rs. 31,000 crore. To promote international tourism new marketing strategies are being studied and enforced as also more international airlines are allowed to operate through India. Most of these carriers see a great future in the Indian market and for that reason want more frequencies and landing rights.

Thus, tourism has come into its own in India. International agencies forecast the Asia-Pacific region as the centerpiece of tomorrow's tourism and India is part of it. It opens up new challenges and opportunities. As part of the ongoing economic liberalisation, foreign investment from 51 to 100 per cent has been allowed in tourism related projects. Nonetheless, for such expanding multidimensional activity new directions and fresh initiatives are constantly called for particularly for up gradation of the product. A central tourism authority with powers to coordinate policy decisions by a multiplicity of agencies at the centre and in the States is called for. Strong political will and commitment is also an imperative for the tourism sector to fulfil the expectations from it.

Centre for Cultural Resources and Training (CCRT) was set up in May 1979 as an autonomous organisation by the Government of India. The CCRT took over the scheme 'Propagation of Culture' among college and school students which was being implemented by Delhi University, since 1970. The Centre is under the administrative control of Department of Culture, Ministry of Human Resource Development.

The broad objectives of the CCRT have been to revitalise the education system by creating an understanding and awareness among students about the plurality of regional cultures of India and integrating this knowledge with the education. The main thrust is on linking education with culture and making students aware of the importance of culture in all development programmes. The training being imparted stresses on the role of culture in science and technology, housing, agriculture, sports, etc. An important component of training is creating an awareness amongst students and teachers of their role in solving environmental pollution problems and conservation and preservation of the natural and cultural heritage. To fulfil these objectives, the Centre organises a variety of training programmes for teachers, educators, administrators and students throughout the country. It has also been organising academic programmes on Indian art and culture for foreign teachers and students. Workshops are conducted in various art activities lilke drama, music, narrative art forms, etc., to provide practical training and knowledge in the arts and crafts. In these workshops, teachers are encouraged to develop programmes inwhich the art form can be profitably utilised to educational curriculum.

The CCRT organises various educational activities for school students, teachers and children belonging to governmental and non-government organisations under its extension and community feedback programmes, which includes, educational tours to monuments, museums, art galleries, craft centres, zoological parks and gardens, camps on conservation of natural and cultural heritage, camps on learning crafts using low cost localilty available resources, lectures and demonstrations by artists and experts on various art forms, demonstrations by artists and crafts persons in schools.

The CCRT collects materials on the arts and crafts of the country in the form of audio recordings, slides, photographs, films and written texts in order to disseminate the information on culture and provide participants and other research institutions with material on the arts of India. The Centre also aims to disseminate information and foster an understanding of Indian culturre amongst teachers, administrators, educators and students. Publications for institutions and members of the community are prepared on topics related to aspects of Indian culture and ecology and the natural environment.

The CCRT implements the Cultural Talent Search Scholarship Scheme, which was taken over from the Department of Culture in 1982. The scheme provides scholarships to outstanding children in the age-group of 10 to 14 years studying, either in recognised schools okr belonging to families practising traditional, performing or other arts to develop their talent in various cultural fields particularly in rare art forms. The scholarship continues till the age of 20 years or first year of university degree. The Centre has also instituted CCRT Teacher's Award which is given every year to selected teachers in recognition of the outstanding work done by them in the field of education and culture.

Zonal cultural centres have been conceptualised with the aim of projecting cultural kinships transcending territorial bounds. The idea is to arouse and deepen awarreness of the local cultures and how these merge into zonal identities and eventually into the rich diversity of India's composite culture. Besides, these are also intended to document, preserve and to sustain the vanishing art forms and oral traditons. The involvement of artists and creative people has been in built in the set-up through a system of autonomous governance.

The seven zonal cultural centres established under the new scheme are: (i) North-Zone Cultural Centre, Patiala; (ii) East Zone Cultural Centre, Santiniketan; (iii) South Zone Cultural Centre, Thanjavur; (iv) west Zone Cultural Centre, Udaipur; (v) North-Central Zone Cultural Centre, Allahabad; (vi) North East Zone Cultural Centre, Dimapur and (vii) South-Central Zone Cultural Centre, Nagpur. The participation of states in more than one zonal cultural centre according to their cultural linkage is a special feature of the composition of the zonal centres.

The Ramakrishna Mission Institute of Culture, Calcutta is engaged in the promotion of thought, knowledge and education. Apart from being engaged in cultural activities at national and international level, the Institute also maitains several schools of instructions.

Indira Gandhi National Centre for the Arts (IGNCA) was established to commemorate the memory of the late Prime Minister, Mrs Indira Gandhi. This Centre launched on 19 November 1985 as a fully funded autonomous trust, is visualized as a centre encompassing the study and experience of all the arts-each for its own integrity, yet within a dimension of mutual interdependence, inter-relatedness with nature, social structure and cosmology. Through diverse programmes of research, publication, training, creative activities and performance, the IGNCA seeks to place the arts within the context of the natural and human environment. the fundamental approach of the Centre in all its work is multi-disciplinary and inter-disciplinary.

The Indira Gandhi National Centre for the Arts, comprises five main divisions viz. (i) Kala Nidhi; (ii) kala Kosa; (iii) janapada Sampada; (iv) Kala Darshana and (v) Sutradhara. During 1994-95, the reference library of Kala NIdhi Division added 2,204 selected works of eminent authors to its collection, 478 rolls of microfilms of rare Indian manuscripts from abroad and 1,532 microfiches from SMPK, Berlin University of Vienna were also added to its collections. The Kala Kosa Division under its programme of Kalathttvakosa, a lexicon of fundamental concepts of Indian arts, is engaged in the preparation of its volume engaged in the preparation of its volume III and IV. The institution organised a 17 day workshop on 'Manuscriptology and Palaeography' in collaboration with Shri Lal Bahadur Shastri Rashtriya Sanskrit Vidyapeetha as part of training programme for younger generation of researchers from within IGNCA and outside. During the year, the janapada Sampada Division under its Loka Parmapara programmes, recieved interim reports on various projects including Santhal Perception of Sound", "Seed and Eaarth in Oral Tradition of Vraja", etc. Under its publication programme, a number of manuscripts were assigned to the co-publishers. The first and second issues of IGNCA Newsletter, Vihangama, have been brought out during the year and the third issue is under publication. The Kala Darshana Division organised a number of exhibitions abroad in collaboration with Mr. Jacques Pimpaneau of Musee Kwok On, France, photographic exhibition of photographs by David Ulrich titled Hawalii Landscape of Transformation; and Raja Deen Dayal Exhibition at Bombay and Bhopal. The IGNCA also co—sponsored a session on "Cave art of India and China" at Dunhuang (China), and deputed three delegates to participate in the International Seminar held there as a part of the Dunhaung Academy Golden Jubilee celebrations.

One of the important activities undertaken by the Government of India has been the commemoration of the centenaries ofdistinguished Indians who have left an indelible impression on the history and life of our country. National committees are set up for centenaries which are considered to be of such importance. Year long programmes are drawn up by the committees for implementation during the centenary year. These programmes normally include organisation of national seminars, installation of statutes, other functions, stamp release, publications and exhibitions. The Department of Culture also provides financial assistance to registered voluntary organisations for celebrating the centenaries of outstanding personalities which are not taken up for celebration by the Government of India. Another mode of organising centenaries is where one or more state governments are requested to set up the centenary committee and the Government of India on its part organises a few programmes like release of commemorative postage stamps, seminars/lectures, publication, etc.

Gandhi Smriti and Darshan Samiti (GSDS) was set up by the Department of Culture in 1948 primarily to maintain and look after the national memorial where gandhiji was assisinated and now called 'Gandhi Smriti', and a permanent photo exhibition at Rajghat called' Gandhi Darshan', which was created at the time of Gandhiji's birth centenary in the year 1969. The institution has brought out a number of books on Gandhi, communal harmony and national integration. It also publishes a quarterly newsletter to create awareness about the GSDS and also organises annual Gandhij Memorial Lecture by an eminent scholar both in India and abroad.

The year 1994-95 happens to be the 125th birth anniversary year of Gandhiji and, therefore a series of programmes commenced with an inaugural function at Vigyan Bhawan on 2 October 1994 chaired by the President. The Samiti has since organised a programme of painting by the children, a photo exhibition put up at Paris on the eve of the 1st UNESCO Gandhi Memorial Lecture delivered by the Prime Minister; a massive programme of creating awareness for the youth in all the districts of Kerala; another programme involving several thousand youths and others for creating awareness about the literature on Gandhi. Programmes have also been organised for women, especially for those elected for Panchayats. Orientation programmes comprising discussions, film shows, visit to an exhibition and cultural programmes in several rural settings were the other highlights. The GSDS also participated and collaborated in the regional Conference organised by UNESCO on tolerance in April 1995 at New Delhi.

Maulana Abul Kalam Azad Institute of Asian Studies, under the administrative control of the Department of Culture is the centre for research and training of the life and works of Maulana Abul Kalam Azad and with the study on social, cultural, political and economic movement in Asia from the middle of the 19th century. The Institute also maintains library of books, newspapers, still photographs and materials on the secular traditions of modern India and events of the 19th century which is suitable for the public to collect papers and library sources for study and research from India and abroad. It also maintains personal museum at the former residence of Maulana Abul Kalam Azad. The Museum highlights the life and works of Maulana Abdul Kalam Azad as a distinguished national leader and thinker.

Festival of India

All festivals have a common purpose of creating a greater awareness amongst the people of the receiving country of India's rich cultural heritage and contemporary development in vrious spheres of modern India. This helps to generate an appropriate climate of goodwill and understanding for mutual exchanges in different spheres including technology, commerce and tourism on a more permanent footing. The main thrust of the Festival of India has been to project its multifaceted cultural life, while also highlighting scientific and technical progress and advancement through a series of exhibitions, programmes of performing arts as well as through seminars, readings, workshops, youth meetings, sports festivals etc.

The Festival of India in China was inaugurated on 9 May 1994 at Ply Plaza at Beijing by the Human Resource Development Minister and his Chinese counterpart. The inaugural ceremony consisted mainly of performing art event with the underlying theme 'Harmony'. Eight Indian films were screened at different venues in China during the Festival of India. The National Institute of Fashion technology mounted fashion shows during the festival.

The Performing Arts programme for the Festival of India in China was the single largest component among the festival events. About 75 performers visited China during the period of festival. Indian handicrafts combine varied styles and colours, fine workmanship, profound traditions and have a distinctive national flavour, Karigari provided a glimpse of these patterns of handicraft traditions that have survived in India for many thousand years. It was inaugurated on 10 May 1994. In this exhibition, an effort was made to give the viewers an impression of Indian science as a whole, in all its rich diversity through Indian experience in science and technology in its long history of 4500 years.

Around 1500 titles, mostly recent and some old titles of perennial value, brought out by almost 150 publishers were displayed at the exhibitions in China. The books selected for the exhibitions in China covered a wide range of subjects such as arts, history, biography, literature, philosophy, religion, social sciences, technology and books of general reference.

Education about India's common cultural heritage has been identified in National Policy on Education as one of the core areas under the national system of education. While spelling out the cultural perspective in education, the policy has stressed on the need to bridge the schism between the formal system of education and India's rich and varied cultural traditions. It has called for enriching the curricula and processes of education in as many manifestations as possible and laid considerable emphasis on value education by highlighting the need to make education a forceful tool for cultivation of social and moral values.

Within these overall objectives, a Centrally-sponsored scheme of Assistance for Strengthening Culture and Values in Education has been designed for providing assistance to Government agencies, educational institutions, Panchayat Raj institutions, registered societies, public trusts and non-profit making companies. The scheme has two broad components (i) strengthening cultural and value education inputs in the school and non-formal education system and (ii) strengthening the in-service training of art, craft, music and dance teachers. A total grant of Rs. 98 lakh has been approved for sanction to 33 organisations during 1994-95.

National Open School (NOS) was established in November 1989 as an autonomous organisation with the objective to provide quality education through distance education mode upto secondary stage for the school dropouts and children who cannot attend formal schools. This school is vested with the authority to examine and certify students registered with it upto pre-degree level courses. The certificates issued by this school are recognised for admissions for pursuing higher education and also for employment. The students have the freedom to choose the set of subjects according to their needs, interests and abilities and are also encouraged to choose vocational subjects in combination with academic subjects. The marginalised groups, viz., rural youth, girls and women, SC and ST, handicapped, ex-servicemen are given priority by NOS.

The NOS provides student support services through a network of study centres known as accredited institutions (AIs) for academic courses and accredited vocational institutions (AVIs) for*. As on 31 March 1994, 306 AIs were functioning under NOS.

The number of students enrolled by the National Open School during the years 1992-93, 1993-94 and 1994-95 for its secondary and senior secondary courses was:

Year	Secondary	Senior Secondary
1992-93	31,375	20,932
1993-94	35,098	25,777
1994-95	36,766	29,054

It is proposed to extend the open learning facilities in a phased manner at the secondary level in all parts of the country. In order to facilitate setting up of state open schools, the NOS provides consultancy services to the state goverments and serves as an agency for effective dissemination of information related to distance education and open learning.

The National Council of Educational Research and Training (NCERT) was established in September 1961 in New Delhi as an autonomous body. Qualitative improvement and excellence in school education and teacher education are some of its major objectives. They maintain effective liason with state education authorities for providing academic inputs to school education system.

The NCERT develops curricula, syllabi and prepares textbooks for classes I-XII which form the basis for prescription of schemes of studies by Central Boaard of Secondary Education (CBSE) for the schools affiliated to the Board. It also develops instructional material for childhood education and training packages for teacher educators and supervisory personnel. It provides technical assistance for national population education programmes designed to introduce population education in the formal education system. NCERT also provides its expertise to states/UTs. It also designs courses and material, generates software systems and sets up resource centres for computer literacy and studies in school project. NCERT organises Jawaharlal Nehru National Science Exhibition every year in which a large number of school students from all over the country participate. The Council produces science kits for the use of school students. It prepares comprehensive guidelines for curriculum evaluation and school industry linkages as well as for pre-service education of teachers on vocationalisation of education. Training courses for the officials involved in the Integrated Education Programme for Disabled Children are also conducted.

The NCERT is providing very useful assistance to the Department of Education in implementing the District Primary Education Projects (DPEPs) in several states towards fulfilment of the recommendations made in Education For All (EFA) Summit of nine high population countries held in New Delhiin December1993.Oneof the major projects entrusted to the NCERT is the Sixth All India Educational Survey which the Council is implementing in collaboration with the National Informatics Centre (NIC).

The objective of inculcating the message of small family norms and other population related issues in the minds of school and college students and the clientele of adult and non-formal education is being achieved through National Population Education Project.This project is now being implemented through school and non-formal education, higher education and adult education.

Since its inception in 1980, NPEP has done much

towards achieving its main objective of institutionalising population education through the school education system. During the second cycle (1986-1990) the main focus was on consolidation of the project's multidimensional activities and further expansion of its network. During the third cycle, special attention was paid to girls and SCs/STs through various curricular activities with an emphasis on community participation. The process of interweaving population education elements into the syllabi, textbooks and of instructional and training materials will continue.

One of the main factors responsible for slow pace of growth of enrolment of adolescent girls of rural, tribal and other remote areas is the traditional social inhibitions against their movement outside the family precincts. Moreover the high/higher secondary schools in schools in such places are sparsely located. In order to actualise the recommendation in POA 1992 for formulating a special enabling plan to ensure increased enrolment of girls in secondary education and the NPE directive for encouraging NGO participation in education, the scheme for strengthening of boarding and hostel facilities for girl students of secondary/higher secondary schools was launched in 1993-94 with the objective of providing the following types of assistance to the existing hostels run by the NGOs: (i) Non-recurring assistance as non-time grant for provision of essential furniture, utensils and meeting basic recreational needs at the rate of Rs. 1,500 per boarder: and (ii) recurring assistance for food, emoluments of cook and bearer at the rate of Rs. 5,000 per annum per boarder.

Khuda Bakhsh Oriental Public Library, Patna established in 1891 was declared as an Institution of National Importance in 1969 by an act of Parliament. It has a rich collection of over 18,000 Arabic and Persian manuscripts and over 2,000 Mughal and Rajput paintings besides 1,70,000 printed books. More than 850 audio and 550 video tapes of eminent persons have been prepared. It brings out a quarterly research journal. The Library has published critical editions of 64 rarities.

The Library has instituted a few fellowships at par with UGC. It has been recognised by seven universities as a centre of research for awarding the degrees of Ph.D./D.Litt. The Library has also instituted a prestigious award which carries an amount of Rs. 1,00,000 and a citation. The first Khuda Bakhsh Award was conferred on Shri B.N. Pande, the noted historian and former Governor of Orissa.

The Thanjavur Maharaja Serfoji's Sarasvati Mahal (TMSSM) Library, Thanjavur is one of the few medieval libraries that exist in the world. It symbolises a priceless repository of culture and time defying treasure house of knowledge, built up by the successive dynasties of Nayaks and Marathas of Thanjavur. The Library was made a public library in 1918 by the Madras Government and was registered on 9 July 1986 as a society under the Tamil Nadu Societies Registration Act. Now the Library is administered by both the Government of India and the Government of Tamil Nadu. The Library has 46,695 manuscripts in Sanskrit, Marathi, Telugu, Tamil and other languages both in palmleaf and paper form. More than 35 volumes of descriptive catalogues for these manuscripts were brought out. Miniature, paintings,colour drawings, atlases, maps, charts and rare prints in its collection are very attractive which reflects the Tanjore school of painting. Besides, it has 47, 100 books in Indian languages covering various disciplines and a rare collection of about 4,500 books in European languages collected by Raja Serfoji. The Library published more than 360 books from the unpublished manuscripts. It also publishes a quarterly journal.

The Rampur Raza Library housed in Hamid Manzil in the fort of Rampur is as autonomous body under the MInistry of Human Resource Development, Department of Culture, Government of India and was set up under the Rampur Raza Library Act, 1975. It has the priceless collection of about 51,000 printed books and 15,000 manuscripts, besides a large number of miniature paintings and specimens of Islamic calligraphy and Bhoj Patras etc.

The Asiatic Society, Calcutta was founded in 1784 by Sir William Jones (1746-1794), eminent indologist with the objective of inquiring into the history, science, arts and literature of Asia. This institution proved to be the inspiration behind all literary and scientific activties in the country. Directly or indirectly it has contibuted to the growth and development of most of the major antiquarian, scientific and lilterary institutions in India. The Society was also the model for all other Asiatic Societies of the world. Its historic imortance was recognised and the Government of India declared it as an "Institution of National Importance" by an Act of Parlilament in its bicentenary year, 1984.

The Society maintains a museum which includes an Ashokan rock edict and copper plates ranging from third century BC and important documents, and coin collections for the study of Indian history and culture. It contains approximately 65,000 MSS in various languages. With its library of printed books, archives and the collection of MSS, it is one of the leading centres of study of indology in the world. Recently the Society has expanded its activities considerably in the sphere of establishing intercultural relationships with various countries of the world. It has been chosen by the UNESCO as one of the institutions for its 'Memory of the World Programme'. It has undertaken the Encyclopaedia

Asiatic Project in eight volumes. A new art gallery is soon going to be opened at the historic Metcalfe Hall recently acquired by the Society.

Libraries are the keepers of our history and culture. Development of libray system is an important component of the scheme of non-formal and continuing education. Constitutinally the subject 'libraries' is included in the State List. The Centre has jurisdiction only over libraries establilshed by it and institutions of national importance as declared it. There are more than 60,000 libraries in the country.

National Library, Calcutta serves as a permanent repository of all readings and information material produced in India as well as printed material written by Indians and concerning India written by foreigners, wherever published and in whatever language. Under the Delivery of Books Act, 1954 the National Library is entitled to receive one copy of each publication published in the country. It is also a repository of the United Nations publications. It renders multi-faceted services and extends different types of bibliographical assistance to numerous readers and scholars, ministries, national and international organisations. Over 23 lakh books, besides periodicals, maps, manuscripts, newspapers and microfilm/microfiche totalling several million items are housed in the Library. Invaluable and prestigious personal collections like Asutosh Collection, Jadunath Sarkar Collections, Buhar Collection and some others are in its possession.

The Central Reference Library, Calcutta, is responsible for the compilation, publication and sale of the Indian National Bibliography. This is a monthly/annual bibliography conatining the entries of the current Indian publications in major Indian languages and in English received under the Delilvery of Book Act, 1954.

The Library is also compiling and publishing Index Indian an annual index to select articles appearing in current Indian periodicals in six major Indian languages. During 1994-95, it had published annual volume upto 1991 and monthly upto 1992 of Indian National Bibliography and Index Indiana upto 1984-85.

The Delhi Public Library, established in 1951 with financial and technical assistance from the UNESCO, has since developed into metropolitan public library system consisting of a central library, a zonal library, 55 branches/sub-branches and community libraries, a braille lilbrary, 12 braille mobile service points, seven braille deposit stations, 32 resettlement colony libraries and reading rooms, three sports libraries, two hospital libraries, a prisoners library in Central Jail and a network of mobile services stations serving 70 areas and 22 deposit stations, all over the Union Territory of Delhi.

Raja Rammohan Roy Library Foundation has taken long strides in promoting library services in the country since its inception. Currently it operates two types of schemes of assistance i.e. Matching and Non-Matching. Matching schemes are operated from the fund created with state government's contribution along with equal share from Foundation whereas Non-matching schemes are operated fully from Foundation. During 1994-95, Foundation rendered assistance to the tune of Rs 193.61 lakh under Non-matching schemes to about 1,100 libraries all over the country.

The Central Secretariat Library originally known as Imperial Secretariat Library was established in 1891. The Library has a collection over eight lakh volumes. The main objective of the library is to provide facilities for reference and research to Central Government offices/ organisations, employees, general readers and research scholars. The Library has a centralised membership system for the library complex. The Library has a separate Hindi and regional language wing-Tulsi Sadan at Bhawalpur House, New Delhi and a branch library at R.K. Puram, New Delhi.

Under the Delivery of Books and Newspapers (Public Libraries) Act, 1954, four libraries are entitled to receive a copy of every new book and magazine published in the country. These are the National Library, Calcutta; Central Library, Bombay; Connemara Public Library, Madras and Delhi Public Library, Delhi. There are also specialized libraries for researchers. Prominent among them are Nehru Memorial Museum and Library, New Delhi; Indian Council of World Affairs, New Delhi; Indian Statistical Institute, Calcutta; Gokhale Institute, Pune; Theosophical Society, Madras; National Council of Applied Economic Research, New Delhi and Indian Institute of Public Administration, New Delhi. Apart from these, some of the bigger universities also have sizable libraries.

Indian scholars, many centuries ago took arduous journeys across the Himalayas to Tibet and with them they carried Indian philosophy and thought. Evolution to Tibetan thought and culture was consequence of this intention. After Independence, a number of institutions have been set up in the country for preservation of Tibetan culture, philosophy, literature etc. Government is also implementing a scheme of financial assistance to such organisations.

The Central Institute of Higher Tibetan Studies, Varanasi, an autonomous organisaton fully minanced by the Centre was established with the objective of preservation of Tibetan culture and tradition, restoration of ancient Indian literature preserved in Tibetan languages and providing higher education in Buddhist studies to the border area students. The Institute prepares students fo rvarious courses. It has been given the status of deemed-to-be-university with effect from April 1988. The Central Institute of Buddhist Studies, Leh was established in 1959 to train students in Buddhist philosophy, literature and arts. It is affiliated to Sampurnanand Sanskrit Vishwa Vidyalaya, Varanasi.

The Sikkim Rsearch Institute of Tibetology,l Gangtok is an autonomous organisation set up for research and studies in Tibetology. The Institute has done significant work in promoting research in CHHO (Tibetan for Dharma) and associated subjects like iconography, medicine, astrology, history, etc. It publishes a quarterly journal, a Bulletin of Tibetology. The Institute receives maintenance and development grants from the Government of India. Library of Tibeṭan Work and Archives, Dharamsala acquires and preserves Tibetan books and manuscripts. The main activities of the library are to provide research facilities to run regular courses on Buddhist philosophy and Tibetan languages, classes on Tibetan traditional woodcarving and thanka paintings etc.

The Anthropological Survey of India is a scientific research organisation under the Department of Culture, Ministry of Human Resource Development with its headquarters in Calcutta and seven regional centres, a subregional centre and eight field stations located in different parts of the country including a camp office in New Delhi. Being established in December, 1945, the Survey is in the threshold of completing its glorious and eventful existence of fifty years. Since its inception as a nodal organisation of scientific research in anthropology and allied disciplines, it has the eviable records of conducting bio-cultural research covering the entire range of human surface of the country.

The Survey under its Seventh Plan programmes

commissioned a national project 'People of India' which has since been completed. The material so far generated has produced 11 national volumes and 32 volumes under state/union territory series containing anthro;ological profile of all the communities of the country. After successful on time accomplishment of the aforesaid project, the major thrust of research activities of the Survey, during 1994-95, was to complete other 12 Plan projects within the committed time frame. As a part of dissemination activities, the Survey organised several exhibitions and film shows in different parts of the country depicting bio-cultural heritage of our populations.

Indira Gandhi Rashtriya Manav Sangrahalaya, Bhopal, an autonomous organisation under the Department of Culture, Government of India is dedicated to the depiction of an integrated story of humankind in global perspective with special focus on India. The Sangrahalaya is being developed in a picturesque 200 acres site as a predominantly open air museum, supported by an indoor display related to three broad fields; (a) human evolution and variation; (b) culture and society in pre and proto-historic times and (c) contemporary cultures. It has already developed four open air exhibitions depicting tribal habitat, life in coastal villages, life in desert village and heritage of Indian pre-historic rock art through life size exhibits in authentic environmental settings. Regular educational activities and live programmes related to tribal and folk life are conducted in the setting of these exhibitions. There is an indoor facility of periodical and special exhibition. The Sangrahalaya is also developing an indoor museum. The other programmes being carried out by this organisation are salvage of anthropopogical objects of national heritage, research projects and multimedia documentation of cultures.

Live demonstration of techniques, fold ways, folk and classical music are also organised periodically in the open air setting. For the dissemination of recent information on various themes in human evolution pre-history, contemporary culture, museum methods etc., the Sangrahalaya organises lectures, seminars, colloquia, etc. The museum also undertakes audio, video, photo,cine and textual documentation and research and field projects on various aspects of Indian society and culture for better understanding, salvage and revitalization of the rich cultural heritage of the country.

India initiated underwater archaeological research in 1981 by establishing Marine Archaeology Centre in the National Institute of Oceanography, Goa. The main objectives of the Marine Archaeology is to reconstruct the history of past seafaring activities from the material remains and study of submerged archaeological sites.

Since 1983 underwater archaeological explorations have been carried out almost every year in Dwarka waters. The successive investigations of Dwarika in about 4 to 12 m water depth have revealed the presence of a number of submerged stone building blocks. The explorations during 1992 to 1995 were carried out mainly to demarcate the limits of the submerged ancient Dwarika and also to document properly the submerged structures and objects noticed. At Dwarka approximately 9,80,000 sq m area was explored between the water depth of 3 to 12m off Samudranarayana temple. The important findings were documented mainly with still photography, underwater video filming and underwater drawings. The on-shore explorations at Bet Dwarka revealed the presence of late Indus seal depicting three headed animal, earthen vessel inscribed in the characters of Indul-Brahmi transition phase of about 1500 BC and the large variety of pottery similar to Lostrous Red Ware bowl and the Red Ware dishes, dish-on-stand, perforated jar and incurved bowls which are datable to 160-1500 BC in Dwarka,l Rangpur and Prabhas.

Preliminary underwater explorations off Somnath were carried out during 1992 and 1995. The findings were a three-holed triangular stone anchor and a three-holed prismatic stone anchor measuring in length about a meter and a one holed circular stone object similar to that found in Dwarka.

Marine archaeological explorations are being carried out since 1991 in Poompuhar waters in collaboration with the Department of Archaeology, Government of Tamil Nadu. The main objective of this survey was to delineate the submerged extension of the ancient town of Kaveri-poompattinam, north of present river Kaveri and to explore the deep water where an U-shaped structure was noticed during the earlier explorations. Diving and airlifting operations were undertaken north of the river Kaveri at a water depth of 5-7 m. Deeper waters were also explored to confirm whether the U-shaped structure was man-made. Diving at shipwreck site became esential to ascertain the country of which it belonged. Off-shore exploration was carried out in shallow waters, north of river Kaveri and south of the present Poompuhar village. A few dressed stone blocks were found in various water depths. One of them was semicircular with an L-shaped cut Airlift operations yielded building blocks of stone and a number of potshaerds of the early historical period (300 BC to 300 AD).

Explorations carried out in deeper waters (23 m depth) revealed presence of an U-shaped stone structure which was located about 5 km seaward of Kadaikkadu. The structure lies in north-south direction. In the centre of the object there is a hollow which is filled with sand. Maximum height of structure on the outer side is about 3 m, while on the inner side it is less than 1 am. On the northern side of the object an opening was noticed. The height of object is greater in the south than in the north. The corcumference of this object is 140 m. Maximum length is 40 m and its width is 20 m. About 40 m north of this structure two smaller objects of the same material were found which seem to be related to the main structure. It is belived thatthese are man-made structures, perhaps, pertaining to a Buddhist relic?

Geophysical explorations carried out with the sub-bottom profiler revealed a submerged palaeochannel of the river Kaveri in the north of Poompuhar. The width of the channel varies from 300 m to 500 m and it is buried 20 m below the sea bottom. This channel extends upto deeper water structures, suggesting that the ancient shoreline was about five km seaward of the present shoreline.

Poompuhar wreck seems to have belonged to the Dutch rulers in India and might have sunk during a war against the French in 1792-93 as indicated by a few lead ingots from the wreck. Two of them bear the symbols of a crown below which is the letter 'D'. This symbol of crown over 'D' is engraved on the coins issued by the Dutch in India.

The on-shore explorations of Lakshadweep revealed the presence of significant potsherds of red ware, red-pollished ware, dull red ware, red and black ware and buff ware from Kavaratti, Androth and Amini. Two Buddha heads (one 95 cm and the other 55 cm high) carved out of locally available coral rock found earlier by inhifitants of Androth, were examined and assisgned to the 6th-7th century AD. The presence of red polished ware suggests the earliest habitation on these islands to the 100-500 AD. Four shipwrecks located in Lakshadweep waters, one was at the reef of Suheli Par and three at

Minicoy. Part of the first wreck seems like a tank part lying on the reef along with some tyres, which may be a warship belonging to the 1st or 2nd World War. Two shipwrecks explored by diver-archaeologists at a water depth of 4-15 m is about 100 m long. In one of them the steam engine is intact with a 27 m long shaft attached between engine and propeller blade. An anchor chain more than 100 m long was also observed at a depth of about 15 m. In the other wreck the engine is disintegrated, however two boilers can be clearly noticed.

From the information gathered from hydrographic charts, Marine Archaelogy Centre of the National Institute of Oceanography, Goa has located thewreck at Grandy island off Goa waters in 1987. This wreck is a steel julled cargo vessel with cabin, hatch, bridge and accommodation. It is more than 60 m long. This ship might have sunk ina furious storm after it lost anchor and drifted towards the shore. The Marine Archaeology Centre has been again resumed exploration in November 1994. This wreck can be an excellent training base for Marine Archaeologists.

In December 1989 the Marine Archaeology Centre discovered a historical shipwreck at Amee Shoals in Mormugao waters. The shallow depth suggesting that the vessel must have run around on the rocky shoals. The wreck revealed large and well dressed granite blocks. Other finds are a cannot and an iron anchor.

Established in 1861, the Archaeological Survey of India (ASI) conserves and preserves archaeological monuments and sites located in different parts of the cuntry and maintains site museums which display antiquities mainly relating to the same site. It is also as an academic body entrusted with the task of promoting scholarship byway of explorations and excavations, epigraphical research, study of secular and religious architecture and scientific studies and investigations. With headquarters at New Delhi, ASI discharges its responsibilities through various circles and branches. The Institute of Archaeology at New Delhi functions as the training wing of theASI wherein service officials and those from states and fresh university post-graduates are imparted extensive training in all aspects of archaeology leading to Post-graduate diploma in Archaeology. The Institute also organises short-term courses on conservation and preservation of monuments and sites epigraphy and numismatics, administration and accounts.

During 1994-95, 500 monuments were programmed for conservation. Some of the important conservation works carried out by the Survey during 1994-95 are Agra Circle-(i) Taj Mahal, Akbar's Tomb, Sikandra, Agra Fort, Jama Masjid, Fatehpur Sikri; (ii) Aurangabad Circle - Ajanta Caves, Daulatabad Fort, Ellora Caves, Elephanta Caves, Markandadeo temple, Vijaydurg Fort; (iii) Bangalore Circle - Monuments at Badami, Galaganatha temple, Monuments at Bijapur, Hampi, Naryana temple, Tipus' place - Bangalore, Monuments at Srirangapatnam, temple at Mandya; (iv) Bhubaneswar Circle - Vimana of Lord Jagannath temple, Sun Temple - Konark, Lingaraja temple - Bhubaneshwar, Jagannath temple - Puri; (v) Bhopal Circle - Monuments at Khajuraho, Fort, at Ater, Bhind, Kankanmath temple, Monuments at Dhar, Mandu, Chanderri, Bhojpur Fort, Sas-Bahu temple - Gwalior; (v) Calcutta Circle - Maharshi Bhawan, Kalna Palace Complex, Hazarduari Palace, Monuments at Bishnupur and Sikkim, Cooch Behar Palace, (vii) Hyderabad Circle - Monuments at Bidar, Temple complex in Chandragiri, Chittoor, Golkonda fort, Charminar, Temples at Srikakulam, Papanasi, Nataraja cave; and (viii) Madras Circle - Fort and temple Gingee, Fort at Cannaere, Fort at Pallikera, Group of monuments at Kanchipuram and Mamallapuram.

Chemical conservation works have also been taken up by the ASI, a few important works being Venkateshwara Vishnu temple, Srinivasa Mangapuram Chittoor in Andhra Pradesh; Diwan-e-Khas, Diwane-e-Am, Red Fort in Delhi; Bom Jesus Church, Viceroy Gate, Lady Rozari Church, Velha, Goa; Tabo Monastry, Lahaul Spiti, Sun temple, Konark, Ratnagiri Museum, Buddhist Monastry-Cuttack, Orissa;; Shringar Choli temple, Chittorgarh, Suraj Bhawan, Deog; Kailashnath temple, Kanchipuram, Mukteswara temple, Mahabalipuram, Tamil Nadu; Taj Mahal, Itmaduddaula, Khas Mahal, Agra Fort, Agra; Museum objects of Hazardwari Palace, Murshidabad and many other places in West Bengal.

A large number of sites and remians ranging from pre-historic to the medieval times have been discovered by the Survey in different parts of the country. Exploration work is continuing in KLarnataka, Kerala, Ghaggar river basin of Haryana, Kali Sindh river valley in Rajasthan, South West Kutch of Gujarat, and in the area to be submerged on account of the construction of dams in Gujarat, Maharashtra and Madhya Pradesh, under the Sardar Sarover Project. The Clearance Operation of Gingee fort in South Arcot district of Tamil Nadu has revealed a palace of 16th century sub-terranian passage and throne platform. The excavation at Barabati Fort, Cuttack has brought to light remains of a palace debris of temple, darabara hall, a citadel, a pillared hall and a platform. The excavation at Sannati has provided significant information pertaining to the general cultural sequence of the area. The Epigraphy Branch of the Survey has collected about 200 inscriptions from various parts of the country like Maharashtra, Gujarat, Karnataka, Uttar Pradesh, Andhra Pradesh, etc.

The museum branch of Archaeological Survey of India looks after 31 site museums located all over the country. Setting up of site museum at Piprahwa in UP is approved during 1994-95. Opening kof museum for commemoratory the history of Freedom Struggle at Salimgarh, Red Fort is also in progress.

Museums

Museums are repositories of our cultural heritage and are meant for acquisition, conservation and preservtion of historical, technical and other materials against decay and for their transmission to posterity as records of history. They also serve as important audio-visual means of education. The development of museums in all their ramifications is considered important as they promote national integration and international understanding. Great emmmphasis is laid on the documentation of the existing collection in Government and private museums, preservtion of the collections by using latest scientific aids and publication of the catalogue of the existing collection.

The National Museum, established in 1948, is one of the premier museums of the country and its main activities are in the field of acquisition, exhibition, conservation, education and publication of art objects. During 1994-95, a jewellery gallery was set up permanently which was inaugurated by the Hon'ble Prime Minister of India on 26 April 1995. This gallery is first of its kind in India. Coincidding with the World Archaeological Congress held in India, the National Museum had organised four exhibitions in its premises during December 1994. Under Inter Museum Exhibition Scheme, an exhibition of Pahari paintings was mounted in October 1994 at Bhopal and Ahmadabad. Under the Cultural Exchange Programme, the National Museum had received four exhibitons from Italy and three exhibitions have been organised abroad. Besides an exhibition entitled "Buddha in India: Early Indian

Sculptures" was sent to Vienna in March 1995. The Museum conducted its 26th short-term in-service training course in museology and an intensive in-service course on conservation of Manuscripts.

Indian Museum, Calcutta founded in 1814, but established under Indian Museums Act, 1910 is a statutory body fully funded by the Department of culture, Ministry of Human Resource Development. It is one of the prenmier museums in the country. Its Board of Trustees is headed by Governor of West Bengal in ex-officio capacity. During 1994-95, the Museumorganised international exhibition on Indian Bronzes - Sacred Images from 9th-12th centuries in the Art Gallery of New South Wales, Sydney form 16 April to 1 May 1994 and at National Gallery of Australia, Canberra from 5 May to 5 June 1994 as a part of the India Today, 1994. On 16 December 1994, an International exhibition was also organised in collaboration with National Gallery of Modern Art, New Delhi. The Museum organised jointly with Eastern Zone Culture Centre an exhibition on Marks of Eastern India. On the birth centenary of an Italian Tibetologist, Prof. Giuseppe Tucci, the Museum organised an exhibition on Art of Tibet in the collection of Indian Museum from 24 November 1994 and a three day seminar on this occasion. Indian Museum, Rabindra Bharati University and Chintan jointly organised an exhibition on Art of Mukul Dey and his contemporaries on 14 February 1995 and a day long seminar on this occasion.

The National Research Laboratory for Conservation of Cultural Property, Lucknow, a subordinate office of the Department of Culture, was established in 1976. Its activities include carrying out research in the field of conservation, technical assistance to museums and other related departments, conducting short-term training for curators and directors in the care and upkeep of museum collections, long-term course of six months duration in the conservtion of art obects, imparting practical training in conservation to museilogy students from vrious universities, etc. The NRLC Library has a unique collection of books and reprints on various subjects like conservation, art, history and related pure and applied sciences. It extends its documentation services like abstracting, indexing, reprography, etc., to the desirous institutions. A regional centre of the Laboratory for south has been opened at Mysore which is fully operational and providing assistance to the institutions of the region in the conservation of their collections. A major project on the conservation of miniature paintings in different museums in the country has been initiated. In this direction, miniatures belonging to Bharat Kala Bhawan,and Allahabad Museum have been examined, A project on the survey, documentation and identification of methods and material of wall paintings has also been undertaken. In this context, survey of wall paintings at Quila Mubkarak, Patiala, has been completed. Survey of some sites in Kerala will also be done. A joint project on the conservation of Ajanta wall paintings is also under way. Conservation of Thankgkas belonging to Tawang Monastery, Arunachal Pradesh, was done besides conservation of other different types of objects like coins, palm-leaves, manuscripts, books, lithographs and oil-paintings received from different museums and institutions. The Laboratory undertook conservation work at the Fenfushi Mosque, Fenfushi (Maldives). The Laboratory had completed conservtion work on another Mosque in Male in the past. An orientation workshop for curators and directors was conducted in August 1995. The course on the conservation of art objects started in September 1995.

The National Council of Science Museums (NCSM), an autonomous organisation under the Department of Culture, is primarily engaged in the task of popularising science and technology among students in particular and the masses in general through a wide range of interactive programmes and activities. the Council has completed and made open to public the Engine Hall, an addition to the Museum at Bangalore. The Mobile Science Exhibition "Man, the Tool Maker" was also completed and is now on the road under the centre at Delhi. This centre has also taken up fabrication of a large animated exhibit 'Dinosaur' which is to be completed shortly. Work is in progress for Regional Science Centre at Calicut with a planetorium, District Science Centre at Vijayawada, District Science Centre and National Science Camp at Digha. NCSM is going to set up for the first time a full fledged Zeiss Planetaria at Nagpur and Calicut during this year. Science City is a unique venture of NCSM and is planned to be a Major attraction to the residents of Calcutta as well as to the visitors to the metropolis. Set up on a 40 acres plot of land, it is expected to be one of the largest and finest in the world, presenting science and technology to the people through gigantic and thrilling experiences.

The National Gallery of Modern Art organised 26 sketch club meets for two different age groups - Junior and Senior. They were given on-the-spot practical guidance by reputed artists. the Gallery is organising film shows on Sundays, second Saturdays and working days. The Gallery organised four exhibitions titled "100 years from NGMA Collection", "Rajiv Gandhi Landscape of Man", "Paintaings of Nicholas Roerich" to commemorate his 120th Birth Anniversary and 'Punjab 1994", an exhibition of photographs by the Forum of Contemporary Artists. The Nehru Memorial Museum and Library organised a symposium on "Economic

Reforms, the public sector and the Trade Union Movement" besides 14 seminars/lectures on the themes relevant to the understanding and transformation of Indian Society. Seven occasional papers written by the fellows of the Museum were mimeographed and circulated among the universities and other research institutions. Two publications titled "Towards understanding the Post Colonial World - Theory and Method" and "Selected Works of Motilal Nehru" Vol.VI were brought out. The Museum added 2,346 books to its Library during the year bringing the total number of publications in the Library tomore than 1.81 lakh.

The Salar Jung Museum together with the Salar Jung Library at Hyderabad was declared as an institution of National Importance by the Salar Jung Museum Act (26 of 1961). It is managed by the Salar Jung Museum Board constituted under the Act. The Salar Jung Museum, Hyderabad, as a part of celebrations for the World Heritage Day, organised a special exhibition titled "Structures: Indian Heritage" in collaboration with National Council of Science Museum. To coincide with the celebrations of Sadbhavana Diwas in the country, a month long exhibition titled "Paintings of European Masters in the Salar Jung Museum" was organised. The paintings shown in the exhibition are copies of Italian, Flemish, Dutch, French and Spanish scholars. As part of its educational activities, the Museum organised three illustrated lectures on "Heritage and Science Museums", "Asokan Inscription from Nizams Dominion" and "World Heritage Monuments in India". Six gallery talks were also organised on varied subjects including Jade and other Minarels, Persian Carpets, and French Art etc.

The National Museum of Institute of History of Art, Conservation and Museology, New Delhi, set up by the Government of India under administrative control of the

Department of Culture is a society registered with the Register of Societies. Delhi Administration. The Institute offers M.A. and Ph.D degrees, besides courses like Art Appreciation, Indian Art and Culture, Kala Nidhi Kosh (Hindi).

The Allahabad Museum has got a rich collection covering the subjects of art, archaeology, numismatics, epigraphy and natural history,. During 1994-95, in addition to the routine museological activities, the Museum organised many academic and research activities, like lectures, seminars, courses, etc.

The collections of Victoria Hall, Calcutta include Indian miniatures, Indian arms and armours of late Mughal period as well as illustrated and illuminated historical, literary and religious manuscripts. There are a large number of oil paintings of portraits, landscapes and historical monuments of the Indian sub-continent, besides a very good collection of water colours, graphic prints, photographs and various other artefacts associated with Indian history of 18th, 19th and 20th century.

National Archives of India (NAI), known until Independence as Imperial Record Department was established on 11 March 1891. It is the official custodian of all non-current records of permanent value of the Government of India and its predecessor bodies. It is the premier organised record repository in Asia with its holding running over 30 km of linear shelf-space. The newly constructed annexe has become functional. National Archives of India is an attached office of the Department of Culture. It has three regional repositories at Bhopal, Jaipur and Pondicherry.

Major activities of the Department include: (i) accessioning of public records and making such records accessible to various government agencies and research scholars; (ii) preparations of reference-media; (iii) preservation and maintenance of records and conducting of scientific investigations for the said purpose; (iv) evolving records management programmes; (v) rendering technical assistance to individuals and institutions in the field of conservation of records; (vi) imparting training in the field of archives administration, records management, reprography and repair and conservation of records, books and manuscripts at professional and sub-professional levels and (vii) creation and promotion of archival consciusness in the country by celebrating 'Archives Week' every year. The Archives also provides financial assistance to state archives, voluntary organisations and other custodial institutions.

During 1994-95, more than 4,200 visits were made by scholars to the Research Room and Library of the National Archives of India. Of these, 44 scholars were from foreign countries. Holdings of this Department were further enriched by acquisitions of public records/private records/microfilm copies of records. A few important records being: Private Papers (i) 226 xerox copies of the letters and extracts ofa book Christian Action (Gandhi century Issue), Summer 1969 from E.S. Reddy, New York (USA); (ii) 14 xerox copies ofthe letters (1835-80) written by Pandit Jawaharlal Nehru, Smt Indira Gandhi and Shri Lal Bahadur Shastri; (iii) 1,893 items of Dr. Y.S. Subbarooj Papers (1922-1955) relating to experiments and treatment of cancer, invention of folic acid, tetracycline and details of experiments on animals and humans; (iv) 174 items of Gandhi-Holmes Papers (1924-1987) relating to philosophy, freedom movement , economic and political situation, etc.; (v) A book entitled Indian Currency (2nd Edition, 1898) written by Henry Dunning Macleod and Journal of the Institute of Actuaries (1912) received from the Institute of Actuaries Library, Oxford (U.K.) and (vi) nine photocopies of the papers (in Malayalam and English) on the massacre in Jallianwala Bagh in 1919, and also on the execution of Sardar Udham Singh in 1940. Microfilms: (i) five rolls of Dr. Y.S. Subbarow Papers (1948) relating to his correspondence with Dr. E.L. Milford; (ii) 104 rolls of Panda Records containing Hindu Pilgrimage Registers from Genealogical Society of Utah, USA; (ii) Five rolls of PREM-8 Series (Prime Minister's Office), 1945, relating to freedom movement/Indian indepedence and containing correspondence of national leaders received from Public Record Office, London (UK); and (iv) 23 rolls (1920-1949) relating to transfer of power, trade in Muscut, Defence Affairs, etc., received fromthe British Library, London (UK).

To commemorate the 75th anniversary of Jallianwala Bagh episode of 1919, an exhibition entitled "Lahuluhan Baisakhi" was mounted at the Jallianwala Bagh complex, Amritsar during 1949-95. This exhibition was as well taken to eight states/union territories capitals/ headquarteers. On the same occasion, an exhibition entitled "Archives and Jallianwala Bagh: A Sage of Independence" was inaugurated by Dr. Shanker Dayal Sharma, Hon'ble President of India on 28 April 1994 in the Natonal Archives of India. As part of Archives Week, the National Archives of India organised an exhibition entitled "Archives and Mahatma Gandhi: A Satyagrahi in South Africa" on 16 September 1994. An "Open House" programme was organised and documentary display relating the theme "Indian Postal System: Down the Memory Lane" depicting the early stages in the evolution of postal system in India was as well made from 17-20 November 1994.

School of Archival Studies of the Archives conducts one year Diploma Course in Archival Studies and a number of short term certificate courses. Significant publications brought out by the National Archives of India during 1994-95 includes (i) The Indian Archives, volume XL, No. 2 (July-December 1991): Volume XL I, No. 1 (January-June 1992); (ii) Guide to the Source of Asian History, volume 3.6: (iii) Proceedings of the 39th Meeting of the National Committee of Archivists Proceedings; (iv) Proceedings volumes of 54th session of Indian Historical Records Commission; (v) Catalogue of Revenue Maps, Volume III, (vi) Index to Papers Read at the Indian Historical Records Commission Part III (1977-92); (vii) Elements of Records Management and Conservation; (viii) Eshob, (in Urdu) Volume I; and (ix) Descriptive list of Mutiny Papers in the National Archives of India, Bhopal, Volume VII.

Literary Art

Rediscovery of ancient and medieval Indian literature and development of modern literature in major Indian languages and English mark literary activities of present-day India. A large number of literary periodicals and magazines, literary institutions and All India Radio have given impetus to the growth of modern Indian literature.

Sahitya Akademi was set up by the Government on March 1954. Being an apex national body for the promotion of literature, the Akademi has all through devoted itself to recognise men of achievement in letters, to educate public taste and to improve standards of literature and literary criticism. With this Akademi has a big publication programme and some of the major publication projects which are continuing are publication of series of Markers of Indian Literature, series of Histories of Indian Literature, publication of a bi-monthly journal entitled Indian Literature in English, a quarterly journal entitled Samkaleen Bharatiya Sahitya in Hindi and a periodical journal entitled Sanskrit Pratibha in Sanskrit. The six volume project of Encyclopaedia of

Indian Literature is now complete. During 1994, 22 Akademi awards to writers and 19 translation awards to translators were given by the Sahitya Akademi and it published 143 books and organised 46 book exhibtions and workshops.

The national Bibliography of Indian Literature published by Sahitya Akademi in four volumes hitherto covered Assamese, Bengali, English, Gujarati, Hindi, Kanada, Kashmiri, Malayalam, Marathi, Oriya, Punjabi, Sanskrit, Sindhi, Tamil, Telugu and Urdu for the period from 1901-1953. Its fifth volume covering Dogeri, Konkani, Maithili, Manipuri, Rajasthani and Mepali for the period 1901 to 1980 has been brought out in 1990-91. It is now proposed to publish a second series of the National Bbliography of Indian Literature form 1954 to 1980/90 for all the languages covered in the first series.

To provide financial support to outstanding artistes for creative work in various fields of performing, plastic and literary arts the following schemes are being implemented by Government.

The scheme of Emeritus Fellowships has been formulated to extend financial support to artists who have achieved a high degree of excellence in their respective fields but have since retired from the profession to enable them to continue experimentation in the spirit of financial freedom. Nine fellowships are awarded every year for a period of two years. The rate of fellowships is Rs. 5,000 per month. In addition to this fellowships amount, Rs. 10,000 as annual incidental grant for fellowship is also granted.

A fellowship in memory of Pt Kumar Gandharv has been instituted from 1992-93. The fellowship is conferred to distinguished senior artistes in various fields every year.

The scheme gives financial assistance to young artistes of outstanding promise for advanced training in the fields of music, dance, painting, sculpture, book illustration, design, etc. The duration of scholarship is two years and the value is Rs. 1000 per month, while the number of scholarship is 200 per year.

The scheme provides for financial assistance to persons distinguished in letters, arts, etc., who may be in indigent circumstances and are above 58 years of age and in certain cases, to their dependents who are left unprovided for. Under the scheme, expenditure is shared by the Central and the respective state governments. The maximum assistance that could be given to an individual is Rs. 1,500 per month.

The scheme provides for the award of Senior Fellowships of the value of Rs. 3,000 per month and Junior Fellowships of the value of Rs. 1,500 per month each. Fifty Senior Fellowships and 150 Junior Fellowships are awarded every year. The duration of fellowship is two years and in exceptional cases, this can be extended a year more.

Financial assistance is being given to institutions of all India character, engaged in the development of cultural activities, to meet part of their expenditure on maintenance and development activities. The institutions assisted include the Institute of Historical Studies, Calcutta; Numismatic Society of Inda, Varansi; Institute of Traditional Culture, Madras; Bharatiya Vidya Bhawan; Bombay and the Institute of Numismatic Studies, Nasik.

The Government encourages development of all Indian languages including classical, modern and tribal. Its policy lays emphasis on training of teachers in relation to adoption of the three-language formula and production of university-level textbooks with ta view to facilitating media switch over from English to regional languages. In order to assist non-Hindi speaking states/ union territories to effectively implement the three-language formula, support for provision on facilities for provision on facilities for teaching of Hindi in these states/union territories is provided by sanctioning financial assistance for appointment of Hindi teachers in schools and for establishment of Hindi teachers training colleges in these states/union territories, under a Centrally-sponsored scheme. The grant-in-aid is provided mainly to assist the consolidation and further development of Hindi teacher training colleges in non-Hindi speaking states/union territories and to a limited extent, to assist the setting up of a new institution in such areas which are in need of such assistance. Assistance is also given to voluntary organisations for enabling them to hold Hindi teaching classes, conducting research on methodology of its teaching and providing Hindi books to various organisations. Various schemes are in operation to promote and develop tribal, calssical, modern Indian languages and prepare and publish books, dictionaries, research and instructional material besides training of teachers in Hindi. Through the kendriya Hindi Sansthan, Agra the Government of India promotes development of improved mentodology for teaching Hindi to the non-Hindi speaking students. A full-fledged academic course for teaching Hindi to foreigners is being conducted by the Sansthan under the scheme 'Propagation of Hindi Abroad'. Central Hindi Directorate runs programmes relating to pruchase and publication of books and their free distribution to non-Hindi speaking states and to the Indian missions. The Directorate also brings out Hindi journals like UNESCO DOOT, Bhasha and Sahityamala. It is also implementing a scheme of teaching Hindi through correspondence courses in the media of English, Tamil, Malayalam and Bengali.

The Commission for Scientific and Technical Terminology, New Delhi, prepares and publishes definitional dictionaries and terminology in various disciplines and Pan-Indian terminology. Hindi-English glossaries in Basic sciences, humanities, social sciences, university level textbooks in agriculture and engineering and other subjects are also published. Fifty scholarships are awarded every year to foreign students for studying Hindi in Kendriya Hindi Sansthan, Agra.

Modern Indian Languages

Financial assistance is given to voluntary organisations and individuals to bring out publications like encyclopedias, dictionaries, books of knowledge, original writing on linguistic, literary, indological, social anthropological and cultural themes, critical editions of old manuscripts etc., for the development of modern Indian languages. Grants are also given for holding literary conferences, seminars and exhibitions besides purchasing copies of printed publications. States are given special help for the production of university level books in the regional languages. the Bureau for Promotion of Urdu was set up in 1969. Apart from working as a secretariat to Taraqqie-Urdu. Board which has been converted into an autonomous body known as National Council for Promotion of Urdu Language to advise the government on development of Urdu, it also develops educational literature in Urdu. It gives financial assistance to calligraphy centres. A National Council for promotion of Sindhi language has been set up as an autonomous body.

Government also provides facilities for study of language other than mother tongue. For this the Central Institute of Indian Languages (CIIL), Mysore conducts research in the areas of language analysis, language pedagogy, language technology and language use. Study of tribal languages is one of important functions. It runs six regional language centres at Bhubaneswar, Mysore, Patiala, Pune, Solan and Lucknow to help meet the demand for trained teachers to implement the three-language formula and one extension centre at guwahati to do research for development of tribal languages of north-eastern region.

The Central Institute of English and Foreign Languages (CIEFL) Hyderabad, set up as an autonomous body n 1958 is engaged in bringing out qualitative improvement in teaching of English. Subsequently, teaching of major foreign languages viz., Russian, Germani, French and Arabic and their literatures was also included in its activities. In 1973, it was declared to be an institution of higher learning deemed-to-be a university. It has two regional centres at Shillong and Lucknow.

Financial assistance is also provided to states for setting up CIEFL's district centres for English with a view to improving the standard of English language, teaching and learning. So far 28 district centres have been set up. These centres aim at imparting training to teachers of English in their areas through orientation course. Under another scheme, financial assistance is given to regional and state institutes of English for strengthening their programmes of training with respect to improving standard of English language teaching.

There are many schemes for propagation, popularisation and development of Sanskrit and other classical languages like Arabic and Persian. These include schemes for financial assistance to state governments and voluntary sanskrit organisations and their development into Adarsh Sanskrit Pathshalas, for incentives to retired scholars as Shastra Chaudamani pandits, for publication of original writtings of contemporary authors, editing and publication of rare manuscripts and catalogues of manuscripts, reprinting of important out-of-print Sanskrit texts, promotion of oral vedic tradition, vocational training to products of Sanskrit Pathshalas, national awards to eminent Sanskrit, Arbic and Persian scholars and preparation/publication of Sanskrit dictionaries.

Registered organisations engaged in the development and propagation of Sanskrit are given recurring grants for salary of teachers, scholarships to students, construction and repair of buildings, library books, research projects etc., upto 75 per cent of the approved expenditure. About 550 voluntary institutions conducting courses on traditional Sanskrit education and about 200 institutions working in the field of propagation and promotion of Arabic, Persian are benefitteed under this scheme every year. Institutions having potential for greater development are identified and brought under the scheme of Adarsh Sanskrit Mahavidyalayas and Shodh Sansthans. So far, 14 post-graduate Sanskrit Mahavidyalayas and two research institutions have been brought under the purview of this scheme. To encourage more students to learn Sanskrit, the amount of scholarship under the voluntary organisation scheme has been increased from Rs. 100 per month to Rs. 300 per month with effect form 1 April, 1995.

Department of Education also conducts an all-India Vedic Convention through Maharishi Sandipani Rashtriya Ved Vidya Pratishthan and an all-India Sanskrit elocution every year where scholars in different Shastras and a team of eight contestants from all states are invited with a view to identifying the rare Veda Shakhas and their repositiories, devising ways and means for preserving the ortal traditions and encouraging extempore speech on classical subjects. As a special measure to preserve oral tradition of Vedic studies, a scheme was introduced in 1978 under which each Swadhyayin is required to train two students each below 12 years, in a particular Veda Shakha. The scholar gets an honorarium of Rs. 1250 and the student Rs. 175 per month. At present, 18 such units are functioning. During 1994-95, five more units were selected. Annual Elocution contest was held at Sadashiv Kendriya Sanskrit Vidyapeetha, Puri from 26 to 28 February 1995 in which about 90 students from 13 states participated.

Maharishi Sandipani Rashtriya Veda Vidya Pratishthan had been set up in 1987 with the objective of preserving and developing all aspects of Vedic studies. During 1994-95 the Pratishthan organised one all India and six Regional Vedic Sammelans, seminars and workshops on different topics, gave financial assistance to Vedic institutions, aged Vedic Pandits and Nityagnihotris, stipend to Veda students, fellowships, conduct of vedic classes for general public, tape recording of Vedic recitation etc.

To encourage scholars in Sanskrit, Arabic and Persian a scheme for awarding "Certificate of Honours" with a suitable monetary grant to eminent Sanskrit, Arbic, and Persian scholars was introduced in 1958. Eminent scholars of Pali and Prakrit languages are also considered for the award. A monetary grant of Rs. 10,000 per annum for life is granted to each scholar and a Sanad and a Robe of honour (Shawl) is also presented when the distinction is conferred by the President at the investiture ceremony. The award money has been enhanced from 10,000 to Rs. 20,000 per annum from 1995-96.

Rashtriya Sanskrit Sanstha, an autonomous organisation under the Ministry of Human Resource Development with its headquarters at Delhi, exercises academic and administrative control over seven Kendriya Sanskrit Vidyapeethas at Jammu, Allahabad, Guruvayoor,

Puri, Jaipur, Lucknow and Sringeri where Sanskrit education in traditional shastras and research in various fields is conducted. Vidyapeethas of Delhi and Trupati were declared deemed-to-be universities in 1987. The Vidyapeethas located as Sringeri and named after late Shri Rajiv Gandhi was inaugurated by the President of India on 5 March 1992. Rashtriya Sanskrit Sansthan also plans to open more Kendriya Sanskrit Vidyapeethas at Madhya Pradesh (Bhopal), Himachal Pradesh and Maharashtra (Bombay) during 1995-96. The Sansthan also conducts examination for prathma to Vidyavaridhi (Ph.D.) and Vachaspati (D.Litt) and in addition to its own institutions over 50 other institutions all over the country are affiliated to it.

Under the Centrally - sponsored scheme of development of Sanskrit, cent per cent grant is given to the state governments/uhnion territories for: (a) financial assistance upto Rs. 4,000 per annum to eminent Sanskrit scholars in indigent circumstances, (b) for appointment of teachers for teaching selected modern subjects in the traditional Sanskrit pathshalas; (c) for providing facilities for teaching Sanskrit in high and higher secondary schools; (d) for scholarships to students studying Sanskrit in order to attract good students in IX to XII classes and (e) for their own schemes for promotion of Sanskrit.

Under a scheme, registered voluntary organisations working for the promotion of Arabic and Persian are given financial assistance towards salary of teachers, scholarships, furniture, library, books etc., and other activities which are conducive to development of Arabic and Persian. Financial assistances is available to the extent of 75 per cent of the approved expenditure. About 150 voluntary Arabic and Persian institutions were sanctioned financial assistance during 1994-95.

A new scheme, modernisation of 'Madrasa

Education; has been introduced in 1993-94. The objective of the scheme is to encourage traditional institutions like Madrasas and Maktabs by giving financial assistance to introduce science, mathematics, social studies, Hindi and english in their curriculum. However, the process of modernisation of traditional madrasas and maktabs is entirely voluntary. The scheme provides opportunities to students of these institutions to acquire education comparable to the national eduction system. Assistances is given to these traditional institutions for the activities which contribute to this objective. In the first phase, modernisation will only cover about 250 educational institutions providing primary education.

Performing arts

Two main schools of classical music Hindustani and Carnatic continue to survive through oral tradition being passed on by teachers to disciples. This has led to the existence of family traditions called gharanas and sampradayas.

Dance in India has an unbroken tradition of over 2,000 years. Its themes are derived from mythology, legends and classical literature, two main divisions being calssical and folk. Classical dance forms are based on ancient dance discipline and have rigid rules of presentation. Important among them are Bharata Natyam, Kathakali, Kathak, Manipuri, Kuchipudi and Odissi. Bharata Natyam though derives its roots from Tamil Nadu has developed into an all India form, Kathakali is a dance form of Kerala and Kathak is a classical dance form revitalised as result of the fusion of Mughal influence with Indian culture. Manipur has contributed a delicate, lyrical style of dance, Manipuri, while Kuchipudi is a dance form owing its origin to Andhra Pradesh, and Odissi from Orissa, once practised as a temple dance, is today widely interpreted by artists. Folk and tribal dances are of numerous patterns.

Both classical and folk dance owe their popularity to institutions like sangeet Natak Akademi and training institutes and cultural organisations. The Akademi gives financial assistance to cultural institutions and awards fellowships to scholars, performers and teachers to promote advanced study and training i different forms of dance music especially those which are rare.

Theatre in Indian is as old as her music and dance. Classical theatre survives only in some places. Folk theatre can be seen in its regional variants practically in every region. There are also professional theatres, which are mainly city-oriented. Besides, India has a rich tradition of puppet theatre, prevalent form being puppets, rod puppets, glove puppets and leather puppets (shadow theatre). There are several semi-professional and amateur theatre groups involved in staging plays in Indian languages and English.

Sangeet Natak Akademi, the national academy of music, dance and drama, was set up in 1953 to promote performing arts in collaboration with states and voluntary organisation. It seeks increased public appreciation of these art forms through sponsorship, research and dissemination. It holds seminars and festivals, presents awards to outstanding performing artites, gives financial assistance for theatre productions, extends financial help to traditional teachers and grants scholarships to students. It operates a scheme of inter-state exchange of troupes to promote national and cultural integration through regional festivals and bringing rare art forms of the regions to the fore.

The Akademi has set up a special unit for surveying and docmenting various theatrical, musical and dance forms in the country. Its disc and tape unit has the largest collection of Indian classical, folk and tribal music, dance and theatre items. The Sangeet Natak Akademi runs two zonal institutions for training in dance, Kathak Kendra, New Delhi and Jawaharlal Nehru Manipuri Dance Academi, Imphal. It took over the Rabindra Rangshala as the third unit with effect from 2 April 1993. It gives subsidy for publication of books in various Indian languages and English on music, dance and drama and confers awards and fellowships to distinguished artistes and scholars. The fellowship carry a purse of Rs. 40,000 and the awards Rs. 25,0000 and a Tamrapatra.

The National School of Drama (NSD) - one of the foremost theatre training institutions in the world and the only of its kind in India was set up by Sangeet Natak Akademi in 1959. Later in 1975, it became an autonomous organisation, financed entirely by Department of Culture, ministry of Human Resource Development, Government of India.

NSD gas produced a galaxy of talents - actors, directors, script writers, designers, technicians, educationists who work not only in theatre but in film and television also - winning several awards, national and international. The training in the School is based on a thorough, comprehensive, carefully planned syllabus. The systematic study and practical performing experience of Sanskrit drama, modern Indian drama, traditional Indian theatre forms, Asian drama and western drama give the students a solid grounding and a wide perspective in the art of theatre. In order to establish links between traditional theatre forms of India and modern expressions, the School brings experts to train the students in these forms and also sends students to regional centres for training in traditional theatre. The School has also attracted to its training faculty some of the finest creative talents from within the country and abroad. The school has a Repertory Company and

Theatre-In-Education Company in Delhi and Regrional Resource-cum-Research Centre at Bangalore. NSS's extension programme seeks to extend and diffuse its activities in all regions of the country. A programme for research, documentation and publication is recently added to the School's record of academic activities.

For want of good opportunities in India, talented young men and women are now seeking employment with American software firms. We seem to have an edge in the field of software, which is internationally recognized. The Ninth Plan should provide a framework to utilise the talent within the country. There is no use in simply appealing to the young people in the name of national interests without giving them an opportunity and a fair deal to utilize their talent.

It is comforting that the Ninth Plan approach has spoken of the need to nuture and support fully scientific talent with exceptional capabilities. The approach paper says that facilities comparable to international standards will be offered to them so as to enable them to carry out outstanding research within the country. More Centres of Excellence will be created and they will be encouraged to function in close co–ordination with institutions of higher learning to supply future manpower needs for thenational S & T programme.

The preoccupation with the demands of the rising middle class has led to an obsession with consumer goods in the production pattern of the country. While there is nothing basically wrong in catering to this market, the needs of the majority of the people below the poverty line have been given less importance. This is a pity because many of the CSIR laboratories have done excellent work that is relevant to the poor in the villages but is should be applied on a large scale.

The late Dr. Y. Nayudamma pleaded for a social bias in scientific applications. He pointed out that it is fashiionable (and paying) to do research in frontier areas. But not all frontier areas are relevent or urgent to the needs of our country. While no one denies the right of a talented person to contribute to the world's pool of knowledge whithout any national inhibitions, it is essential that the major emphasis should be to make life a bit easier for the underprivileged among us. This calls for a change in the value system. At present, none would rate a researcher n say, cowdung utilization high. AddressingWestern–oriented priorities gives better recognition!

When Dr Nayudamma assumed charge of the CSIR, he drastically reduced hundreds of needless procedures that had only delayed matters. He proved to be an excellent administrator.

However, red tape has great attraction for scientists, who want to become administrators. Even Fellows of the Royal Society have succembed to the lure of power, though, thanks to our ministers, powers to such technocrats have been effectively reduced.

Frustration: This brings out a deeper problem. The lure of easy money in banking and management has drained S & T areas of young talent. This has led to a lot of frustration among scientists. It is a pity that only a handful of science talent marit scholars end up with science degrees or as scientists. To be a scientist is no longer socially, financially or intellectually attractive. Our scientific establishment, with a few exceptions, lack in good public relations. Most scientists cannot communicate their work and ideas in a user—friendly manner. They generally (with some exceptions) look down upon those who try to popularize their work. Their sights are set elsewhere. Humility, which is the halmark of a true scientist has become a rare quality! Their dialogue is addressed to ever—narrowing circles of a few highbrows!

In sum, the main issues in S & T involve several hard choices.

First, the lion's share now going to Space and Atomic Energy calls for a review. People are disillusioned why Space should continue to get so much money. However many big rockets are needed, for instance, to launch our INSATs which in any case last for more than seven years now—a days? If there is no scope for exports of rocket subsystems, where is the rationale for the huge outlay on big rockets? A credible answer is called for to justify the status quo. While remote sensing satellites and rockets for launching them may be justified, it is difficult to convince the common people about the need for large boosters, when such rockets are commercially available elsewhere at reasonable prices (which are only occasional expenses). In Atomic Energy also, there has been no convincing answer to the problem of safety. If it is a rocket or a plen, the damage from failure is limited. In the case of nuclear waste contammination,l the consequences affect generations and are simply too tragic for words. With all the massive investments, nuclear power accounts for an insignificant portion of the power supply. The position may change but as of now, people do not have high hopes about it.

Second, agriculture needs a new deal in terms ofinfusing environmentally—friendly technologies particularly in reducing the use of chemical fertilizers.

Third, let the industry pay for R & D useful to it. There is no justification to protect obsolete industries. This is a false patriotism. The government can then concentrate on socially significant research where profit—

driven industries hesitate to go in. Foreign technology for consumer items should be limited to upgrading items of mass consumption. The Western culture of creating non–essential wants (through advertising) need not be encouraged.

Above all, there should be a wider debate (not confined to scientists only) on the S & T issue. The worst scenario would be public indifference, making it easy for a few scientists (with their own selfish agenda) to call the shots.

The immediate environment of man comprises air on which depends all form of life. It has been estimated that a man can live for 5 weeks without food, for 5 days without water, but for only 5 minutes without air. Normally the air is composed of 78.1 part Nitrogen, 20.93 part oxygen and 0.03 part carbondioxide. The balance is made up of other gases which occur in traces. In addition to these gases air also contain water vapour, and suspended matter such as dust, bacteria, pores and debris. Therefore, the term air pollution is applied when there is excessive concentration of foreign mater in the outdor atmosphere which is harmful to man or his environment. Pollution of air has resulted in sickness and deaths. More than 100 contaminants have been identified. The important ones are carbonmonoxide, sulphur dioxide, Nitrogen dioixide, Ozone, Lead, etc. Air pollution is a growing menace to health through out the world.

Most of the pollutants are associated with fossil fuel consumption. Two main categories of outdoor air pollutants are recognised. Industrial smog predominatc in large industrial areas. It is a combination of smoke and fog and results from combustion of fuel and consists primarily of sulfur dioxides and particulate complexes. Combustion of coal, oil and other fuel is another source of smoke, dust and sulphur dioxide. Photochemical smog occurs in areas shich a high density of motor vehicles. Motor vehicles, truck, trains, aircraft and other forms of transport emit hydrocarbons, carbonmonoxide, lead, nitrogen dioxide and particulate matter. In strong sunlight certain of these hydrocarbons and oxide of nitrogen may be converted into photochemical pollutant of oxidising nature. Burning of refuse, agricultural activities e.g. crop spraying, pest control and nuclear energy programmes also contribute to air pollution.

Sulfur dioxide is a major atmospheric pollutant in many urban and industrial areas, produced by the burning of sulfur content of coal and crude oil. The major source of environmental pollution are poer plants, oil refineries, and industries such as smelters, paper pulp mills and wineries. The sulfur dioxide released in the atmosphere is oxidized to sulfur trioxide in the presence of sunlight and high humidity which immediately combines with water to form sulfuric acid. Sulfur trioxide and sulfuric acid are much more irritant than sulfur dioxide.

Nitrogen dioxide is a pollutant generated in the outdoor environment mainly from automobile exhaust. In the presence of flame temperature oxygen combines nitrogen to form nitric oxide, a gas of litlle significance as an air pollutant. However when nitric oxide is vented into the air and cools rapidly, a fraction is converted into nitrogen dioxide. At home wood burning, fireplaces, kerosene heater and improperly vented gas stoves give rise to nitrogen dioxide pollution.

Ozone is a gas which is a key component of a complex mixutre of photochemical oxidant and fine particles called "Smog". It is formed by a series of sunlight driven reactions of nitrogen oxides and volatile organic compounds arising from combustion sources.

Indoor sources of ozone include air "purifiers" and ion generators and office equipment with electric motors or ultraviolet lights, such as photocopy machines. In indoor environment (e.g. home, work, school) concentration of ozone are generally lower than outdoor.

Carbon monoxide (CO) duduced in ambient air comes mainly from vehicular exhaust with a bimodal peak corresponding to the morning and evening rush hours. Catalytic converters on motor vehicle decreases CO in exhaust. Indoor air can be contaminated by cigarette smoking and outdoor air that enters building from the street traffic. High exposures are relatively rare and are primarily associated with certain occupations (e.g. fire fighting) and from exposure to the product of combustion in an enclosed space from improperly vented combustion appliances and of charcoal briquettes for barbecuing and space heating. Combustion from fires, stoves, and motor vehicles generates CO at concentrations of 1% to 6% (10,000 to 60,000 ppm).

Lead: The leaded gasolines/petrol is the main source of wide spread dispersion of this metal throughout the biosphere. A marked reduction in the ambient levels of airborne lead resulted since 1970s with the use of unleaded gasoline. In countries where leaded gasolilne is still used airborne lead from automotive emissons continues to accumulate in the environment.

In most cities and towns of India there are NGOs whose focus is the improvement of the urban environment and the condition of the urbanites.

The Bombay Environmental Action Group's efforts have been focused on Bombay and Maharashtra, but the fallout is expected to be experienced in many urban centres. The group has used environmental advocacy and public interest litigation to bring about a rethinking on siting of failities, unplanned growth and pollution.

The Ahmedabad Study Action Group's activities include programmes for slum children, income supplementing programmes for women, low-cost housing, biogas plants and policy research on poverty-related issues.

The Self Employed Women's Association, Ahmedabad, represents a merger of labour, cooperative and women's movements and has promoted cooperatives of rag-pickers, roadside vendors and hawkers, and has been campaigning for the rights of unroganized workers in the non-formal sector.

The Society for the Promotion of Area Resource Centres (SPARC), Bombay works in training and mobilization of the urban poor.

The KKNSS, Bangalore, is a federation of slum dwellers, one of the few peoples' organizations of thi kind.

The Government has taken several initiatives to cope with the burgeoning problem of urban housing. Slum upgrading became a part of official housing policy in 1972. The rationale of slum upgrading is that in situ improvement of existing communities is socially preferable to relocation or redevelopment. Under the scheme of Environmental Improvement of Urban Slums, water supply including drinking water taps, open sewer drains, storm water drains, street lighting, etc., are provided to notified slums.

In 1986 the Scheme of Urban Basic Services was launched as a centrally sponsored scheme with teh objective of promoting woman and child survival and development, low-cost water supply and sanitation, and other community welfare activities through community participation.

The Government seeks to completely eliminate the practice of manual scavenging by conversation of dry latrines and construction of low cost sanitation units.

The Government has recently announced a comprehensive Pollution Abatement Policy which seeks to combine regulation with fiscal incentives, encourage clean technologies, make voluntary action attractive and promote people's participation.

A whole economy runs on recycling in Indian cities. In Ahmedabad alone, a hundred factories are exclusively involved in converting plastic picked from the roadside into recycled products. Apart from the used paper which is sold to old paper dealers, 60 tonnes is picked up an recycled. Foundry wastes are ground, undergo magnetic extraction and are made into manhole covers. Rags are sold on a large scale for cleaning machines in factories. The total amount of recycling in Ahmedabad by the informal sector alone is estimated to be 200 tonnes per day, providing employment to 100,000 people, at Rs. 20 to Rs. 30 a day, which is higher than the minimum wage.

Premature infants, newborn, and elderly and people with chronic disease of the lungs or heart are at higher risk. Pre-school and school children appear to be sensitive to air pollution health effects. The traffic policeman, the automobile mechanics, the drivers may have unusually high risk from exposure to community air pollution due to substantial exposures in association with their occupations.

Cigarette smoking is the predominant risk factor in producing respiratory diseases and lung cancer. Air pollution have a more than additive effect. This means that cigarette smokers are at unusual higher risks if they live in areas with substantial air pollution and that the effects of air pollution on chronic disabling pulmonary diseases are more likely to occur in cigarette smokers. During periods of low winds and still weather dissipation of domestic pollution due to heating and cooking will be impaired. In such condition if smoking or cooking occurs indoors, exposures to carbonmonoxide and nitrogen oxides may be quite high.

The problem of air pollution was first brought to a sharp focus when air pollution epidemics took place in the middle of 20th century. In 1952 London Fog epidemic, many people became ill and some 4000 deaths occurred. Since these episodes evaluation of exposed populaltions, have been performed in urban areas around the world to examine the impact of air pollution on human helath. Overall, these studies show a consistent pattern of association between increased sulfur dioxide and particulate concentrations and mortality. The acute bronchonstrictor effects of sulfur dioxide have been well established for more than 20 years. Patients with asthma represent a susceptible subgroup responsive to the effect of SO_2 and H_2SO4 at a concentration that have no effect on normal subjects. Sulfur dioxide is highly soluble in water, nearly all the inspired gas is absorbed in the nasal mucosa and very little reaches to the lungs undernormal resting conditions. Oral breathing reduces the uptake of sulfur dioxide in the nose, but increases pollutant delivery to the lungs. In some patients of asthma oral breathing predominates because of associated nasal obstruction.

Ozone is a powerful oxidant. The respiratory system is the primary target of the ozone toxicity. Inhalation of ozone can result in damage to almost all parts of the respiratory tract, depending upon concentration. Studies on animals have documented the inflammation of the respiratory tract, damage to epithelial cells and marked increase in susceptibility to bacterial infection following acute ozone exposure. Redness and swelling of the airways has been observed after ozone exposure the cytotoxicity of ozone may be largely due to its interaction with unsaturated lipids which generate damaging free radicals. Moreover, long lived radicals could enter the blood stream and exert effects on body temperature of blood pressure or remote organs such as the liver.

The evidence that ozone is determental to health is increasing. The concentration that sometimes occur in urban areas cause modest reductions of lung function both in children and exercising normal adults. There is a wide variation of susceptibility to these effects. Increased symptoms and lung function decrement usually occur in the same subjects. The major mechanism of ozone induced reduction in lung function is the inability of the exposed individual to inspire fully. Ozone exposure potentiate the allergic response and is harmful to asthmatics.

Nitrogen dioxide is less potent than ozone as an oxidant. According to intensity and duration of exposure, respiratory illness ranges from slight irrigation, burning an pain in the throat and chest to violent cough and shortness of breath. Acute Nitrogen dioxide poisoning leading to pulmonary odema and deaths has been recognized. There is a great paucity of information on chronic Nitrogen dioxide exposure because damage develops slowly. Moreover nitrogen dioxide is usually associated with other pollutants, which renders assesment of its action difficult. Indoor sources of combustion add NO_2 to indoor air. The use of gas for cooking might have a small effect on children and asthmatics. Sulfur dioxide has an additive effects on lung functions on healthy individuals.

The exposure to nitrogen dioxide in indoor air might increase the occurrence of respiratory infections because both short and long—term exposures to notrogen dioxide exposures impair the ability to clear inhaled infectious organisms. An increased incidence of respiratory illnesses during childhood predisposes to the development of chronic respiratory diseases in adults. Nitrogen dioxide is also an ingredient of cigarette smoke. Smokers employed in an environment polluted by automobile exhaust are believed to be particularly vulnerable to harm from nitrogen dioixide.

The toxic properties of CO are attributed to its high affinity for oxygen carrying protein (haemoglobin) to form a chemical complex called carboxyhaemoglobin (COHb). The exposure to CO is expressed as percentage of total haemoglobin bound to CO. In healthy individuals who do not smoke or are not otherwise exposed to CO, COHb level ranges from 0.3 to 0.7%. Inhaled CO is thought to be responsible for the further elevation of COHb levels to about 1% in non smokers. A significant proportion of the urban non smokers population has COHb level in excess of 1.5%, suggesting widespread exposure to environmental Co. Cigarettes, cigars and pipe smoking commonlyu commonly result in blood COHb levels of 2-14%. Patients of obstructive airways disease who continue to smoke tend to have higher COHb levels than smokers free of cardiiopulmanary disease.

Acute CO poisoning, with COHb levels over 30 to 50%, results in damage mainly to the heart and brain because less oxygen is carried on haemoglobin secondary to the formation of COHb. Patients with Ischemic heart disease, are particularly sensitive to CO. Earlier onset of angina and ECG changes indicative of myocardial ischemia have been documented during exercise in such pateints at COHb level in the range of 2 to 6%. The adverse effect of maternal smoking on foetal growth and development are now well accepted. CO a major component of cigarette smoke, interfers with the transport of oxygen to the developing tissues. Similar effects have been postulated for ambient CO exposures.

The route of exposure of lead is through both inhalation and ingestion. Most of the lead deposited on the airways is cleared by mucociliary blanket of the lungs and swallowed. Approximately 10% is absorbed in the gastro intestinal tract and gets deposited in the bones. Women with previous lead exposures may have elevated blood levels during periods of high bone turnover (e.g. pregnancy, lactation, or hyperthyroidism). Their urborn children may be exposed transplacentally, and newborns through breast milk to high levels of lead. Foetuses, infants and children are considered to be particularly susceptible to the adverse effects. Early childhood lead exposures has neurobehavioral effects such as various learning dosorders, reading disabilities, poor vocabulary and grammatical reasoning.

Inspite of decades of laboratory clinical and epidemiologic research, however the health effects of exposure of humans to pollutants remain incompletely characterized. Finally most environmental exposures involved multiple pollutants. Control of exposures in life is an important component of appropriate preventive action. Escape of toxic substances into the ambient air can be prevented by an variety of engineering methods such as enclosure, ventilation and air cleaning. A major contribution in this field is the development of arrestors for the removal of contaminants like convertors to reduce automobile exhaust. Use of technology that reduces pollution like use of electricity and natural gas in place of coal. The control of an air pollution is ultimately an engineering problem.

Human rights are a extensive as human life and,

whether or not enshrined in national constitutions or bills of right or in international covenants to which nations are signatory, first order rights are inherent and inalienable. As Jefferson said, "the God that gave us life, gave us liberty at the same time". These rights are not gifted and cannot be taken away except by due process of law. To act otherwise is to violate Human Rights. There are, however, a whole series of rights, other than the basic or fundamental freedoms, which are statutory or derive from subscription to international or regional covenants.

Human Rights may be broadly classified as civil and political (so-called civil liberties and democratic rights), and social, economic and cultural. The latter include rights to development, the rights of women and children, a whole new family of environmental rights, rights to education and health, and to employment and to enjoy the fruits of labour. Both sets of rights are growing. Thus, freedom of speech and expression has developed to encompass the right to information. Privacy is now increasingly protected. There will be refinements and new situations will bring forth new rights such as now, in some societies, of pays, and may be for victims of AIDS.

A comparison of South Asian constitutions will probably indicate a broad similarity in the basic rights enunciated. Interpretations and implementation might vary. Derogations are permitted in emergency situations and these instances have been extensive in all parts of South Asia and have sometimes continued long after the proximate cause, perhaps well justified in some cases, has passed. The Indian Emergency (1975-77) and martial law or emergency regimes in Pakistan, Nepal, Bangladesh and Sri Lanka can also be cited. Many statutes contain preventive laws (preventive detention in India), and special laws may be invoked in given circumstances such as declaring certain areas to be disturbed and applying therein summary procedures (such as the Armed Forces Special Powers Act in India).

The South Asian nations are members of the United Nations and have variously subscribed to a number of international instruments including the international Covenants on Civil and Political Rights/Economic and Social Rights, the Geneva Conventions, ILO conventions and so forth. However, retification has not always followed speedily or at all. For instance, India took a long time to ratify the Convention on the Rights of the Child and has yet to ratify the Convention Against Torture. The record of the other South Asian governments would probably reveal similar lags or omissions which need to be overcome. Even where ratifications has taken place it is not certain whether governments have cared to create public awareness about national adherence to these conventions and to explain their implications or to examine whether national laws need to be upgraded, expanded or created to give them an enforceable statutory basis. This is an exercise national governments should be asked to undertake and could be the subjects of a report of SAARC.

While human rights are proclaimed, newly-independent nations have sometimes been prone to stress sovereign or national rights, the rights of the state, over individual human rights. This was true worldwide until the second world war and in some ways continue to be so even in the more industrially advanced and politically older or mature societies because of the fears and compulsions of the cold war. With the end of the East-West divide, the West has given more emphasis to human rights and democratic governance and has come to attach trade and aid conditionalities for "good performance". While this may be justified at one level, the question that arises, as it does in the domestic domain, is who will police the policeman? Also, how far observing is the human rights record of smaller and weaker countries. Such conditionalities are also creeping into the field of environment, the rights of so-called indigenous people, a misnomer when applied to South Asian societies, and so on.

Development, gender, minority, regional and environmental rights, among others, are of great importance to South Asia where poverty, gender inequalities, disparities, illiteracy, bonded labour and child labour are widespread. Poverty robs the individual of dignity and, often, children of their childhood. While, therefore, development rights are vitally important, there are no hierarchy of rights. All rights, political, civil cultural, social and economic, are indivisible and mutually reinforcing. This is a normative value that South Asia must accept and proclaim so that one right is not used to supersede and thereby deny another.

South Asia has a number of human rights organisations, statutory and voluntary. In India, for scheduled castes and tribes and statutory bodies such as the Press Council, the Minorities Commission, the National Commission for Women, and the Commissioner for Linguistic Minorities. A statutory Human Rights Commission has been brought into being by ordinance and incorporates many improvements in relation to an earlier Bill. Pakistan has a very active non-governmental Human Rights Commission whose reports merit wider distribution in the region. The Human Rights Organisation of Nepal (HURON) played an important part in securing the change-over from the panchayati system to the vigorous multi-party democracy that was established in 1991. Bangladesh has a Coördinating Council for Human Rights (CCHRB) which aims to publish annual reports.

All the countries of South Asia are in transition and there is much ferment: violence, terrorism, ethnic discords, the rise of religious fundamentalisms, basic rights, but the exploitation of religion for partisan political ends, can be dangerous as India has discovered. Likewise caste. With the process of nation-building still underway, individual and state rights tend to clash. A more careful study of events and trends and a sharing of experience could promote clarity and wisdom in dealing with highly complex and volatile situations.

Human rights violations regrettably occur everywhere around the globe in greater or lesser measure. What matters, however, is that violation, aberrant action and derogations are brought to light by the media, the law enforcement agencies and human rights groups or by the community at large and the guilty are brought to book. While human rights mechanisms need to be strengthened or even created where necessary, human rights problems most often begin where due process and the criminal justice system break down. This then leads to false cases, torture, custodial death, extortion, rape, corruption, et al. The public preception of a breakdown in the local criminal justice system led to the Bhagalpur blindings in Bihar in the 1980s when there was widespread public approval of known criminals being blinded while in detention for fear that they would otherwise be bailed out or released and continue with their depredations.

The restoration of the efficacy, integrity and speed of the criminal justice system (including the working of the police and jails) is perhaps the single most important item that should be on the South Asian human rights agenda. For prevention is better than cure. Political interference with the police, the politicisation of crime and the criminalisation of politics have played havoc.

Dealing with human rights violations then becomes a case of trying to shut the stable door after the horse has bolted. The understaffing of courts, mounting arrears and costs, and dilatory procedures are discrediting the rule of law.

Yet the judiciary has been innovative. In India, for example, public interest litigation has opened new doors, overriding former impediments of locus standi in relations to the cause of action and treating a single case as a class action. Judicial verdicts have also amplified Article 21, the Right to Life, to embrace "rights to livelihood, health, education, shelter, dignity, minimum wage, environment" (Upendra Baxi).

Environmental issues have come to the fore in South Asia with poverty, population and livestock pressures leading to deforestation, erosion of common property resources and environmental degradation generally. The land can no longer support burgeoning numbers and the region is spawning its share of inadvertent cities and threatens to (and does) explode with crime and violence. Water and energy shortages confront us and industrial, pollution and development blight are increasingly visible, though yet in the early stages. The warning signals are there.

South Asia's environmental problems are largely related to the economics of survival, poverty in a broad sense being the worst polluter. Population control and ensuring an early demographic transition are of the highest importance. Primary education and health and improving the status of women hold the key as Sri Lanka, and Kerala and Goa in India have well demonstrated. The pace of development must be hastened and the fruits of development more equitably shared. There have to be alternative sources of fodder and fuel, improved land-use patterns, better land and water management and greater emphasis on biofertilisers and integrated pest management so as to avoid incremental toxicity entering the food chain. Rivers are becoming sewers. The Ganga Action Plan, now being extended to the Yamuna, Damodar, Gomati and other rivers, represents the largest river clean-up operation ever undertaken anywhere. Conservation, substainability and maintenance of bio-diversity have become key ideas.

South Asia is setting new pollution standards and seeking to upgrade technology and maintenance systems, but there is a long way to go. Environmental groups are active and environmental awareness is spreading. Indian courts have ordered the closure of polluting industries for failure to ensure minimal emission of effluent standards despite being allowed resonable time, access to credit, and technical assistance to upgrade their technology. Environmental tribunals are contemplated.

Two problems will have to be confronted. One is internal pressure from local groups and communities to adopt alternative strategies of development: decentralised, low-energy, appropriate technology, small-is-beautiful, back-to-nature systems. While the opposition to ostentatious consumption, crass consumerism and waste is widel'y shared, there will be reservations about nostalgia, romanticising the past, overlooking the tremendous growth of population which is likely to double or triple again before it stabilises in South Asia, and ignoring the demand for minimal life styles and national infra-structure in a globalised setting. There has to be a practical via media. At the other end of the scale, the North would like to globalise tropical forests and bio-diversity and points to population growth as a looming ecological threat, leading to green house warming, a possible sea-rise, and destablising climate changes. This ignores the unsustainable life styles of the North and its massive contribution to global warming since the industrial revolution, but more particularly, in the past few decades. Global conferencing and the Rio meet have brought about some convergence, but maybe not nearly enough.

South Asia, as a clearly demacrated monsoonal geopolitical entity, should concert action on both the regional and global planes. The Himalayan-Karakoram barrier constitutes a critical watershed the greening of which should be worth something as a global carbon sink and oxygen bank. Debt-for-nature swaps and debt forgiveness by the North, linked to environmental improvement and technological upgradation in South Asia, should be jointly explored. The natural disaster study undertaken by SAARC (1989-91) marks a beginning towards collective action on environmental issues and optimal harnessing of shared natural resources such as rivers and bio-diversity.

There could be joint studies and research programmes in South Asia to meet the challenge of global warming and sea-rise effects, to fight locusts and study seismicity.

On the human rights plane, it is perhaps not widely known that a South Asian Forum for Human Rights was formally set up in Kathmandu in February, 1993, a spinoff from a suggestion mooted at the World Human Rights Congress in Delhi in 1990. This is a non-governmental body that plans to promote networking and interaction among human rights groups in the region. All the SAARC nations other than the Maldives are represented. It is still at an embryonic stage but could grow. The setting up of SAARC observer groups to monitor elections in the region represents another initiative. Perhaps the time has come to moot the establishment of a human rights cell within SAARC or more informally to gather information, liaise and sensitise governments on issues and opportunities that call for concerted action.

Human rights and environmental issues are very much on the national, regional and international agenda today. These concerns have wide linkages and need to be properly understood and fully internalised in national and regional policies and instruments.

Hotels

The Department of Tourism classifies functioning hotels under the 'star system' into six categories from one to five-star deluxe and the newly introduced category of heritage hotels. The Department also reclassifies these hotels after every three years to ensure that the requisite standards are maintained by these hotels. The Hotel and Restaurant Approval and Classification Committee (HRACC) set up for the purpose has representatives from Central Department of Tourism, stae governments and hotel and travel industry associations. By the end of 1994, there were 912 hotels with 55,455 rooms on the approved list of the Department of Tourism. The classified hotels included 103 in one star, 240 in two star, 163 in three star, 58 in four star, 56 in five star, 35 in five star deluxe and 22 in heritage hotel category. During 1994, 113 hotel projects with 6,011 rooms were approved and are at various stages of construction. The speed up the work of functioning hotels pending classification/reclassification, four regional committees have been set up in Delhi, Bombay, Calcutta and Madras to conduct inspections of the hotels in one to three star and heritage category hotels. These regional committees became functional with effect from 1 January 1993.

A new classification standard of heritage hotels has been introduced to cover functioning hotels in palaces, havelie, castles, forts and residences built prior to 1950. As the traditional structure reflect the ambience and lifestyle of the bygone era and are immensely popular with the tourists, the scheme is aimed to ensure that such properties, landmarks of our heritage are not lost due to decay and disuse; at the same time by bringing such properties into the approved sector, they will become financially viable besides providing additional room capacity for the tourist. Twenty-two properties have been classified in the heritage hotel category providing a room capacity of 682 rooms. Another 27 heritage hotels projects comprising of 590 rooms are in the pipe line. Guidelines have also been formulated for conversion of heritage properties into heritage hotels and their approval at project planning stage.

To augment the room requirements at the major tourist centres, Paying Guest Accommodation Scheme has been introduced. In all 1,476 units have been registered. This scheme is open to the house-owner having lettable rooms of requisite standard. In this connection, a Paying Guest Accommodation Committee has been constituted. A directory of paying guest accommodation units has also been brought out by the Departement.

Travel Trade Tourist Service Division of the Department of Tourism is to extend support to the travel trade both national and international and to coordinate with various Central and state governments with the aim to facilitate to tourists and promotion of travel trade. It also interacts with travel trade associations, Travel Agent Association of India (TAAI), Indian Association of Tour Operators (IATO), Toursit Transports Association (TTA) which are national bodied and also with India Convention Promotion Bureau, Pacific Asia Travel Association (PATA), National and International Chapters, ICCA International, etc., for promotion of tourism.

Department of Tourism has streamlined and simplified the rules from April 1992, regarding the grant of approval to travel agents, tour operators and tourist transport operators so that their service to tourists is standardised and is more broad-based for both international and domestic tourists. Upto 1994, there were 232 tour operators, 168 travel agents and 128 transport operators. Approval once granted is valid for all time provided no complaints are received about them and the necessary papers are submitted annually. With a view to attract more tourist charter flights to India, the system of granting clearance has been liberalised. *The new rake is already operational in Rajasthan. Another special tourist train 'Orient Express' has been introduced in Gujarat sector and one more covering the temple towns of Tamil Nadu will become operational soon. In addition, five more such trains with private sector participations connecting major tourist centres will become operational soon.

Tourism Promotion

In recent years, the Indian Railways have shown an interest in assisting and promoting the country's rich tourism industry. A beginning in this direction was made with the introduction of the Palace on Wheels trains on the Rajasthan sector. Now special trains are run to centres of both tourism and pilgrimage. Lately, the private sector has also been invited to aid the tourism efforts of the Indian Railways.

With the Government deciding to open up the economy in a big way, the private sector has been invited to assist the Indian Railways. Two major schemes are "own your wagon" and "build, operate lease and transfer (BOLT)" schemes.

Not every effort of the Indian Railways in improving

its performance has been successful. For instance, there continues to be concern over the failure to lure back sufficient goods traffic from the road transport sector. Despite all the measures, the safety record of Indian Railways is not examplary. The woes of ordinary passengers hve not declined to any considerable extent. Despite its excellent work, the research and development activity also need to do better to meet newer callanges. On its own part, the Ministry of Railways continues to pine for higher budgetary support which has dropped to 15 per cent from a high of 75 per cent in the Third Plan, while some of its actions are seen as reckless by economists.

The Indian Railways, however, feel confident of meeting the needs of the 21st century. Its Corporate Plan, for the year 1985-2000 A.D., has outlined seven broad strategies: Optimise investment and improve productivity of assets; upgrade technology; bring down costs by reducing fuel consumption, material costs etc.; adopt cost-based tarrif policy; rehabilitate and maintain assets, particularly track and rolling stock; develop human resource and divest auxiliary activities. Perhaps a pursuit of this strategy might ensure a better ride for the Indian Railways in the next century.

Spain hosts 50 million tourists annually, double that of its population. Tiny Hong Kong received 9.5 million visitors and even communist China, opened its doors to 23 million tourists in 1995. That year, as many as 567 million tourists crossed international boundaries. And what was India's share of the cake? As little as 0.4 per cent.

Does this reflect a lack of potential/ With a physical, historical and cultural variety that few can match, this would hardly seem so. Inadequate and unfocused marketing of product India is quoted as a major reason for lack of interest in the country. Further, India's image management requires a serious overhaul. An incident occurring in one corner is all that it takes to initiate a travel advisory against visiting the whole country.

The greater problem lies at home. There has been a clear failure of public relations in tourism. Allocations to tourism over various plan periods has never exceeded 0.5 per cent of the total. Though tourism ranks as the third largest foreign exchange earner (and the second largest net foreign exchange earner) the annual allocation stands at just one per cent of the total income. Tourism was not mentioned in the budget of 1996097, nor in the economic survey. In a list of 52 priorities once drawn up by the Planning Commission, tourism occupied the 51st place, the 52nd being occupied by lighthouses!

In a strategy paper suggesting an investment of over Rs. 30,000 crore to put to tourism on the rapid growth path, former secretary of tourism, Mr G. Sundaram lamented the "persistent lack of awareness about the real benefits of tourism, on the part of the Planning Commission and finance ministry."

"It's really a question of mindset," says former director-general of tourism, Mr Ashok Pahwa. "Tourism has come to be associated with elitism, with a five-star culture." "Small wonder," says tourism expert, Mr Rabindra Seth, "that a country of 900 million people has only 58,000 rooms in its hotels, while Las Vegas alone has close to 100,000. Even Bangkok city has as many rooms if not more than the whole of India."

"Tourism has not been projected in a proper manner," says Mr Subhash Goyal, president of the Indian Association of Tour Operators. "We keep talking of economic liberalisation, but this is not necessarily going to increase employment, in fact it could be the reverse.

Tourism is the one exception—it is labour-intensive industry. One out of every nine workers in the world is employed in this industry which both the World Bank and the IMF have recognised as the world's largest.

"One of India's problems is the migration from rural areas to cities. If tourist destinations and circuits are developed away from cities—as has been done at Bekal in Kerala and Shivpuri in Madhya Pradesh—the economy of such places changes. It really can be a catalyst for growth," he says.

At 1985-86 prices, the labour-capital ratio for a million rupees investment in the hotel and restaurant sector is 89 jobs against 44.7 in agriculture and 12.6 in manufacturing industries.

This is definitely an industry to be encouraged. Yet at all the major conventions of the travel trade, the minister for tourism is absent. Why has tourism been relegated to the periphery? Why do decision-makers brush it aside?

A major responsibility for this lies with the travel trade and its failure to present a strong case for tourism. There have been some efforts, by Assocham's expert committee on tourism and Pacific Area Travel Association (PATA) which helped create a better understanding, but by and large, these have been isolated. That apart, the industry fails to present itself as a cohesive body. The different segments, hoteliers, travel agents, transporters, etc are more keen on pushing their own case and resolving their individual problems than ironing out their differences and presenting themselves as aunified body to the government. Several years ago, a bureaucrat remarked, "First, let them get their act together, then talk about resolving the problems of the industry."

And there are a number of issues that concern them all—rationalisation of taxes, institutional changes in laws, single-window clearances for projects. Recently, there was some move towards an apex body—the National Tourism Council, which would be the industry's single voice, but that, predictably has yet to get off the ground. If tourism is to get its due, the industry will have to get their act together.

The 1997 travel scenario is depressing. In over two decades of analysing the Indian travel scene we have never seen anything more dismal than the outlook today. In the last 12 months rail accidents have occurred with hurtful regularity. An IGIA terminal was burst down, an aircraft collided in midair, a number of near-collisions were reported, but, again, no one has done anything discernible about them. Political survival, apparently, is more important than pinning responsibility.

Air-India is, seemingly, so broke that it did not print calendars this year and the minister painted a morbid picture of the financial state of our airlines. But he also refused to allow the superbly efficient Singapore International Airlines to enter into a collaboration with the Tatas to upgrade our civil aviation standards. The control of patronage and power, apparently, is more important than efficiency.

Our roads, particularly the important tourist highways out of Delhi, are disgraceful stretches of vehicle-destroying potholes; and they're getting worse. Moreover, the power situation is dark and getting darker; pollution chokes our cities; shaky governments opt for prohibition making the dishonest richer and the visitor poorer. People after all don't come to India to drink, but then people don't come to India to travel in cars, so must we ban motor vehicles just because of traffic accidents?

The oil-pool deficit has touched a whopping Rs. 15,500 crore, l so a hike in petrochemical prices is inevitable, the cost of travel will soar. Business traffic and foreign investments are falling, while inflation-is rising. The criminalisation of the bureaucratic-political nexus has reached such hideous dimensions that influential criminals are trying to put themselves above the law; this also seems to be one reason for the setting up of the central board for bank frauds.

In other words, the foundations of travel, the basic life-support systems of the economy, have been weakened by neglect. All this happens because, in an age when national economies are going global to survive, many of our legislators haven't the education, background or the vision to rise above their regional concerns. Consequently, since tourism is, essentially a global business it was ignored in the budget. And if the industry doesn't make its presence felt now, it will continue to be ignored.

For years politicians and bureaucrats ignored the opinion of defence experts, skulking behind the veil of the Official Secrets Act. Then the retiring chief of naval staff, Admiral V P Shekhawat, spoke out blaming the bureaucrats and the politicians for the deplorable state of our defence planning. The result? There has been a sudden flurry of activity with the purchase of sophisticated aircraft and talk of buying and aircraft carrier; and many brave statements from our hitherto arrogant *netas* about how our defence needs will never be compromised.

The industry must do for travel and tourism what Mr. Shekhawat did for defence. It must concentrate on a single-point programme. It must make the people of India aware of the fact that tourism is the only industry, that can give them jobs, food, houses and a better quality of life within the next 10 years. It worked this economic miracle for Austria after the Second World War, it can do it for India today.

To create this awareness we must set up a Confederation of Indian Travel Industries (CITI). Every Indian organisation which earns more than 51 per cent of its income from the movement of people should be eligible to enroll its CEO as a member of CITI. In other words, CITI will be the national equivalent of the extremely powerful 7—member World Travel and Tourism Council (WTTC).

According to the WTTC, tourism creates more than 10 per cent of the global economic output and one in nine jobs today; is expected to grow at real rate of 5.5 per year through 2005; will add one new job every 2.5 seconds, stimulate US $ three billion of capital investment every day and drive US $ 3.4 trillion of output every year. Consequently, the mission of CITI should be "... to make travel and tourism a strategic economic development and employment priority, to promote competitive environmentally sustainable markets and to eliminate barriers to growth; in the process creating wealth, jobs, trade and investments in India". We cannot afford to let on ill-informed government drift away from opportunities any more.

2

Ministry of Tourism and its Functions

The department of tourism has been declared as an independent Ministry i.e. the Ministry of Tourism w.e.f. 23rd May, 1998. The Ministry which includes the offices of Director General of Tourism functions as the nodal agency for the formulation of national policies and programmes and for the coordination of activities of various Central Government Agencies, State Governments and the Private Sector for the development of Tourism in the country. It is headed by a Cabinet rank Minister i.e. the Minister of Parliamentary Affairs & Tourism who is assisted by a Minister of State for Tourism.

The administrative head of the Ministry is the Secretary, Ministry of Tourism. The Ministry is assisted by an attached office headed by the Director General in the rank of Additional Secretary to Government of India. The office of the Directorate General of Tourism provides executive directions for the implementation of various policies and programmes. The office of the Directorate General of Tourism has a field formation of 21 offices within the country and 18 offices abroad. The overseas offices are primarily responsible for tourism promotion and marketing in their respective areas and the field offices in India are responsible for providing information services to tourists and to monitor the progress of field projects.

The Ministry of Tourism is also having under its control a public sector xi) undertaking viz. The India Tourism Development Corporation and the following autonomous institutes:

i) Indian Institute of Tourism and Travel Management (IITTM).
ii) National Council for Hotel Management and Catering Technology and the Institutes under its control (NCHMCT).
iii) National Institute of Water Sports (NIWS).
iv) Indian Institute of Skiing and Mountaineering (IISM).

Role and function of the ministry of tourism

The Ministry of Tourism functions as the nodal agency for the development of tourism in the country It has to play a crucial role in coordinating and supplementing the efforts of the State/Union Territory Governments, catalysing private investment, strengthening promotional and marketing efforts and in providing trained manpower resources. The functions of the Ministry in this regard mainly consist of the following:

i) Policy Formulation and Planning
ii) Coordination
iii) Infrastructure and Product Development
iv) Regulation
v) Human Resource Development
vi) Publicity, Marketing and Facilitation
vii) Research, Analysis, Monitoring and Evaluation

viii) International Cooperation and External Assistance

ix) Public Sector Undertaking and Autonomous bodies

x) Legislation and Parliament Work

xi) Establishment, Welfare and Vigilance Functions and Progressive Use of Hindi.

3

Policy, Planning and Co-ordination

Tourism policy

Recognising its importance as an instrument for economic development, a comprehensive tourism policy highlighting the objectives of tourism development in the country was promulgated by the Government during 1982. The policy envisaged the conversion of the many attractions of India for tourism into a reality through well planned, well defined and fully integrated national programmes. It specified the responsibility for tourism development as a common endeavour of all the agencies vitally concerned with tourism at Central and State levels including public and private sector enterprises; airlines, railways and road transport systems; municipal and local bodies as well as cultural and educational institutions. Further, it provided an action plan based on a 'travel circuit' concept to maximise the benefits of tourism. The plan proposed to achieve intensive development of selected circuits, dispel the tendency of concentration in a few urban centres, encourage the diversification of tourist attractions and opening up economically backward areas, which hold many tourist attractions. Manpower development and training were also given due weightage to ensure efficient services and effective management of tourist facilities.

Tourism was recognised as an industry by 1986 and became eligible for several incentives and facilities including tax incentives, subsidies, priorities in the sanctioning of loans by the State Financial Institutions and preferences in providing electricity and water connections. In July, 1991, tourism was also declared as a priority sector for foreign investment. In order to take advantage of the liberalised economic regime and the developments taking place around the World, a new National Tourism Policy has been drafted and the same is under the consideration of the Government.

National action plan for tourism

A National Action Plan for Tourism was drawn up in May 1992 and it included a set of strategies for achieving a phenomenal growth in tourist arrivals, foreign exchange earnings and employment generation through tourism. These strategies consisted of:

(a) Improvement of Tourism infrastructure;
(b) Developing areas on a selective basis for integrated growth along with marketing of destinations to ensure optimal use of existing infrastructure.
(c) Restructuring and strengthening of the institutions for development of human resources.
(d) Evolving a suitable policy for increasing foreign tourist arrivals and foreign exchange earnings.

Travel circuits and destinations

As stipulated in the National Action Plan for Tourism, 25 circuits and destinations have been identified for development through the joint efforts of Central and State Governments and the Private Sector. These are:

Travel Circuits

(a) Kullu-Manali-Lahul/Spiti-Leh-Monastic Circuit
(b) Gwalior-Shivpuri-Orchha-Khajuraho

(c) Bagdogra-Sikkim-Darjeeling-Kalimpong

(d) Bhubaneswar-Puri-Konark

(e) Hyderabad-Nagarjunasagar-Tirupati

(f) Chennai-Mahabalipuram-Kancheepurarn-Vellur-Thiruvannamalai Ginjee-Pondicherry (Southern Heritage Circuit)

(g) Rishikesh-Narendranagar-Gangotri-Badrinath

(h) Bhopal-Sanchi-Indore-UjjainMaheshwar-Omkaresh-war-Mandu (Bhopal and Sanchi)

(i) Jaisalmer-jodhpur-Bikaner-Barmer

(j) Bangalore-Mysore-Hassan

(k) Raigad Fort-Janjira Fort-Kuda Caves-Sirivardhan-Harihareshwar-Sindhudurg

(l) Varanasi/Sarnath-Gorakhpurl Kushinagar- Sunali-Piprahwa (Kapilvastu),-Sankisa-Kausambi- Sravasti-Lucknow (Buddhist Circuit)

(m) Patna-Bodhgaya-Nalanda-Rajgir-Vaishalin (Buddhist Circuit)

(n) Bhubaneswar-Lalitgiri-Ratnagiri-Udaygari-Kendraparha-Chand Bali Bhadrak (Sun Temple)

(o) Cochin-Thekkady-Madurai-Rameswaram

(p) Harishankar-Narsinghanath-Hirakud-Sambalpur-Bed Vyas (Gandhamardhan Circuit)

(q) Swaranchuda Circuit-Chandipur-Chandaneshwar-Panchelingeswar-Simlipal Sanctuary- Khiching. ArakuValley-Nandapur-GupteshwarRayagada (Panchabati Circuit)

(r) Guwahati-Kaziranga-Shillong-Tawang

Destinations

(a) Ajanta-Ellora (Aurangabad)

(b) Andaman Islands

(c) Bekal Beach
(d) Diu (Damn & Diu)
(e) Kangra (Pong Dam)
(f) Lakshadweep Islands
(g) Manali (Solang Nalah)
(h) Muttukadu-Mamallapuram
(i) Puri
(j) Sindhudurg

Pilgrim Centres

Nineteen Pilgrim Centres in 12 States and 2 Circuits in U P have been identified for development:

Sl. No.	State	Centre
1.	Assam	Kamakhya
2.	Bihar	Bodhgaya and Patna
3.	Gujarat	Dwarka, Palitana and Odwada(Near Vapi)
4.	Himachal Pradesh	Paonta Saheb and Jwalaji
5.	Jammu & Kashmir	Mata Vaishno Devi
6.	Karnataka	Gulbarga and Sringeri
7.	Kerala	Guruvayur
8.	Madhya Pradesh	Ujjain
9.	Maharashtra	Shirdi, Nanded Jyotiba (in Kolhapur District)
10.	Orissa	Jagannath Puri
11.	Rajasthan	Ajmer Shateef

12.	Tamil Nadu	Rameswaram
13.	Uttar Pradesh	(i) Badrinath - Kedarnath - Gangotri - Yamunotri -
		(2) Barsana - Nandgaon - Brindavan - Gowardhan

Special tourism areas

The State Governments of Kerala, Tamil Nadu, Orissa and Maharashtra and Union Territory administration of Daman and Diu declared Bekal Beach (Kerala), Puri-Konark Area (Orissa), sindhudurg (Muttakadu - mamallapuram (Tamil Nadu) and Diu as special tourism area for integrated development.

Eighth five year plan

The Planning Commission had approved an outlay of Rs. 240 crores excluding Rs. 32 crores to be generated by ITDC as internal resources and borrowings for the plan activities of the Department of Tourism during Eighth Plan against an outlay of Rs. 138.68 crores for the Seventh Plan. The break up was as given below:

Annual plan allocations during eighth plan

The allocation provided by the Planning Commission for each of the years of Eighth Plan so far and the expenditure are as given below:

(Rs.in crores)

Year	DOT		ITDC		Total	
	Outlay	Exp.	Outlay	Exp.	Outlay	Exp.
1992-93	76.00	73.57	4.00	5.00	80.00	78.57
1993-94	80.20	78.24	5.00	5.00	85.20	83.24

1994-95	92.81	92.81	-	-	92.81	92.81
1995-96	92.00	92.00	-	-	92.00	92.87
1996-97	90.00	89.25	-	-	90.00	89.25
Total	431.01	425.87	9.00	10.00	440.01	436.74

Thrust areas during the Eighth Plan

With a view to accelerate the overall growth of tourism, the following activities were given considerable attention during Eighth Plan period:

— Development of selected tourist places/ areas.
— Diversification of tourism to include holiday and leisure tourism
— Development of trekking, winter sports, wildlife and beach resort tourism.
— Exploring new source markets in regions and countries having cultural affinity.
— Restoration of National Heritage Projects.
— Launching of national image building and marketing plans in key markets.
— Providing inexpensive accommodation in different tourist centres.
— Improving service efficiency in public sector corporation.

Strategy in the Ninth Plan

The basic strategy during the Ninth Plan is to establish effective co-ordination with all the relevant agencies so as to achieve synergy in the development of tourism.

The specific components of the development activity during the Ninth Plan have been outlined as:

— Infrastructure development
— Product development and diversification including development of mega tourism resorts.

— Entrepreneurship development and promotion of self employment opportunities.
— Enhanced tourist facilitation.
— Human resources development.
— Environmental protection and cultural preservation.
— Provision of incentives
— Monitoring and evaluation.
— Strengthening of organisation.

The approach during the ninth plan would be to concentrate on a few selected centres and circuits to achieve balanced development of infrastructure in an integrated manner. As a result, the Central Government assistance to State/U.T. Governments for infrastructure development would be confined to such identified centres and circuits each year till they are saturated. The projects which are commercially viable will be funded under the equity scheme except in the North Eastern States, Sikkim and hill districts of West Bengal and Uttar Pradesh. The normal funding scheme would be generally applicable only to purely promotional and product development projects and the above areas where the equity funding pattern is not insisted upon. In general, emphasis would be given to integrated development projects and mega tourism resorts rather than spreading the resources too thinly over a number of small projects in a multitude of locations. However, in the case of North Eastern States, Sikkim and hill districts of Uttar Pradesh and West Bengal, the existing pattern of assistance would be continued. The strategy outlined above would be applicable only in the case of centrally assisted schemes and projects. The State/UT Governments would decide their own strategies and priorities in respect of funds provided under their own budget. It would be, however, insisted that centrally assisted projects are given due attention.

And the necessary linkages with sectoral schemes are established. The Planning Commission has approved an outlay of Rs. 511.32 crores as budgetary support during the Ninth Plan period excluding Rs. 319.23 crores to be generated by ITDC through internal and extra budgetary resources. The gross break-up of approved outlay is given below:

Sl. No.	Name of the Scheme	Rs. in crores
1.	Infrastructure Development	100.00
2.	Product Development	20.00
3.	Mega Tourism	5.00
4.	Tourism Development Fund	5.00
5.	Marketing & Publicity	300.00
6.	Manpower Development	60.00
7.	Incentives	15.00
8.	Research, Computerisation & Monitoring	3.00
9.	Organisation	2.00
10.	External Aid through Budget	1.32
	Total	511.32

Annual Plan Allocation provided by Planning Commission for the first two years of the Ninth Plan is given below:

	Ministry of Tourism Plan Outlay	ITDC	Total
1997-98	110.35*	70	180.35
1998-99	160.50	70	230.50

Plan Outlay was reduced to Rs 100.35 crores at the time of Revised Estimates.

Co-ordination

Tourism comprises the activities of persons travelling to and staying in places outside their usual environment for not more than one consecutive year for leisure, business and other purposes. These persons invariably seek a pleasant and delectable experience on their trips. The most desired tourism product should therefore consist of:

— an environment of peace and stability
— an assurance of safety and security an affable host society an industry and a Government that provide the requisite services with a smile.
— absence of extortions and hostility
— accessible tourist attractions, and an integrated system of physical infrastructure that does not fail. These include:
— international air seat capacity
— internal transport system
— hotels and restaurants
— entertainment and recreational avenues
— shopping and communication facilities
— well preserved monuments with tourist amenities
— basic amenities like drinking water, toilets, snack bars, etc. at the tourist sites

Just like raw materials get converted into finished products by moving through various machines in a processing system, the different components of tourism supply should be so organised that the expectations of the tourist while planning the trip get converted into full satisfaction and pleasant memories on his/her return. It means there should be perfect coordination and linkages in the availability and performance of all components of tourism infrastructure.

Tourism development is thus a composite subject and does not necessarily mean the development of only the tourism facilities like hotels, restaurants, recreational activities, etc. In fact, creation of tourism infrastructure will be meaningful only if the area has the minimum basic amenities and infrastructure like roads, water, electricity, sewerage and telecommunication facilities. This aspect was given importance in the Tourism 'Synergy' programme and it was the first attempt in this regard. Subsequently, the State Governments were asked to prepare master Plans for the development of tourism based on the same concept.

A National Strategy for the Development of Tourism was drawn up during 1996 for achieving a greater realisation of the importance of tourism, a consensus on the developmental needs, positive contribution of all the infrastructural departments in a co-ordinated manner, higher plan allocations and introduction of new schemes for the accelerated development of tourism. The strategy has been endorsed by the Government and a 'Board of Tourism Industry and Trade' has been set up for coordinating the activities of different departments for tourism development. Considering the importance of ensuring co-ordination and synergy in tourism development, a Group of Ministers under the chairmanship of the Minister of Tourism and a Standing Committee of Secretaries under the chairmanship of the Cabinet Secretary have been set-up by the Government.

Constitution of task force

The Department of Tourism also constituted Special Task Force for the promotion of schemes/projects for the development of tourism in North Eastern States, Sikkim, Jammu & Kashmir, Himachal Pradesh and Hill districts of Uttar Pradesh and West Bengal. Senior Officers of the Department along with representatives of respective State Governments and industry visited these areas and action plans for North Eastern States and Jammu & Kashmir have been prepared.

4

Infrastructure and Product Development

Pattern of assistance

Since most of the tourist attractions and delivery systems are within the purview of State/UT Governments, a large part of the Central Government investment for the improvement and creation of tourist facilities is channelised through the State Governments on a cost sharing basis. The State Governments generally meet the cost of land and its development while the Central Department meet the cost of construction, etc. This method of central assistance has been continuing since Second Five Year Plan and is most popular with the State Governments. It is found to be very useful in achieving a coordinated development of tourist facilities. The schemes assisted through this method include:

(a) Construction of budget accommodations, tourist complexes, forest lodges, tented accommodation, tourist reception centres, etc.

(b) Development of special tourism areas, pilgrim centres and other centres identified for intensive development.

(c) Development of adventure and sports tourism facilities.

(d) Development of tourist transport facilities.

(e) Promotion of fairs and festivals and rural craft melas and flood lighting/ Sound and Light **Shows in** monuments, etc.

A new method of funding by way of grant-in-aid towards project cost was introduced during 1992-93. As per the scheme, 28 per cent of the project cost is provided by the Central Government and 12 per cent is provided by the State Government. The balance 60 per cent has to be raised as loan from financial institutions or banks. This method of funding is applicable to bankable projects requiring large investments. It is expected that the State Governments would be able to mobilise more resources from financial institutions for investment in tourism projects through this method. In the initial years, the State Governments did not show much interest in this method of funding as they were generally not interested in availing loan facilities for putting-up developmental projects. It was, therefore, proposed to reallocate a major part of the funds provided for the scheme to normal funding schemes. The remaining budget was proposed to be used to meet the committed liabilities in respect of already sanctioned projects. However, some of the State Governments became aware of the significance of the scheme and came up with new projects for financial assistance. The scheme is, therefore, being continued along with the normal funding scheme. All bankable projects with substantial financial requirements are funded under this scheme while the developmental projects not requiring heavy investments are funded under the normal scheme. Procedure for Central Financial Assistance The State Governments desirous of availing of the central assistance prepare a list of projects proposed to be taken up during a particular year and discuss the same with the Central Department of Tourism during the beginning of each financial year. On the basis of these discussions, a number of projects which conform to the norms of approved schemes and useful from the point of view of tourism are short-listed or prioritised. The State Government/Union Territory Administration are required to submit the project proposals in prescribed'C'form along with following documents:- A certificate to the effect that the developed piece of land is readily available and the same is in possession of the State Government (State Tourism Department) and the land/title of the land will be transferred in favour of Govt. of India free of charge and free of cost. The certificate should also indicate the exact location of land with site measurement, name of the place and district, etc. along with an undertaking in prescribed format from the State Government, as given in'C'form. Blue prints, drawings, details of the proposed facilities to be created with rate per sq. metre and estimated cost of each of the facility. Estimates, prepared / vetted by the CPWD/State PWD (approved Civil Engineering Wing), as the case may be. Location map of the proposed project along with tourist map of the state. Description about the tourist Centre along with tourist traffic for the last three years, facilities already available, if any, and full justification for creation of the proposed facility.

The projects and proposals received with the above details are scrutinised with reference to the norms of approved schemes, their desirability and availability of resources. The projects satisfying the existing guidelines are then approved for financial assistance. The actual releases against the sanctioned projects are made in 3 to 4 instalments. The first instalment is normally released as an advance and the subsequent instalments are released on submission of utilisation certificates in respect of the funds already released. The total release made to any State Government in a year thus depends upon the efficiency of that State in executing the project.

Criteria for grant of assistance

The criteria for grant of assistance to State Government for the development of tourism include the following:

(a) The Demand Criteria: The number of popular tourist destinations in the State/UT and volume of tourist traffic to them.

(b) The Supply Criteria: The feedback received from the overseas offices, travel intermediaries and tourists regarding shortage of tourist facilities in respective centres.

(c) Past Performance and Capacity Criteria: The capacity of the State/UT to absorb assistance.

(d) The unique attractions of the State.

(e) The destinations and circuits identified in the National Action Plan for intensive development of tourism

Special tourism areas

The National Action Plan 1992 envisaged the intensive development of some of the tourist circuits and destinations in coordination with the State Governments and the private sector. A number of new circuits and destinations were thus identified and emphasis was given for the development of these circuits and areas.

Bekal in Kerala was identified as a special tourism area and a Development Authority for the Bekal Beach has been set up. The State Government also established a Bekal Resorts Corporation.A master plan for the development of the area has been prepared and land acquisition as well as development work have been taken up.

The Government of Maharashtra constituted an administrative body under the Chairmanship of Chief Secretary of Maharashtra for the development of Sindhudurg as a special tourism area. The State

Government also declared a stretch of 84 km between Sindhudurg and Vijaydurg as special tourism area and a concrete plan for the development of the area has been prepared.

The Puri-Konark Beach was initially identified as a special tourism area. However, due to the non clearance of the project by the Ministry of Environment and Forest in the specified area, the State Government identified an area South of Puri for the establishment of the special tourism area. The Central Department of Tourism has prioritised a project for the preparation of the master plan of Puri 3.16 special tourism area.

The State Government of Tamil Nadu constituted a State *Level Authority* for setting up a special tourism area in the Muttukadu-Mamallapuram beach. The State Government is yet to prepare the master plan for which the Central Department of Tourism has *agreed to* provide financial assistance.

An amount of Rs.1.25 crores was released to various State Governments during 1997-98 for the intensive development of various circuits and destinations.

Budget accommodation

The Department of Tourism is laying special emphasis on the creation of facilities for domestic tourist and is particularly keen that there should be more movement of people from one region to another. To provide budget accommodation for domestic and foreign tourists, Yatri Niwases, Tourist Complexes, Tourist Lodges, Tourist Hostels/Homes are being provided at a number of places in the country.

Wayside amenities

Recognising the importance of a well-knit network of wayside amenities to *keep* pace with the fast developing highway tourism in the country, the construction of wayside facilities on the roads leading to or connecting important tourist centres has been taken up for implementation. These include tourist reception *centres*, cafeterias, restaurants, motels, public conveniences, etc. During 1997-98, an amount of Rs.3.23 crores was released to State Governments for creation of wayside amenities in the country.

Refurbishment of Monuments

The mainstay of Indian tourism is cultural tourism around the magnificent monuments and heritage centres located in different parts of the country. Both foreign and domestic tourists visit these monuments and derive intense pleasure by experiencing the journey back to the ages. With a view to retain the glory of these monuments and to provide visitor facilities around them the Department has taken up a scheme for the refurbishment of monuments and improvement of their environs. The scheme was started during 1995-96 and a sum of Rs.1.22 crores was released during the Eighth Plan period. During 1997-98, an amount of Rs.1.77 crores was released under the scheme tc various executing agencies.

Integrated Development of Tourist/Pilgrim Centres

In order to ensure integrated development of the infrastructural facilities including basic amenities in the identified tourist/pilgrim centres, it has been decided to provide financial assistance to the State/Union Territory Governments for the implementation of composite projects in 50 selected centres. The maximum assistance will be Rs one crore, subject to matching contribution by the State Governments, and it will be provided over a period of two years at the rate of Rs. 50 lakhs per year.

Adventure tourism

As a part of the policy for the diversification of tourism product of India, special attention is being given for the development of eco-tourism and adventure tourism. Ministry of Tourism thus formulated a comprehensive Eco-tourism Policy and Guidelines in consultation with all the concerned 3.22 agencies. A set of guidelines on adventure tourism has also been formulated by the industry.

The Ministry of Tourism is also continuing to provide financial assistance to State/Union Territory Governments to put up infrastructural facilities for trekking, rock climbing, mountaineering, aero-sports, winter/water related sports, trekkers' huts, wildlife viewing facilities, etc.

Trekking equipments were provided to Himachal Pradesh, Mizoram, Nagaland and Uttar Pradesh. Financial assistance for provision of water sports equipments consisting of kayaks, canoes, paddle boats, fiberglass boats, hovercrafts, water scooters, etc. have been extended to Tripura, Mizoram, Kerala, Delhi and Goa. In most of the cases, balance funds were released during 1998-99 on completion of the projects.

The Gulmarg Winter Sports Project (GWSP) was established in 1968 to popularise Kashmir as a tourist destination and develop winter sports with a view to attracting tourists during the lean winter season and to provide gainful employment to the local people. During 1998-99, funds have been released for conducting ski courses for 1998-99 season.

Since 1992, the promotion of other destinations such as Patnitop (Udhampur District, J&K), Sanasar (Doda District, J&K) and Auli (Garhwal Hills, UP) for winter sports have also been taken up. Para-gliding courses were conducted at Solang Nallah through Indian Institute of Skiing and Mountaineering.

Earlier surveys were conducted to open up new centres for Skiing Resorts in Himachal Pradesh. Based on the survey report received from Government of Himachal Pradesh, proposal for setting up Of Ski Resort at Pabber Valley was examined. This will be considered during the Ninth Five Year Plan. Detailed proposal is awaited.

Regular heliskiing operation took place in Manali region and Government of Himachal Pradesh and the organizers were extended required assistance. Similarly, Department of Tourism extended support for successful operation of Himalayan Run and Trek; Annual event in Darjeeling (West Bengal) from 6th -16th November, 1998.

For promotion of aero-sports, aero-sports, equipments (para-sailing equipments/accessories) have been provided for running aero-sports at Jolly Grant, Dehradun (UP), Manipur, Mizoram, Nagaland, etc. In some of these cases, balance funds were released based on utilization certificates.

Special efforts were made by the Department of Tourism to promote Inland Water Tourism by providing necessary infrastructural facilities. Financial assistance was extended for purchase of boats at Sukhna Lake, Chandigarh; Dadra & Nagar Haveli; for purchase of boats and shikaras for Naini Lake, etc.

For promotion of water sports activities, funds were released for purchase of water sports equipment at Kerala, Lakshadweep, Manipur, Watersports complex at Mahe, Pondicherry; Watersports Centre at Kulavai Lake, Tamil Nadu; River Rafting equipment for J&K, etc.

Son-et-Lumiere/Floodlighting

In order to make some of the tourist destinations more

attractive for the tourists, the Ministry of Tourism in collaboration with the Archaeological Survey of India (ASI), has formulated schemes for SEL/Floodlighting of monuments. The Ministry of Tourism provides financial assistance to State Governments/Union Territories to meet the equipment cost of such facilities. So far during 1998-99, funds have been released for Son-et-Lumiere at Gurudwara Anandpur Sahib, Punjab; Khajuraho; Tirumalai Nayak Palace, Madurai (TamilNadu); Neer Mahal Palace, Tripura; Ajmer, Jaipur; etc. Funds have also been released to State Governments of Punjab, Delhi and Bihar for floodlighting/high-mast lighting of various monuments.

Himalayan Tourism Advisory Board (HIMTAB)

Certain decisions had been taken at the HIMTAB Meet held in Mussoorie, UP in 1996. Most of the member-States have taken actions according to the decisions taken.

5

Development and Regulation of Tourism Industry

Tourism Industry has been defined to include the following segments:

(a) Hotels, restaurants, resorts and other tourist complexes providing accommodation and/or catering and food facilities to tourists.

(b) Travel agencies, tour operators and tourist transport operators.

(c) Units providing facilities for cultural, adventure and wildlife experience to tourists.

(d) Surface,water and air transport facilities for tourists.

(e) Leisure,entertainment, amusement,sports and health units for tourists,and

(f) Convention/Seminar units and organisations.

Tourism as a Priority Sector

As a consequence of economic restructuring and liberalisation policies, the tourism industry was declared as a priority sector for foreign investment. The horizons for foreign investment in the tourism sector were widened and it is eligible for automatic approval of direct foreign investment up to 51 per cent of the equity since July 1991. Higher foreign equity participation in specific cases is also allowed on a case to case basis. Non-Resident Indian investment is allowed up to 100%. Automatic approvals are given for foreign technology agreements and management contracts within specified parameters. Under these revised guidelines, 311 proposals involving foreign investment of Rs.34885.10 (Million) were approved till the end of August,1998.

Investment Facilitation Cell

An "Investment Cell" was set up in August, 95 to undertake the following activities:

(a) Formulation of national investment policies in respect of tourism industries.

(b) Co-ordination and integration of State policies on tourism.

(c) Prepare investment profiles for each State in collaboration with the respective State Governments. These profiles will include information on identified priority centres for tourism development, details of existing infrastructure, expected demand, availability of land and other support services, agencies to be contacted, etc.

(d) Regular interactions with prospective entrepreneurs both within the country and abroad to promote investment in tourism.

(e) Establishing linkages with the Ministry of External Affairs to highlight investment opportunities in tourism abroad through their investment cell.

(f) Process investment proposals received from both local and foreign investors and obtain approvals and clearances from various agencies like FIPB, SIA, Environment Ministry, etc.

(g) Assist the entrepreneurs in getting import licenses, finance, land etc. by co-ordinating with the respective agencies and the State Governments.

(h) Provide technical assistance wherever required.

(i) In consultation with State Governments, devise a "Single Window System" to facilitate investors to obtain various clearances speedily.

(j) To formulate a statutory framework for identification, creation and establishment of Special Tourism Area and Mega Tourism Projects for development Of tourism infrastructure.

(k) To co-ordinate with the 'Investment Promotion and Infrastructure Development Cell' in the Ministry of Industry with regard to infrastructural requirements, facilitation and monitoring of investment in the tourism sector.

Since its inception, three years ago, the investment cell has attended to over 16000 postal inquiries, met individually several hundred prospective investors in Delhi, Agra, Mumbai, Chennai, Thiruvananthapuram, Bhubaneswar and Jaipur; organised and participated in the Investor 95' in Jaipur and at Hyderabad in 1997. The cell with the assistance of National Informatics Centre (NIC) has designed software in the 'ORACLE' system to specifically meet the information needs of the investor. This cell is in correspondence with all the investors and provides guidelines for setting up of tourism units and investment opportunities in various states with the contact addresses of the state departmental officials.

Incentives for Tourism Industry

Tourism is the second largest net foreign exchange earner by way of invisible exports. Tourism creates more jobs than any other sector for every rupee invested. It also creates the jobs at the local level, dispersing with the need of migration to distant places for earning of livelihood. In fact, tourism plays a major role in promoting large-scale employment opportunities. Keeping in view all this, the Government has accorded

Export House Status to tourism industry. Hotels, Travel Agents, Tour Operators and Tourist Transport Operators are now entitled for recognition as Export House/ Trading House/Star Trading House/Super Star Trading House on earning free foreign exchange in accordance with prefixed slabs and shall be entitled to certain benefits. This would definitely go a long way in the promotion of and investment in Tourism.

The endeavour of the Government is to achieve sustained growth of tourist facilities in the private sector and to ensure high standards of quality in their services. Tourism has been, therefore, given the status of an industry and several incentives have been made available both by the Central and State Governments. The incentives being made available by the Central Government include:

a) Interest subsidy of 3% on loans taken from financial institutions is available to 1 to 3 star categories of hotel projects outside the metropolitan cities of Mumbai, Calcutta, Delhi and Chennai. A subsidy of 5% is available to such hotel projects if they are located in the travel circuits and destinations identified for intensive development as per National Action Plan for Tourism. Heritage Hotel projects are eligible for the higher rate of interest subsidy of 5%.

b) As a fiscal incentive, under Section 80 HHD, 50% of profits derived by hotels, travel agents and tour operators in foreign exchange are exempt from income tax. The balance amount of profits in foreign exchange is also exempt provided it is reinvested in tourism projects.

c) With efforts of the Ministry of Tourism, the Ministry of Finance have reintroduced Section 80 IA (iii a) for the hotel units, which start operating between 1.4.97 and 31.3.2001. The hotels located in the rural areas, hilly areas and places of pilgrimage are allowed 50% exemption in their profits, whereas for hotels located in the other areas under Section 80 IA (iv a), the exemption is 30%. This is however, not applicable to hotels located in the four cities of Mumbai, Delhi, Calcutta and Chennai.

(d) Benefits have also been made available under the Liberalised Exchange Rate Management System (LERMS). 4.9 Hotels, travel agents, tour operators and other tourism industries have been given facility to open and operate Exchange Earners Foreign Currency (EEFC) Account. The procedure for release of foreign exchange for 4.10 specified purposes have been streamlined and liberalised.

(e) Import of special items for hotel industry is permitted subject to import entitlement. Concessional customs duty is charged for import of specified goods required for initial setting up or substantial expansion of hotels.

(f) In terms of the policy announced in the Parliament on 3rd May, 1993, a new Export Promotion Capital Goods (EPCG) Scheme was introduced for the Service Sector which includes hotels and restaurants, travel agents and tour operators. Under this Scheme, capital goods can be imported at a concessional duty of 15 per cent subject to fulfilment of an export obligation over a period of time. The duty has now been reduced to 10%The hotel sector is now eligible for import under Zero Duty also.

National Tourism Awards and Awards of Excellence

Ministry of Tourism presents National Tourism Awards and Awards of Excellence for various segments of travel and tourism industry every year. National Tourism Awards are presented to classified hotels including heritage hotels, approved travel agents, tour operators and tourist transport operators in recognition of their performance in their respective fields and also to encourage healthy competition in order to promote tourism.

Awards of Excellence introduced in 1996 are also presented to various other segments of travel and tourism industry.

National Tourism Awards are given to all the approved segments of travel industry viz: travel agents, tour operators, tourist transport operators, classified hotels including heritage hotels and restaurants independent of hotels.

The criteria for selection of the awards under these categories is as follows:

Travel Agents/Tour Operators

A total of 12 National Awards are given to travel agents and tour operators on the basis of their foreign exchange earnings categorised as under:

Category	Foreign Exchange Earnings
Category - I	Over Rs. 15 crores
Category - II	Rs. 7 - 15 crores
Category - III	Rs. 2 - 7 crores
Category - IV	Rs. 1 - 2 crores

Selection of Awards is considered on the basis of foreign exchange earnings from handling inbound tours. Due weightage is given for the growth rate achieved in foreign exchange earnings.

In addition to the above, there are two special National Tourism Awards, one each in the category of 'Adventure Tourism' and 'Conference Tourism basis for selection of these awards highest foreign exchange earnings respective categories.

Tourist Transport Operators

There are three National Awards under the following categories based on the foreign exchange earnings:

Category	Foreign Exchange Earnings
Category - I	Over Rs. 50 lakhs
Category -II	Rs. 15 - 50 lakhs
Catrgory -III	Less than Rs. 15 lakhs

The criteria is the foreign exchange earning based on business transacted through travel agents, tour operators, hoteliers and FITS, etc.

Classified Hotels

Six National Awards and 18 Regional Awards are presented to the classified hotels as per the following classification:

5 Star deluxe :	One National Award + 3 Regional Awards
5 Star	One National Award + 3 Regional Awards
4 Star	One National Award + 3 Regional Awards
3 Star	One National Award + 3 Regional Awards
2 Star	One National Award + 3 Regional Awards
1 Star	One National Award + 3 Regional Awards

The basis for National Tourism Awards for approved hotels is the foreign exchange earning and foreign tourists handled. The star category classifications are based on the ambience, services, facilities, etc.

Heritage Hotels

Under this category, there are three National Awards; one each for Heritage Grand, Heritage Classic and HeritageHotels. The criteria for selection is based on efforts for preservation and promotion of heritage including ambience, local cuisine, activities and provision of modern amenities, etc.

Restaurants Independent of Hotels

Under this category, there is one National Award and three Regional Awards. Only restaurants approved by Ministry of Tourism, Government of India are eligible. Weightage is given to the ambience, cuisine, services, cleanliness, hygiene, staff, turnover, foreign exchange earned, crockery, cutlery etc.

Awards of Excellence

Awards of Excellence introduced in 1996 are given to various other segments of travel and tourism industry for their meritorious services. For the year 199798, these awards will be given for the following categories:

(a) Excellence in writing/publication (one award each for Hindi and English writing/ publication).

(b) Tourism film / audio visual presentation.

(c) Most India friendly tour operator abroad.

(d) Best tourism performing state with a separate award for the North Eastern Region.

(e) Best maintained tourism friendly monument.

(f) Best maintained tourism friendly National Park/ Wild Life Sanctuary.

(g) Eco-friendly tourism project/ organisation.

(h) Most innovative and unique tourism project.

(i) Best tourism educational institution.

(j) Most innovative use of information technology.

In association with travel industry and other experts, the Ministry of Tourism has evolved certain criteria for each category of the Award of Excellence.

Excellence in Writing / Publication

Under this category there are two awards - one for writer/publication in English language and the other for writer/publication in Hindi language. In case of articles forwarded as entries, these should have been published in the relevant year in a reputed journal/newspaper magazine.

Tourism film/AV presentation

There is one award in this category for the year 1997-98 (April - March). Entries from Indian producers only are to be considered.

Most India friendly overseas tour operators

Apart from one award at the National level under this category, there are five awards called "The Overseas Regional Tourism Awards".

The Regional Awards are presented by the concerned Regional Directors of the Government of India Tourist Offices at (d) special'India Evenings'which would giveimpetus to other operators in the area.

The Regional Director, Govt. of India Tourist Offices abroad would forward their recommendations about the best tour operator in their region. Criteria for selection would include amongst other points:

(a) The number of tourists the country has sent to India vis-vis tour operator in question.

(b) At least three years, business profile in terms of number of tourists handled to determine the growth rate.

(c) Special emphasis would be laid on:

(i) Continued support to tourism to India even during the crisis period.

(ii) Number of years of continued operation to India to assess the long term commitment.

Best tourism performing state

There are two awards in this category viz., one for the North Eastern States including Sikkim and the other for the remaining States. The awards are decided on the basis of the following:

(a) Investment facilitation efforts of the State Government including investment friendly policies on tourism, provision of incentives, identification of investment projects, project clearance mechanisms, sound taxation policies and joint ventures with private sector.

(b) Number of centrally assisted infrastructure projects completed during the previous year and the percentages of completed infrastructure projects sanctioned during the previous two plan periods.

(c) Existing state owned tourist complexes (number of units and number of rooms) and their financial performance in terms of average gross profit per unit.

(d) State plan allocation for tourism sector during the previous year and its share in the total plan allocation of the State and the details of innovative schemes and projects taken up.

(e) Magnitude of international and domestic tourist visits registered in the State during the previous year and the percentage change.

(f) Efforts of the State Government in human resource development in terms of number of State owned training institutes and their intake, guide training and other training courses conducted along with number of trainees and other achievements.

(g) Promotional and marketing efforts in terms of promotional literature, films, audio-visual and materials produced in the previous year, use of computers and multi-media technologies in tourism promotion and participation in tourism trade fairs and exhibitions both within the country and abroad.

(h) Efforts of the State Government in ensuring sustainability in tourism development in terms of protection of ecology and environment and enhancing (a) the attractiveness of heritage sites and their surroundings and educating the local community about the significance of (b) our cultural heritage and environment.

(i) Performance of the State Government is preventing touting and atrocities against tourists.

Best maintained tourism friendly monument

(a) There is one award in this category. The monuments on the list of Archaeological Survey of India, State Archaeological Survey and State Government are considered for the award on the basis of land-scaping, maintenance, public conveniences, monthwise number of visitors, photo/film/transparency and eco/environment friendliness of the monument.

Best maintained tourism friendly national park/ wild life sanctuary

The selection criteria for this award is the following:

(a) Policies and guidelines prepared by the State Parks/UT`s for promotion of Wild Life Tourism.

(b) Best maintained facilities for accommotion/transport, approach roads with their quality.

(c) Signages

(d) Trained guides, wild life viewing facilities, public conveniences,cleanliness, visitor interpretation centre, promotional material, eco-friendly environment, (e) conservation means, etc.

(e) Any other activity which promotes the cause of adventure tourism.

Best eco-friendly tourism project/organisation

The choice of the best eco-friendly project/ organisation is based on the following criteria:

(a) Policies and guidelines prepared by the State/UT Governments for sustainable development of tourism.

(b) Projects implemented by the State/UT Governments and the specific measures taken for ensuring preservation of ecology and environment in the implementation of the project.

(c) The training courses/workshops organised by the State on sustainable development of tourism.

(d) Awareness creation activities among all segments of the tourism population.

(e) Any other activity relevant to sustainable development of tourism.

Most Innovative and unique tourism project

There is one award in this category. The criteria for selection is as follows

(a) Description of the existing environmental scene.

(b) New and original concept. Proper implementation of the concept. Enhancement of the quality of the are a around the project.

(c) Environment modified by the project and how best it matches with the environment Aesthetic impacts.

(d) Any study or research made on water quality impacts, noise impacts, pollution, protection of flora fauna, air quality, carrying capacity, etc. before taking up the project.

(e) Eco-friendly practices adopted in the project affluent treatment, energy saving system, water solar power utilisation, etc.

(f) Environment design adopted -'Land use Plan', use of local material, etc.

(g) Volume of tourists - length of stay - any regulation.

(h) Strength of local culture and local manpower utilisation. How much the project benefits the locals, specially with regard to improvement in the standard of living, local participation.

(i) Publicity and promotional efforts.

(j) Transport facilities.

(k) Check-list maintained for judging different types of impacts / typically associated with different types of physical development.

(1) Efforts to project outstanding natural features for public benefit, education and enjoyment.

(m) Any additional information from the participant.

Best tourism educational institute

There is one award in this category. The criteria for selection would include the following:

(a) The Institute should be imparting education in one of the Tourism disciplines.

(b) Assessment is made on the basis of the qualitative and quantitative data to be provided by the Institute which would cover areas like courses offered, facilities for training, performance of the trainees, placement and campus recruitment, research and development achievements of students/faculty, etc.

Approval and classification of hotels

The Ministry of Tourism approves hotel projects from the point of view of their suitability for international tourists. Various incentives and benefits are linked to such approvals. Till September 1998, 66 hotel projects were approved in various categories, which, on completion, would provide 3418 additional rooms for tourists.

The Hotel and Restaurant Approval and Classification Committee (HRACC) set up by the Ministry classifies the functioning hotels under the star system into six categories from one to 5 Star Deluxe. A new category of Heritage Hotels has also been introduced since 1994. The Ministry also reclassifies these hotels after every three years to ensure that the requisite standards are maintained by these hotels. The Committee set up for the purpose has representatives from Central Ministry of Tourism, State Governments and hotel and travel industry associations.

As on September, 1998, there were 1188 hotels with 65,598 rooms on the approved list of the Ministry of Tourism. The break up of these hotels by different star categories is as given below:

Star Category	No. of Hotels	No. of Rooms
5 Star Deluxe	45	11,160
5 Star	55	7,365
4 Star	76	5,652
Hertiage	48	1,356
3 Star	303	15,498
2 Star	319	11,208
1 Star	145	5,058
To be Classified	198	8,301
Total	1188	65,598

The classification of remaining hotels is in progress. To speed up the work of classification / reclassification of functioning hotels, pending hotels, four Regional Committees have also been set up in Delhi, Mumbai, Calcutta and Chennai to conduct inspection of hotels of one to three star categories.

During the year 1998,113 new hotels were classified and 112 existing hotels were reclassified. In addition, 20 restaurantswere approved and 7 reapproved during the year

Time share/apartment hotels

In a bid to increase budget/moderately priced accommodation, the Ministry of Tourism formulated guidelines for the approval of Time Share/Apartment Hotels. This concept is approximately 30 years old and has been operating successfully throughout the world. In our country, this is likely to attract a large number of middle class foreign tourists apart from catering to the needs of domestic travellers.

Heritage Hotels

The concept of Heritage hotels was introduced with a view to convert the old palaces, havelies, castles, forts and residences built prior to 1950 into accommodation units as these traditional structures reflect the ambience and lifestyle of the bygone era and are immensely popular with the tourists. The scheme is aimed at ensuring that such properties, landmarks of our heritage, are not lost due to decay but become financially viable properties providing additional room capacity for the tourists.

The Heritage hotels have also been sub-classified in the following categories:

— Heritage: This category covers hotels in residences/

havelies/hunting lodges/castles/forts/palaces built prior to 1950 but after 1935.

— Heritage Classic: This category cover hotelsin residences/ havelies/hunting lodges/castle/forts/ places built prior to1935 but 1920.

— Heritage Grand: This category covers hotels in residences /havelies/hunting lodges/castles/forts/ palaces built prior to 1920.

Till the end of September 1998,as many as 48 properties have been classified as Hertiage Hotelproviding a room capacity of 15948 rooms. Guidelines have also been formulated for conversion of Heritage properties into Heritage hotels and their approval at project planning stage. At present, 50 Heritage properties are approved as projects which, on completion, would add 945 rooms in the Heritage category.

The Ministry of Tourism through an advertisement campaign has invited attention of all the owners of havelies /old buildings for converting them into Heritage properties.

Paying guest accommodation and guest houses

As envisaged in the National Action Plan for the Tourism, two new schemes of Paying Guest Accommodation and Guest houses were introduced under Paying Guest Accommodation Scheme. House owners having lettable rooms of reasonable standards are approved and enlisted as Paying Guest Accommodation. Regional Committees consisting of representatives of Central Ministry of Tourism, State Tourism, Departments/ Corporation, tour operators, travel agent,hotels and the district administration were set up to register such accommodations.So far,1440 premises providing 5313 rooms have been approved.

Approval of Travel Trade

The Ministry of Tourism has a participation scheme of approving travel agents, tour operators and tourist transport operators. Under this scheme, from January 1997 till the end of September, 1998, 35 travel agents/tour operators and 22 tourist transport operators have been approved. This brings the cumulative number of approved agencies as under:

Travel Agents	235
Tour Operators	343
Tourist Transport Operators	186

Tourist charters

With the liberalisation of Charter Policy by the Ministry of Civil Aviation, 785 tourist charter flights were received in India during the year 1997 bringing a total of 1,00,711 tourists.

Tourist facilitation and complaints

The Inspection Unit of the Ministry of Tourism continued to handle matters relating to simplification of entry and exit formalities for tourists. Complaints made by foreign and domestic tourists were also handled and settled through Central and State Administrative Department by this Unit.

6

Human Resource Development

Training Programmes in the field of Hotel Management, Catering and Nutrition were first taken up by the Government in the year 1962 when the programme for training of personnel at Supervisory/Middle management level and Craft level were initiated by the Department of Food in the Ministry of Agriculture. To begin with, four Institutes of Hotel Management, Catering Technology and Applied Nutrition were set up at New Delhi, Mumbai, Chennai and Calcutta between 1962 and 1964. In order to meet the training requirements at craft levels in specific disciplines, 12 Foodcraft Institutes were also set up at different places in the country. The orientation of the training programmes, which were in vogue till 1982, underwent a sea change with the transfer of this programme to the Ministry of Tourism in October 1982. It was decided to orient the training towards meeting the requirements, of the accommodation and catering industry to produce a professional work force. In order to harness the resources and provide a central thrust, the Ministry of Tourism established the National Council for Hotel Management and Catering Technology in 1984. The main objectives of the council are:

(i) To advise the Government on coordinated development of Hotel Management and Catering Education.

(ii) To keep updated records of all international developments in this area and serve as a Technical Store house for use in framing suitable Training Programmes to affiliate institutions and prescribe courses of study and instructions leading to examinations conducted by it.

(iii) To standardise courses and infrastructure requirement.

(iv) To prescribe educational and other qualifications, experience, etc., for members of staff in the affiliated institutions and introduce faculty development programmes.

(v) To give certification and accredition at the national level.

As a result of the above changes that have taken place for expanding and modernising the training capabilities of the Hotel and Catering Education Programme, the profile of students of these institutions has undergone a change as also the reaction of the industry to their acceptance. At present, there are 20 Institute of Hotel Management and 14 Foodcraft Institutes functioning in the country, which include two such Institutes set up by the Government of Rajasthan. A list of *these Institutes* is given in Appendices IV and V, The proposed Institute of Hotel Management at Shillong in the State of Meghalaya is under active consideration. In order to strengthen the existing training infrastructure, Educational Grid consisting of National Culinary Institute, an Advanced Hotel, Management Institute, IITTM chapter and headquarters of National Council, are also proposed to be set up at Faridabad and Noida respectively. The current intake of candidates for the first year of the 3-year

Diploma Course in Hotel Management is 2275. In view of the increased demand for the courses, efforts are on to augment this number to 2500 or more by the next year.

Recognition of the diploma awarded by the national council

The Diploma Course in Hotel Management and Catering Technology has been recognised by the All India Council of Technical Education. The Diploma awarded by the Council has also been recognised by the international School of Hotel and Tourism Management of Luccerne, Switzerland and possibilities of tie-ups with other international Institutes are also being explored.

Affiliation of other institutes

Scheme for affiliation of privately run Institutes of Hotel Management and those set up by the State Governments including Foodcraft Institutes set up by the National Council for Hotel Management and Catering Technology has been finalised and will be implemented after clearance of Ministry of Law.

Management Pattern

All the Hotel Management and Foodcraft Institutes are registered under Societies Registration Act, 1860 and have separate Boards of Governors consisting of representatives of the Central Government, State Governments concerned as well as representatives of the industry.

The Institutes of Hotel Management, Catering Technology and Applied Nutrition and the National Council for Hotel Management and Catering Technology are funded by the Central Government through Grants-in-aid. Grants are released to these Institutes to cover their net revenue expenditure and capital expenditure for purchase of equipments, etc. and construction of the Institute building, staff quarters and students' hostel. The possibilities of funding the Institute through non-budgetary sources are also being explored. Land for the construction of these institutes which are located in different parts of the country, is given free of cost by the respective State Governments. In the case of Foodcraft Institutes, the financial responsibility rested with Central Government only for the first five years of their operation and thereafter with the respective State Governments.

Guide training

The institution, of guides is a very basic component of the tourist services both for international and domestic tourists. There has been a steady increase in the international tourist arrivals in the country. Further, as a result of increasing affluence, domestic tourist movement. In order to meet the increasing demand for guides both for international and domestic tourists, a 3-tier system of guides has been introduced so as to serve different market segments with effect from February, 1996. These are as under:

a) Regional Level Guides

To be trained by the Ministry of Tourism, Government of India through their tourist offices or by the Indian Institute of Tourism and Travel Management or their Chapters or by the Indian Institute of Hotel Management under the Ministry of Tourism, Government of India.

b) State Level Guides

To be trained by the State Governments.

c) Local Guides

To be trained under the supervision of the State Government/Local Administration.

Government of India Tourist Offices are requested to assess the requirement of fresh guides in the region from time to time and to take necessary action for conducting training courses in coordination with IITTM.

Refresher courses for approved Regional Level Guides have been made compulsory and these courses are conducted by IITTM in coordination with the concerned Government of India Tourist Office. In 1998-99, guide training courses have been conducted in Hyderabad and refresher courses have been conducted in Varanasi, Patan and Thiruvananthapuram. In addition, language courses and orientation programmes for customs/immigration officers and various service providers such as taxi drivers, porters, etc. have also been organised by Government of India Tourist Offices in Varanasi and Mumbai. It is proposed to conduct similar training courses for service providers in southern region by Regional Tourist Office in Chennai. As such, adequate emphasis is being laid on human resource development in this sector.

Indian institute of tourism and travel management (IITTM)

IITTM was established as a registered society in New Delhi in 1983. The Institute is fully funded by the Ministry of Tourism, Government of India and has been set up to meet the needs of higher education and training of the travel and tourism industry and as a centre of excellence in the field. It has also been entrusted to perform the role of nodal agency for developing tourism education facilities in the country. In August 1992, it was shifted to Gwalior where the State Government transferred 20 acres of land free of cost for constructing its permanent building. ITDC was entrusted to do the construction work. The IITTM moved from its rented premises to the new campus in February 1996. The full time courses, which were introduced viz. Diploma in Tourism Management (14 months full time) and Diploma in Destination Management (8 months), were started from the new campus. The course on Destination Management has been suspended for the time being due to insufficient demand. Other courses, which are programmed for 1999, include Tourism Orientation Course for officers of Central and State Governments holding tourism portfolios, Basic Course on Tour Operation Services Management, Introduction to Eco-Tourism, Wildlife Tourism Management, etc. The last two programmes are sponsored programmes of the Ministry of Personnel, Public Grievances and Pension (Training Division).

The Eastern Centre of IITTM, which was established at Bhubaneswar in 1997, conducted similar programmes including the full-time Diploma in Tourism Management. The Bhubaneswar Centre has taken up several research projects including "Exploring New Tourism Product", "Gonasika and Environs of Keonjhar district of Orissa" and "Sustainable Development of Chilika".

The part-time 16 months' programme "Diploma in Travel and Tourism Industry Management" was conducted through its Chapters at Thiruvananthapuram, Delhi, Lucknow, Calcutta and Guwahati.

As part of its objectives to conduct workshops, seminars, conferences, etc. on tourism related subjects, IITTM organised a workshop on "Tourism Legislation in India" at New Delhi.

During the year under review, IITTM launched a bi-monthly newsletter "Akhbaar". The newsletter is aimed at highlighting travel and tourism-related activities of the Central and State Governments in regard to human resource development. Publication of an annual journal "IITTM journal of Travel and Tourism" was also launched this year.

IITTM was successful in providing placements to its

students completing the 1997-98 batch of Diploma in Tourism Management from Gwalior and Bhubaneswar with travel agencies and tour operation units in New Delhi, Bhubaneswar and Calcutta.

New classes of DTM (1998-99 batch) commenced on 26th October, 1998 both at Gwalior and Bhubaneswar.

National institute of water sports, Goa

Ministry of Tourism set up a National Institute of Water Sports (NIWS) at Goa in 1990 to promote water sports activities throughout the country. The Institute is proposed to be run as an autonomous registered society under the Ministry on the same lines as IITTM. Government of Goa in 1990 has made available eighteen acres of land for establishing the NIWS, campus. The SFC meeting was held in May 1998 in which approval, in principle, has been accorded for the project. However, the project is being recast to bring in private sector participation in the non-training activities such as amusement park, restaurants, accommodation, marina, etc. Certain essential civil work has already been executed and the Institute has been conducting its training programme from these premises since 1991. The Institute has so far developed 20 training courses covering the entire range of water sports including the technical and management aspects. From March 1998, the Institute has stepped up its training efforts and has conducted 23 courses for 460 trainees earning a course fee revenue of Rs 2,05,400.00 till end October 1998.

The main emphasis of the Institute is to establish safety and quality norms for the Adventure Sports industry and certify the water sports professionals in the field of powerboat handling and lifesaving. In 1998-99, the Institute conducted feasibility surveys for Uttar Pradesh, Tamil Nadu and Kerala and conducted 4-week training programmes for Lakshadweep Tourism, Tamil Nadu Tourism Development Corporation and Allahabad Development Authority. The Institute provided theoretical and practical training in adventure sports to the students of IITTM, Gwalior and Bhubaneswar.

Indian Institute of Skiing and Mountaineering (IIS&M)

Gulmarg Winter Sports Project and the Indian Institute of Skiing and 5.20. Mountaineering was set up in 1968 as a pioneering Institute of the Ministry of Tourism for developing adventure sports activities like mountaineering, skiing, trekking, paragliding, etc. The officers and staff are engaged in promoting winter sports activities in different locations like Auli (UP), Manali (HP), Gulmarg and Patnitop (J&K). The paragliding courses are also being conducted as an adventure sport. Like previous year, during the year 1998-99, Short Ski Courses were conducted at Gulmarg (J&K) and Auli (UP). These courses were held from October, 1998 through the winter season.

To reactivate the Institute and to bring it to full capacity, various plans and programmes are under consideration. Maximum attention is given towards basic amenities to be provided along with latest types of ski equipment, etc. to participants. The youth would be involved in such adventure sports so that young people will come forth to participate in such activities. During off-season, i.e. spring and summer months, the staff is utilized to conduct courses in trekking and mountaineering, etc.

7

Publicity and Marketing

India is a multi-destination country with a variety of tourist attractions and facilities. It, however, suffers from the problems of economic underdevelopment including inadequate basic infrastructure, lack of hygiene and cleanliness in public places, etc. On the other hand, there is fierce competition in tourist generating markets from several nations for attracting a large share of the traffic to their countries. It is, therefore, necessary for India to strengthen its promotional and marketing efforts continuously even to maintain its existing market share. Steps are, therefore, being taken to develop and implement strategic marketing programmes based on market research and market segmentation analysis. Efforts are also being made to tap new segments and niche markets like Korea, South Africa, Israel, CIS countries, etc.

India celebrated 50 Years of her Independence, which culminated on 15th August, 1998. During the course of the year, a number of new initiatives were taken in order to highlight the role of tourism in the socio-economic activity of the country. During the Golden Jubilee celebrations, the Ministry of Tourism made special efforts to publicise the tourism potential of India. Despite the prevailing global situation, we would be able to achieve a growth of 3.8% in our tourist arrivals over the last year, which has also resulted in increase in foreign exchange earnings.

On 25th January, in the year 1956, the tourism was officially recognised as a separate subject by the Government. Therefore, it was decided that starting from the Golden Jubilee Year of India's Independence, this day should be celebrated as "India Tourism Day" (Bharat Paryatan Diwas). The first ever India Tourism Day was thus celebrated on 25th January, 1998. It was also decided that this would now be an annual event. Thus, the India Tourism Week was celebrated in New Delhi from 19.1.1999 to 25.1.1999. The week was inaugurated with a Grand Tourism Ensemble on the Central Lawns, Rajiv Chowk (formerly known as Connaught Place), New Delhi on Tuesday, the 19th January, 1999 by Shri M. L. Khurana, Union Minister for Parliamentary Affairs and Tourism.

As a part of the Tourism Week, the second India Tourism Expo was organised at Pragati Maidan, New Delhi from 22.1.1999 to 24.1.1999. The following seminars were also organised as a part of the India Tourism Week:

(i) A Policy for Tourism
(ii) Investment Opportunities in Tourism
(iii) The Future of Indian Tourism
(iv) Tourism Awareness Creation and Promotion
(v) Marketing Incentives Conferences and Exhibitions
(vi) International Perspectives of India
(vii) German Outbound and the Effect of Euro
(viii) Workshop on Eco Tourism
(ix) HRD in the Next Millennium

Food Festivals were also organised by various participating hotels including private sector hotels throughout the India Tourism Week, in order to popularise the diversity of the Indian cuisine. These were as follows :

Hotel	*Cuisine*
The Ashok	Hyderabadi & Lucknawi
The Surya West Western	Dakshin Cuisine Food Festival
Imperial	Kashmiri Food
Hyatt Regency	Kebabs of India
Le Meridien	International
Maurya Sheraton Hotel & Towers	Culinary Journey Through India
New Delhi Intercontinental	Chicken food Festival
Park Royal	Smoke House & Wine, Yum Cha & Dimsum, Strawberry & Chocolate
Radisson New Delhi	Rampuri Kebab
Hotel Samrat	Rajasthani Food, Sizzler Bonanza
Taj Palace	Goan Food
The Park	Spanish Fiesta Fun Evenings
The Oberoi	Kebabs & Biryani
The Taj Mahal	Barah Handi Seafood from the Coasts of India

For three evenings from 19th to 21st January, 1999, the best in Classical Indian Music and Dance was presented to full houses at Ashok Hotel, New Delhi when maestros like Kishori Amonkar, Tanushri Shankar, Debu Choudhry got standing ovations for their inspired performances.

The Tourism Week culminated in the observation of the India Tourism Day on 25th January, 1999 when the National Tourism Awards **(Appendix VI)** were given away by Hon'ble Prime Minister of India.

On this day, the Foundation Day lecture by Mr. Martin Bracken Bury, President, WTO was also organised by the Ministry of Tourism in New Delhi. The topic was "Role and Responsibilities of Customers, the Public and the Private Sector in Tourism Industry in the 21st Century".

To celebrate "Visit India Year" 1999, the Ministry of Tourism presented a spectacular tableau on "Cultural Heritage of India" at the Republic Day Parade, 1999. The classical dances that were incorporated were Odissi from Orissa; Kathak from Northern India; Mohiniattam from Kerala; Bharatanatyam from Tamil Nadu; Manipuri from Manipur; Kuchipudi from Andhra Pradesh. Each dance was performed with a backdrop of architectural landmarks of the region, promoting Indian monuments. In the last portion, audiences - tourists both foreign and Indian -applauded the performances. The choreography of the classical dances and the music composition was by Padmashree Raja Radha Reddy, well known Kuchipudi dancers. The ITDC produced this tableau for the Ministry of Tourism.

Operational arrangements and publicity efforts

Publicity and marketing of Indian tourism is being achieved through the 18 field offices of Ministry of Tourism located in major tourist generating countries. Their efforts are being coordinated and supplemented by the Marketing Division at the headquarters. Air India and its sales offices abroad also supplement efforts of the Ministry of Tourism by making financial contributions and organising joint promotional events. The publicity efforts of the overseas field offices are also supplemented and integrated with the efforts of Indian Missions and other agencies abroad, travel trade and media agencies. The specific elements of promotional efforts abroad include the following:

a) Advertising
b) Printing of brochures in local languages
c) Brochure support joint advertising with travel agents tour operators
d) Promotion of charters
e) Production of promotional advertisements
f) Multi-vision presentations Organise print media and TV interview.
h) Production of films and audio visuals in local languages
i) Production of lithographic / trade posters
j) Personal contacts
k) Organising seminars, talks, India evenings etc.
1) Direct mail and correspondence
m) Participation in tourism fairs & festivals
n) Market Research
o) Organising food & cultural festivals
p) Publicity budget
q) Organising road show

There has been a conscious attempt to allocate the maximum amount of plan funds for overseas publicity and promotion. The funds provided for this activity during the last five years were :

(Rs. in crores)

Year	Fund Released
1992-93	40.0
1993-94	42.5
1994-95	54.0
1995-96	52.5
1996-97	53.0
1997-98	57.0
1998-99	75.0

Production of publicity material

The tourist publicity material produced by the Ministry has to compete with the best available in the tourist generating markets of the world. In today's highly competitive market place, it is essential that the quality of material produced, whether it be films or publicity material, is of the highest standard.

Tourists, both domestic and foreign, seek information about the places of interest in a country and the need is for authentic data about places of interest, accommodation, accessibility, etc. This need can be fulfilled by producing and distributing authentic and informative publicity literature. During the year 1998, brochures on the following subjects were printed:

1. General Brochure on India
2. Southern Attractions
3. Tourist Charter
4. Investment Brochure
5. North East India
6. Buddhist Sites in India
7. Kangra Valley

8. Delhi/Kurukshetra/Chandigarh/Shimla/Keylong/Spiti/Manali-Kulu.

Work was also initiated on the following brochures:

1. Introduction to the Customs of
2. World Heritage Monuments
3. Lahul Spiti-Ladakh Circuit
4. Natural Health and Meditation Centres
5. Orchids of India
6. Farm & Rural Tourism
7. Medicare & Health Facilities in
8. Brochure on Gujarat, Folder Posters on Gujarat
9. Buddhist Sites in India in lap Thai and Korean Languages
10. Folder on Essentials of Buddhism

Production of films

During the year 1997-98, following three films were completed:

1. Film on Darjeeling/Sikkim Circuit
2. Film on Calcutta/Puri/Konark Circuit
3. Film on Southern Circuit

Work was initiated on production of "A General Film on India".

Production of CD-ROM

CD-ROM on India titled "Destination India" was produced.

Participation in travel mart and exhibitions abroad

The Ministry has taken a conscious decision to encourage travel industry to participate in important Travel Marts and Exhibitions held overseas. The Travel Marts in which the Ministry participated with various other agencies and members of travel trade were, WTM, London; ITB, Berlin; EIBTM, Geneva. Pavilions in these locations were appreciated and substantial business was generated by the travel trade. Cultural shows, seminars were organised in the overseas markets to mark the 50th Anniversary of India's Independence.

Ministry of Tourism organised the first Tourism Export in Pragati Maidan in the month of January 1998 which worked as a platform for exchange of ideas on Tourism and showcasing of Tourism products. For the first time, the Foundation Day of Tourism was celebrated on 25th January, 1998. A foundation day lecture was organised. The lecture was delivered by Dr. Antonio Savgnac, ex-Secretary General, WTO. During the Tourism Week, cultural programmes of music and dance was also organised in Ashok Hotel. A Tourism Run was organised on World Tourism Day, 1997 where people from all walks of life participated. Specially designed T-shirts and Caps were distributed to participants. A special logo was prepared for the 50th anniversary and the same was used in all publications. Buntings and stickers were prepared and distributed. "A March o the Nation" was organised on 15th August, 1997 where 1,000 school children from different States participated.

Domestic campaign

During the year 1998, a number of spot advertisements were issued on different subjects for the promotion of domestic tourism. A consumer awareness campaign was also launched as part of the celebration of 50 Years of India's Independence.

Work was also initiated on launching an advertising campaign in the media to create tourism awareness within the country.

Assistance to states/UT governments

Multifarious fairs and festivals occur throughout the year and are an amalgam of India's rich cultural heritage. They have added a new dimension to the Ministry's promotional efforts. Financial assistance is given to various State Govts. To promote specific extended in the form of publicity support, particularly for releasing advertisements, printing publicity material relating to the fairs festivals and also for creating semi permanent assets. 84 festivals have been identified in various States /UTs for this purpose.

Rural craft melas

Craft Melas, apart from preserving the rural traditional crafts, are also a major attraction for tourists. Ministry of Tourism has been supporting the Surajkund Crafts Mela in Haryana, The Shilpagram Crafts Mela in Rajasthan and the Taj Mahotsav and Crafts Mela, Agra to promote the crafts of India as well as to promote tourism.

Hospitality programme

Hospitality programme is an important element of the marketing process. Under this programme, the Ministry of Tourism invites travel writers, journalists, photographers, TV teams, tour operators, opinion makers etc. to effectively project India as an attractive multi-dimensional destination offering a vast range of tourists attractions. In this work, regular coordination is maintained with overseas Tourist Offices, Tourist Offices in India, Air-India, Indian Airlines, Central Ministries (e.g Home Affairs, Civil Aviation, External Affairs, Information & Broadcasting, Human Resource Development (Department of Culture), Environment & Forests, Railways, Archaeological Survey of India) and other tourism agencies. Special efforts were made to promote the following through the hospitality programme:

a) Ganesh Festival, Pune (Maharashtra).
b) Surajkund Mela during 1st to 15th February, 1998.
c) Buddhist circuits in Uttar Pradesh and Bihar.
d) Other States, which were promoted, include Eastern States like Sikkim, Assam and Arunachal Pradesh.
e) The "Palace on Wheels" train.
f) 50th Year of India's Independence Celebrations.
g) Bauddha Mahotsav.

Bauddha mahotsav

'Bauddha Mahotsav' was organised by the Ministry of Tourism, Government of India in collaboration with the Ministry of Tourism of the Governments of Uttar Pradesh and Bihar from 24th October to 8th November, 1998. The main event of the Bauddha Mahotsav this year was an "International Seminar on Buddhism" on the subject "World Unity in Buddha's Tir-Ratna" which was held on 6th and 7th November, 1998. His Excellency the President of India, Shri K.R. Narayanan inaugurated the Seminar on 5th November, 1998. The Prime Minister was the Chief Guest during the concluding function at Bodhgaya, Bihar on 8th November, 1998.

The celebrations of the Mahotsav began on 24th October, 1998 with the inauguration of the "Rajgir Festival' by Hon'ble Minister of Tourism and Parliamentary Affairs, Shri Madan Lal Khurana. Rajgir Festival holds a special position in the Indian Cultural Calendar as every year from 24th to 26th October, there is an exposition of Indian Classical Performing Arts.

This was followed by 'Ganga Mahotsav" at Varanasi, which was celebrated from 31st October to 4th November, 1998. His Excellency the Governor of Uttar Pradesh, Shri Suraj Bhan inaugurated the Mahotsav, Illustrious traditions, pious surroundings, pulsating excitement, mystical mornings - Ganga Mahotsav unfolded an invigorating experience in one splash. Ganga Mahotsav blended with the symphonies of cultural programmes which left an imprint on one and all.

The most significant feature of the Mahotsav was the "International Seminar on Buddhism", which was inaugurated by His Excellency the President of India. The President was given a rousing welcome at the airport from where he was escorted to the Mulgandha Kuti Vihara. Buddhist Monks received him amid chanting of prayers. He visited the Temple and thereafter was escorted to the 'Anathapindikarama" pandal. During the occasion, the President said "At the present time, when the world needed a new philosophy and a new path of action, the Buddha's principle of tolerence, which was central to India's life, had to be the main principle of the world. Otherwise there will be violence and conflict, not peace and liberation". He also stressed the need to have proper accommodation and good guides for the pilgrims. As the followers of the Buddha in other countries were eager to visit India, we must utilise the great opportunity to the maximum level. The participants in the seminar spoke on the relevance of Lord Buddha's teaching in today's world. The seminar was attended by eminent scholars from many countries.

The fortnight-long celebrations and meditations drew to a close at Bodhgaya, the most revered site in the Buddhist circuit, on 8th November, 1998. At the Kalchakra Maidan, Bodhgaya, Bihar the Hon'ble Prime Minister of India Shri Atal Behari Vajpayee addressed a mammoth gathering that marked a grand finale to the Mahotsav launched with the aim of attracting tourists from Buddhist countries. The Prime Minister announced that funds will not be a problem in developing Buddhist sites. He also used the opportunity to convey the country's commitment to world peace.

The Ministry of Tourism, Government of India together with the Tourism Departments of Uttar Pradesh and Bihar also arranged cultural shows from 5th to 8th November, 1998. These cultural shows presented during the Mahotsav depicted different facets of Lord Buddha's life and were well received by the large number of pilgrims / tourists and the local populace who witnessed these programmes.

Another achievement of the Mahotsav was the inauguration of a special train -"Bauddha Parikrama Express". As a result of the initiative of the Ministry of Tourism and Ministry of Railways, a special train called "Bauddha Parikarama Express' fructified on 23.10.1998. This 5 night / 6 days tour covering Kushinagar, Sarnath, Rajgir, Nalanda & Bodhgaya was flagged off on 23rd October, 1998 by Hon'ble Railways Minister Shri Nitish Kumar. Hon'ble Union Minister of Tourism Shri Madan Lal Khurana was the chief guest during the ceremony. This specially commissioned Holy Train has been tastefully appointed for the comfort of the pilgrims in mind. This train which will be operated by the Indian Railways and Ashok Travels & Tours, the in-house travel agency of ITDC, will go a long way in promoting Buddhist tourism in the region and was the need of the hour.

The Bauddha Mahotsav was very well covered by both the print and electronic media in India as well as overseas. The publicity generated will help in furthering tourism, specially Buddhist tourism to India. It has also been decided that henceforth it would be an annual event. This will go a long way in promoting Buddhist traffic/ tourism to India.

8

Research, Analysis, Computerisation and Monitoring

The Market Research Division of the Ministry of Tourism is responsible for collection, tabulation and dissemination of information on various aspects of tourism in India. The statistics being collected regularly by the Division include data on international and domestic tourist arrivals, occupancy statistics of approved hotels, etc. Periodical surveys are also being undertaken to assess the profiles of international and domestic tourists, expenditure patterns, tourist preferences and satisfaction levels, availability and adequacy of infrastructural facilities at tourist centres, etc. The Division is also coordinating the activities relating to progressive computerisation and Tourist Information Network (TOURNET).

Foreign tourist arrivals

The foreign tourist arrivals during 1998 were 23,61,234 (P) including the nationals of Pakistan and Bangladesh. The tourist arrivals during 1998 registered marginal decline of 0.5 per cent as compared to the corresponding period of previous Year. A statement showing month-wise tourist arrivals during the year 1998 along with the figures for the last two years is as given below:

Foreign tourist arrivals
(Including the nationals of Pakistan and Bangladesh)

Month	Tourist Arrivals			Percentage Change	
	1996	1997	1998	1997-96	1998-97
January	224029	240569	245706	7.4	2.1
February	219635	227458	222089	3.6	-2.4
March	196196	218411	215534	11.3	-1.3
April	158785	154863	174204	-2.5	12.5
May	132833	137536	137868	3.5	0.2
June	133154	143199	140810	7.5	-1.7
July	176347	184324	175322	4.5	-4.9
August	167985	176675	173095	5.2	-2.0
September	160840	160032	160369	-0.5	0.2
October	204126	210798	203903	3.3	-3.3
November	240620	249275	239919	3.6	-3.8
December	273310	270954	272415 (P)	-0.9	0.5
Total	2287860	2374094	2361234 (P)	3.8	-0.5

P = Provisional

Foreign tourist arrivals
(Excluding the nationals of Pakistan and Bangladesh)

Month	Tourist Arrivals			Percentage Change	
	1996	1997	1998	1997-96	1998-97
January	192474	202628	208476	5.3	2.9
February	187260	194406	191979	3.8	-1.2
March	174859	186666	183074	6.8	-1.9
April	129693	122570	141344	-5.5	15.3
May	103564	107320	107655	3.6	0.3

June	107693	114322	113403	6.2	-0.8
July	144559	151488	144575	4.8	-4.6
August	139912	145526	142576	4.0	-2.0
September	132658	130871	131388	-1.3	0.4
October	171686	174785	172897	1.8	-1.1
November	206716	214932	208788	4.0	-2.9
December	232621	228133	228979 (P)	-1.9	0.4
Total	1923695	197364	1975134 (P)	2.6	0.1

P =Provisional

Foreign exchange earnings from tourism

Tourism has become an important segment of Indian economy contributing substantially to its foreign exchange earnings. The estimated foreign exchange earnings during the year 1998 was Rs. 11748.20 crores (P) as compared to Rs. 11051.43 crores during the same period of 1997 and registered an increase of 6.3 per cent.

Domestic tourism

The potential of domestic tourism has grown substantially during the last few years due to increase in income levels and emergence of a dynamic urban middle class. However, there are no precise estimates of total domestic tourist traffic in the country. All the State/ Union Territory Governments were, therefore, persuaded to set up Statistical Cells for the collection of domestic tourism statistics through accommodation establishments and furnish them to the Central Department of Tourism on a monthly basis. As per the figures reported by the State Governments, the domestic tourist visits in the accommodation establishments during 1997 are roughly estimated to be 156.2 million.

Surveys and studies

The following surveys / studies have been completed during the year 1997-98:

i) Tourism potential survey of Pachmari and Khajiar.

ii) International Passenger Survey 1996-97.

iii) Infrastructure development for eco-tourism in Orissa.

iv) Tourism potential study of Orissa.

v) Feasibility study for setting up a Convention Centre at Leh.

vi) Preparation of a concept plan and design for the development of Chumukedima village in Nagaland.

The following surveys/studies are in progress:

i) Techno-economic feasibility study for Island Water Tourism in Brahmaputra.

ii) Master Plan for Tourism Development in Pondicherry.

Computerisation

A computer unit of National Information Centre has been set up in the Department for computerising various activities, including Plan Monitoring, Foreign Tourist Arrival Information System, Hotel Information System, etc.

A Tourism Information Network (TOURNET) is functioning in the Government of India Tourist Offices in the country.

A home page has been established in INTERNET with the following address:

http://www/tourindia.com

The home page contains detailed information on India illustrated with coloured photographs. It is proposed to enlarge the data contents by including information in respect of hotels and travel industry.

Transport and communication network

Existing transport system of the country comprises several modes of transport including rail, road, coastal shipping, air transport, etc. Transport has recorded a substantial growth over the years both in spread of network and in output of the system.

The railways in india provide the principal mode of transportation for freight and passengers. It brings people from the farthest corners of the country and makes possible the conduct of business, sightseeing, pilgrimage and education. Indian Railways have been a great integrating force during the last hundred years.

It has bound the economic life of the country and helped in accelerating the development of industry and agriculture. From a very modest beginning in 1853, when the first train steamed off from Bombay to Thane, a distance of 34 km, Indian Railways have grown into a vast network of 7,050 stations spread over a route length of 62,462 km with a fleet of 7,202 locomotives, 34,088 passenger service vehicles, 5,955 other coaching vehicles and 3,12,405 wagons as on 31 March 1994.

The growth of Indian Railways in the 141 years of its existence is thus phenomenal. It has played a vital role in the economic, industrial and social development of our country. The network runs multigauge operations extending over 62,462 route kilometre. The gauge-wise route and track lengths of the system as on 31 March 1994 were as under:

Table : Respective Gauge Length

Gauge	*Route km*	*Running track km*	*Total track km*
Broad Gauge (1,676 mm)	37,824	53,560	76,295
Metre Gauge (1,000 mm)	20,653	21,643	28,156
Narrow Gauge (762 mm and 610 mm)	3985	3,985	4,469
Total	62,462	79,188	1,08,920

About 18 per cent of the route kilometre, 27 per cent of running track kilometre and 26 per cent of total track kilometre is electrified. The network is divided into nine zones and further sub-divided into divisions. Divisions are the basic operating units. The nine zones, their respective headquarters and the route kilometre for each as on 31 March 1994 are given below:

Table : Track Length Covered

Railways	*Headquarters*	*Route Kilometre*
Central	Bombay	7,158
Eastern	Calcutta	4,303
Northern	New Dehi	10,993
North Eastern	Gorakhpur	5,144
Northeast Frontier	Maligoan (Guwahati)	3,728
Southern	Madras	7,021
South Central	Secunderabad	7,227
South Eastern	Calcutta	7,161
Western	Bombay	9,727
Total		62,462

Cooperation between public and railway administration is secured through various committees including Zonal Railway Users's Consultative Committees and Divisional Railway Users' Consultative Committees. The rolling stock fleet of Indian Railways in service as on 31 March 1994 comprised 911 steam, 4,174 diesel and 2,117 electric locomotives. Currently, the railways are in the process of inducting new designs of fuel-efficient locomotives of higher horse power, high sped coaches and modern bogies for freight traffic. Modern signalling like panel inter-locking, route relay inter-locking, centralised traffic control, automatic signalling and multiaspect colour light signalling, are being progressively introduced to increase the throughput. Indian Railways have made impressive progress in indigenous production of rolling stock and a variety of other equipment over the years and is now self-sufficient in most of the items.

The main objective of railways planning has been to develop the transport infrastructure to carry the projected quantum of traffic and meet the developmental needs of the economy. since the inception of the planned era in 1950-51, Indian Railways have implemented seven Five Year Plans, apart from annual plans in some years. During seven Plans, emphasis was laid on a comprehensive programme of system modernisation. With capacity being stretched to the full, investment in cost-effective technological changes became inescapable in order to meet ever-increasing demand for rail transport. Along with the major thrust directed towards rehabilitation of assest, technological changes and upgradation of standards were initiated in important areas of track, locomotives, passenger coaches, wagon bogie designs, signalling and telecommunication. for long-term requirements, the railways have also prepared a 'corporate plan' covering 15 years period, 1985-2000. It

Table: Progress of Railways Traffic and inputs

Year	Route Length (Kilometre)			Running track (Km.)	Passenger originating (lakh)	Goods originating (lakh tonne)	Number of locomotives			Number of Coaching vehicles	Numuber of wagons
	Electrified	Non-Electrified	Total				Steam	Diesel	Electric		
1950-51	388	53,208	53,596	59,315	12,840	930	8,120	17	72	19,628	2,05,596
1960-61	748	55,499	56,247	63,602	15,940	1,562	10,312	181	131	28,439	3,07,907
1970-71	3,706	56,081	59,790	71,669	24,311	19,65	9,387	1,169	602	35,145	3,83,990
1980-81	5,345	55,895	61,240	75,860	36,125	2,200	7,469	2,403	1,036	38,333	4,00,946
1985-86	6,517	55,319	61,836	77,153	34,335	2,864	5,571	3,046	1,302	38,277	3,59,617
1986-87	7,275	54,538	61,813	77,254	35,937	3,073	4,950	3,182	1,366	37,988	3,54,041
1987-88	8,157	53,819	61,976	77,671	37,921	3,185	4,427	3,298	1,433	37,746	3,46,844
1988-89	8,880	53,105	61,985	77,845	35,003	3,295	3,826	3,454	1,533	37,867	3,45,821
1989-90	9,100	53,111	62,211	78,320	36,531	3,343	3,336	3,610	1,644	37,953	3,49,661
1990-91	9,968	52,399	62,367	78,607	38,576	3,414	2,915	3,759	1,743	38,511	3,46,102
1991-92	10,653	51,805	62,458	78,969	40,486	3,600	2,492	3,905	1,871	39,350	3,46,394
1992-93	11,064	51,422	62,486	79,200	37,494	3,709	1,725	4,069	2,012	39,924	3,37,562
1993-94	11,260	51,202	62,462	79,188	37,080	3,775	911	4,174	2,117	40,043	3,12,405

seeks to provide 370-400 billion net tonne km freight traffic, 310-330 billion non-suburban passenger kilometre and 105-110 billion suburban passenger kilometre by the turn of the century. Progress of railway traffic and inputs is shown in table.

There are five undertakings under the administrative control of the Ministry of Railways viz., (i) Rail India Technical and Economic Services Limited (RITES); (ii) Indian Railway Construction Company Limited (IRCON); (iii) Indian Railway Finance Corporation Limited (IRFC); (iv) Container Corporation of India Limited (CONCOR); and (v) Konkan Railway Corporation Limited (KRC). Centre for Railway Information System (CRIS) was set up as a registered society to design and implement various railway computerisation projects.

The Research, Design and Standards Organisation (RDSO) at Lucknow is the R&D wing of Indian Railways. It functions as a consultant to the Indian Railways in technical matters. It also provides consultacy to other organisations connected with railway manufacture and design.

A substantial part of defence stores needed by the Services is now being developed and produced within the country. The responsibility for this has been entrusted to the Department of Defence Production and Supplies in the Ministry of Defence. The Department directs and coordinates production of material and equipment required by the Armed Forces.

At present, 39 ordnance factories spread all over India operate a wide-range of technologies and product mix. Some of the important products are field guns, anti-aircraft guns, mortars, various small arms and ammunition for weapons and guns, rockets, projectiles, pyro-technics, bombs, grenades, mines, demolition charges, depth charges, infantry combat vehicles, battle tanks, self-propelled guns, transport trucks and petrol vehicles, high-altitude and combat clothing, optical and fire control instruments, engineering equipment, supply dropping equipmet including parachutes, rubberised items, various knitted and woven items like blankets, web equipment and a wide range of general stores are produced by them. Production of 5.56 mm (indigenously designed) weapon system has started in ordnance factories. These factories are also producing bombs required by Air Force. Besides, liquid fuel required for successful flight trials of Prithvi and Agni missiles, igniters and copper liners for the warheads were also supplied in the development of Prithvi missile. The production of Ajeya tank (T-72), Sarath (BMP-II), infantry combat vehicle are carried out at Heavy Vehicle Factory, Avadi and Ordnance Factory, Medak, respectively. A sophisticated opto-electronic production unit has been set up at Dehra Dun to produce the opto-electronic fire control and night vision devices required for Ajeya Tank (T-72-MI and Sarath* infantry combat vehicle is planned from 1994-95. To utilise the sparable capacities, after meeting the services requirements, linear and lateral shift in customer product profiles has been taken up as a major thrust area of operations.

As a part of diversification efforts, Vehicles Factory, Jabalpur (VFJ) has taken up modification and upgradation of Jonga. The vehicle, conforming to military standards, is not only sturdy but also has a very high pick up, high fuel efficiency of 16 km per litre (under test conditions) and a maximum speed of 120 kmph with gradient climbing capability of one in three. It has been decided to launch Jonga in the civil open market. VFJ has a captive capacity to manufacture 20,000 Jonga per annum. Out of this, 10,000 vehicles are to be released in the civil market and remaining 10,000 are reserved for the Army and exports. The release to the civil market would be done without effecting any erosion in the Army requirements.

There are eight public sector undertakings (PSUs) under the Department of Defence Production and Suppliers. These are: Hindustan Aeronautics Limited (HAL), Bharat Electronics Limited (BEL), Bharat Earth Movers* rail coaches, track laying equipments, heavy duty trucks, trailers, diesel engines etc. BEML is a leader in earth-moving industry with over 70 per cent market share. Its equipments and systems are productively deployed in India and over 30 other countries across the globe.

Mazagon Dock Limited (MDL) is the country's leading shipbuilding yard and can build warships up to 6,000 DWT displacement and merchant ships up to 27,000 DWT. It has units at Bombay, Nhava and Mangalore and headquarters at Bombay. At present, its major activities include construction of sub-marines, missile-boats and destroyers etc., for the Indian Navy and off-shore supply vessels and well-head platforms etc., for the Oil and Natural Gas Commission (ONGC). The company also provides diving services as well as services for coating/ laying sub-sea pipes.

Garden Reach Shipbuilders and Engineers Limited (GRSE) is a multi-unit shipyard-cum-general engineering company. It has six units in and around Calcutta and a Diesel Engine Plant at Ranchi (Bihar). Its corporate office is at Calcutta. It has three distinct divisions, namely, ship, engineering and engine divisions. It is presently engaged in the construction of war ships and auxiliary vessels of various types for the Navy and the Coast Guard and to undertake repair of vessels of these two organisations. Other products of the company include a variety of high technology ship-borne equipments, portable Bailey type steel bridges, marines sewage treatment plant, dock-machinery items, turbine pumps for the agricultural sector, diesel engines, etc.

The activities of Goa Shipyards Limited (GSL) located at Vasco-da-Gama, primarily comprise construction and repair-reit of ships/vessels. It has undertaken construction/refit of variety of vessels for the Indian Navy and the Coast Guard as well as for the non-defence sector. It is currently building advanced off-shore patrol vessels of in-house design.

Bharat Dynamics Limited (BDL), established in 1970, is primarily engaged in the manufacture of guided missiles and allied equipments. It has units at Hyderabad and Bhanur (Medak district). Its corporate office is at Hyderabad. It is also the prime production agency for manufacture of four new missile systems, namely, Prithvi, Trishul, Akash and Nag, being developed indigenously. Its activities which had earlier been diversified into a number of Naval projects now proposes to take up manufacture of small arms required for para-military forces of the country.

Mishra Dhatu Nigam Limited (MIDHANI) located at Hyderabad was incorporated in 1973. MIDHANI's product range includes super alloys, maraging steels, heat resistance alloys, controlled expansion alloys, tungsten, molybednum etc., in variety of mill forms.

Surface Transport

Looking back it is noticed that a lot has been done in the post-Independence era for the development of surface transport, the linchpin of the cuntry's prosperity, however much more still needs to be done in this vital sector. Surface transport is a key comment of the infrastructure of sustained economic growth. A well-knit and co-ordinated system facilitates its better utilisation necessary for sharpening the country's competitive edge. Through eight five-year plans progress in developiong the system of transport by land and sea has designed it to operate at peak efficiency. Admittedly, much more needs to be done to attain this goal for a country of continental size like India.

But looking back at the last 50 years one finds the achievements to be in no way in a small measure. With a network of two million kilometres India has now the third largest road network in the world. Similarly, the shipping fleet has increased manifold to attain a strength of 480 ships with a gross registered tonnage of 7.02 million. The post-independence period has seen the country grow as a ship-building nation with four major and three medium size shipyards in the public sector. The total capacity of Indian major ports numbering 11 is estimated at 174 million tonnes in 1995-96.

The growth of the national economy during this period has of course made a quantum leap imperative in all these areas. Since the ushering in the economic reforms there has been a reorientation of shipping policy, liberalisation in acquisition of ships, record handling of cargo and containers by major ports, incentives and facilities to encurage private sector participation in modernisation and development of ports and national highways and mass rapid transit systems.

All these are within the charge of the Ministry of Surface transport which is responsible for the formulation and implementation of related policies and programmes. Easy and speedy movement of commodities for domestic consumption and exports has direct co-relation to its efficient functioning. A measure of the magnitude of the first plan and at present in respect of freight carried by the roads. In 1950-51 roads carried nearly six billion tonne kilometers (btk) of freight and 23 billion passenger kilometers (bpk) of passenger traffic. The current level of estimated freight and passenger traffic are 650 btk and 1500 bpk respectively. Roads have emerged as the preferred mode of transport and the situation in likely to continue for years to come.

Another aspect of the network is that national highways built up to 34,068 km, much of it in the last fifty years carries nearly 40 per cent of the total road traffic. If this is an indicator of the high growth in road transport, it also suggests the colossal nature of the needs of the future as the national highways constitute less than two per cent of the road network. Since the First Plan, the problems of growth in demand for road transport have been addressed to. These cover improvements in the area of road design, construction, maintenance and materials, quantum change in the quality of rural roads, modernisation of construction equipment and transport vehicles, traffic transport management, traffic regulation, multimodel transport, choking urban roads and solutions to the problems of urban transport. Still, 46 years later, on the threshold of the Ninth Plan it has been noticed that development of roads and road transport has still to keep pace with the demands of economic growth.

With the set objective of the removal of those dificiencies, reforms have been initiated and more are contemplated. The Economic Survey for 1995-96 lists among the measures already taken: declaration of the road sector as an industry to facilitate borrowing on easy terms and to permit floatation of bonds; relaxation of MRTP provisions to enable large firms to enter the highway sector; amendment of the national highways Act to enable the levy of a fee on national highways, bridges and tunnels and lowering of customs duties on construction equipment and streamlining of the related procedures. The contemplated reforms are: private sector participation including foreign investors in the development of stretches of national highways and construction of expressways on BOT basis for a period of thirty years, the traffic will be normally regulated by entrepreneurs but to ensure free and uninterrupted flow of traffic, sales tax and barriers will not be established on the expressways and the checks by the authorities will be conducted at the entry and exit points only; the land acquisition and removal of utilities to be done by the government. These reforms underpin the need for expansion of the road network which since the beginning of national planning is up 500 per cent from 0.4 million kilometres. Road transport has increased by 60 to 65 times. It is estimated that road traffic now accounts for 80 per cent of passenger traffic and 60 per cent of good traffic. By 2000 AD, just four years away, passenger and goods traffic will go up to 87 and 65 per cent respectively.

The number of vehicles has gone up to 27.5 million, an increase of 90 times in the past 50 years. Cars sporting all famed international brand manufactured under Indian licence threaten to clog the roads.

National highways constitute the primary network of the road system. A recent study by the Asian Development Bank has noted that the country needs the construction of another 10,000 km of the national expressway network. Obviously, capacity has to go up; payment has to be sufficient; riding quality should be better and bridges should be strengthened, there should be more rail level crossings and more wayside amentities and measures for a safety are to be strengthened. Projections place the cost of attaining these desired objectives at Rs. 52,000 crore. The money is worth spendings as otherwise the country loses an estimated

Rs. 15,000 crore every year because of the bad condition of roads resulting in avoidable excessive use of fuel and an increase in vehicle operating costs. This is again a problem of growth resulting in development driven increase in traffic because of economic activity. A national highway authority of India has since been constituted with a full-time chairman and three members aided by senior and technical official having expertise in various fields. In view of the massive demand for the road network cooperation of the private sector is being mobilised.

Economy's demand on ports has also gone very high. The annual growth in cargo handling has been ranging between 7.6 per cent to ten per cent. Containerised cargo which has come into vogue in recent years recorded the maximum percentage increase in 1994-95 and 1995-96. Calcutta, Cochin and Mumbai have contributed to this phenomenal growth. All the major ports handled around 1.4 million containers during the financial year 1995-96. The 11 major ports are Calcutta, Paradip, Vishakhapatnam, Chennai and Tuticorin on the east coast, and Cochin, New Mangalore, Mormagao, Mumbai and Kandla on the west coast. Development of major ports is constitutionally the responsibility of the Union government. In recent years major investments in port construction have centred on container as well as bulk facilities.

Ministry of Non-Conventional Energy Sources is endeavouring to develop alternatives to diesel and motor sprit in order to reduce their consumption and outflow of precious foreign exchange. The main alternatives are battery-operated vehicles (BOV); use of alcohol, methanol/ethanol as a fuel in diesel and petrol vehicles; and use of compressed natural gas (CNG) as a fuel. In different areas of the country, 235 battery-operated and

105 alcohol-operated vehicles have been taken up for demonstration. Apart from this, a new project to develop 100 alcohol based vehicles has been taken up in Gujarat.

FIPB had cleared in February 1994 a joint venture proposal for manufacture of solar battery car developed by M/s Frazer-Nash, UK, in India in collaboration with M/s Peerless Limited, Calcutta. It has been reported that the performance of the four wheel drive solar battery car is quite compatible to Indian autorickshaws and it can find the market potential in India among educated unemployed for rural and city mass transport, postal department, industrial sectors and various shuttle service applications.

Use of hydrogen as an energy source involves five basic issues i.e. production, storage and transportation, utilisation, safety management and economy. A 100 cc four stroke hydrogen/hydride fuelled motorcycle has been developed and development efforts to increase the range of the motor cycle is under way. The plan for hydrogen fuelled three-wheelers and motor-cars is at planning stage. The other important use of hydrogen energy is in heat pumps and refrigeration. The projects on heat pumps have been progressing well at Indian Institute of Technology, Madras. The production and storage of hydrogen has been pursued at Banaras Hindu University, Varanasi, Osmania University, Hyderabad and Rajasthan University, Jaipur.

The conversion of solar energy into chemical energy is an imortant route for tapping solar energy as it allows storage of solar energy also. As many as 50 research and development projects in the area of photovoltaic chemical cells, photovoltaics and photosynthesis have been funded and good results have been achieved in these areas. The other two areas pursued under chemical sources of energy are duel cell and electro-chemical storage batteries. A 2.5 kw phosphoric acid fuel cell (PAFC) has been developed and is under test. Plan for 200 kw PAFC has been prepared. The programme on storage batteries is for development of storage systems needed for intermittent energy sources like solar, wind, etc., and for vehicular use. Amongst commercial batteries currently available, lead acid battery seems to hold attractive position. However, lead resources in India are rather limited. The other battery systems are such as nickel-cadmium, dilver-zinc, nickel-hydrogen, etc. Materials and construction methods are too expensive fo find application.

A project on 'Development of Sodium Sulphur Batteries' suitable for electric vehicles, satellite communications, photovoltaic energy storage and submarine power etc., has been undertaken at Central Electrochemical Research Institute, (CERI) Karaikudi and NPL, New Delhi

The Ministry is actively pursuing the proposal for setting up a tidal power plant for 900 mw in the Gulf of Kachchh at an estimated cost of Rs. 4,000 crore. The tidal power potential in the country is estimated to be of the order of 8,000 mw to 9,00 mw (approximatley 7,000 mw in Gulf of Cambay, 1,000 mw in Gulf of Kachchh and 100 mw in Sundarbans). A techno economic feasibility report has been prepared by the CEA/NHPC for a 900 mw tidal power plant at Gulf of Kachchh. This project is proposed to be included as a command area development project in the state sector.

India is having large potential of Ocean Thermal Energy Conversion (OTEC) which could be of the order about 50,000 mw. M/s Sea Solar Power Inc., USA, is promoting the use of ocean thermal energy conversion technlogy and the first plant is proposed off the coast of Tamil Nadu with a capacity of 100 mw at a cost of about

Rs. 750 crore, the finance being entirely brought in by the overseas entrepreneurs. The company has signed the MOU for this project with TEDA and TNEB of Government of Tamil Nadu in January 1994.

Wave Energy Potential in India is estimated about 40,000 mw. One wave energy power plant of 150 kw (maximum) capacity based on OWC has been installed in Vzhinjam near Thiruvananthapuram by IIT, Madras under a sponsored project by Department of Ocean Development. The power plant has been commissioned and is under trial. One Swedish organisation Sea Power *(HWPC) concept. Harnessing a wave energy on this principle in India is being explored and a one mw wave energy plant is being set up in the Andaman and Nicobar Islands.

Geothermal manifestations are widespread in India, in the form of 340 identified hot springs localities, many of these having temperature near boiling point at their places of occurrence. There is considerable scope for the development and exploitation of geothermal energy resources. The ongoing activities include the survey and assessment of geothermal potential, utilization of geothermal energy for direct heat and power generation. A five kw geothermal pilot power plant has been commissioned at Manikaran in Kullu district of Himachal Pradesh. The assessment of geothermal power potential in Puga Valley Ladakh in Jammu and Kashmir has been done through Manageto-Telluric surveys and geo-scientific studies. A potential of 4-5 mw geothermal power has been estimated in the Valley. Proposal to explore this potential for power generation and utilization for nearly localities is being finaslised. The use of geothermal energy for space heating and green house effect has been demonstrated. A project on mushroom cultivation and poultry framing using geothermal fluid is under implementation at Regional Research Laboratory, Jammu.

The main objective of Indian Renewable Energy Development Agency (IREDA) is to act as a catalyst agent for accelerating commercialization of new and renewable rources of energy. IREDA has been assigned the main task of administering a revolving fund to promote, develop and finance on soft terms the NRSE technologies. The resources base of IREDA mainly consists of equity support from the Government of India, grants from foreign and international organisations, borrowings and internal accruals. The authorised share capital has been raised from Rs. 25 crore to Rs. 100 crore during 1994-95. In addition, the Government of Netherlands have already given to IREDA grant-in-aid of 17 million Guilders for assisting NRSE projects. It has further committed an amount of 23 million Guilders.

The World Bank has also agreed to provide US dollar 195 million which includes a grant-in-aid component of US dollar 30 million to be contributed by Global Environment Trust Fund and Swiss Development Cooperation for financing projects to generate power through wind energy, small hydro and solar photovoltaic schemes. IREDA has also signed an agreement with the Asian Development Bank to receive technical assistance of US dollar 3.54 lakh and a credit of US dollar 150 million is under finalisation.

The Ministry of Non-Conventional Energy Sources has established a Solar Energy Centre as an institute dedicated to the development and testing of solar energy products. The Centre has state-of-art facilities for the testing of both solar thermal and solar photovoltaic devices. Asia's largest indoor sun simulator for measurements on solar thermal collectors has been dedicated to the Centre in May 1994. In addition, there are specialised simulators for measurements on solar cells and photovoltaic modules as well as equipment for testing of systems for different applications. The Centre is coordinating cooperative activities in solar energy among G-15 countries. It is being developed as a centre of excellence of international standard.

There are 11 major ports in the country apart from about 139 minor working ports along the coastline of about 5,600 km. Major ports are the direct responsibility of the Central Government, while minor ports including intermediate ports fall in the Concurrent List of the Constitution and are managed and administered by the respective maritime state governments.

Kandla, Bombay, Mormugao, New Mangalore, Cochin and Jawaharlal Nehru Port are the major ports of west coast. The Jawaharlal Nehru Port is equipped with modern facilities having mechanised container berths for handling dry bulk cargo and service berth, etc. On the east coast, Tuticorin, Madras, Visakhapatnam, Paradip and Calcutta-Haldia are the major ports. All the major ports are administered in accordance with the provisions of the Major Port Trust Act, 1963. Each major port has a board of trustees representing various interests connected with the port operations and the shipping industry. Among the major ports, Bombay handles over one-fifth of the total traffic of the ports, bulk of which consists of petroleum products and dry cargo. Kandla is a 'Tidal Port'. A free trade zone has been set up here. It handles all types of traffic. Mormugao occupies fifth position in terms of total quantum of traffic handled. Facilities for export of Kudremukh iron ore were specially developed at New Mangalore. Cochin is a natural harbour. Tuticorin port handles mainly coal traffic.

Madras is one of the oldest ports on the east coast. The traffic handled at this port consists mainly oif crude oils and iron ore. Visakhapatnam is the 'deepest port' where an outer harbour has been developed for exporting iron ore and a berth has been constructed for crude oil and also petroleum products as well as a multi-purpose general cargo berth. Paradip handles iorn ore and some quantities of coal and dry cargo. Calcutta is a riverine port handling diverified commodities. A new mechanised dock system at Haldia with provision for deep draft vessels supplements the facilities available at Calcutta. Haldia has fully equipped coal handling oil and containerised berths. All the major ports have generated operating surpluses during 1993-94. However, the financial position of ports of Cochin and Paradip is considered to be weak. All major ports handled a total cargo traffic of 179.3 million tonnes during the financial year 1993-94 and 123.2 million tonnes upto November in the financial year 1994-95.

There are about 139 minor/intermediate ports which are in the Concurrent List of the subjects in the Consititution of India. State governments are responsible for the management and the development of these ports. Accordingly, allocation for the development is provided in the respective state sector plans by the Planning Commission. However, funds for the development of port facilities in Andaman and Nicobar Islands, Lakshadweep, etc., are provided in the Central sector plan.

The Dredging Corporation of India was set up in March 1976 and started its commercial operation from 1 April 1997. The Corporation has been rendering maintenance and capital dredging services in major ports, minor ports, shipyards, shipping harbours, navy, state governments etc. An outlay of Rs. 155 crore has been approved for Eighth Five Year Plan and Rs. 20 crore in the Annual Plan 1993-94 for the Corporation. During

1993-94, the Corporation achieved 98 per cent capacity utilisation by dredging a quantity of 531.60 lakh cu.m. of sand, silt and other material. For 1994-95, the Corporation has targetted to achieve a dredging quantity of 550 lakh cu.m.

There are four major and three medium size shipyards in India in the public sector. Apart from these, there are are about 35 small shipyards in private sector and state government sector which cater to domestic requirements for medium and small craft. Maximum size of vessels that could be constructed in Cochin Shipyard, Cochin and Hindustan Shipyard, Visakhapatnam are 86,000 DWT and 45,000 DWT respectively. Cochin Shipyard Limited has delivered two tankers out of the series of three 86,000 DWT tankers for Shipping Corporation of India, and the work on third tanker has commenced. These were constructed for the first time in the country. Small shipyards are greared up for meeting the country's requirements for small/medium size crafts and fishing vessels. Sixty two fishing vessels have been delivered so far for private entrepreneurs and 26 fishing vessels are under construction in various shipyards.

The ship-building industry is open to private sector irrespective of the size of ship. The following fiscal and financial incentives are available to the ship-building industry; (a) the shipyard constructing vessels incluing fishing trawlers under bond are entitled to duty free import of raw materials, components consumable and spares required in the manufacture of ships; (b) the shipyards registered with the Ministry of Surface Transport for constructing deep sea fishing trawlers above 20 metres in length are entitled to 33 per cent subsidy on the price of the trawler in addition to price preferntial limited to 10 per cent for indigenous trawlers.

Of the 17 dry docks in the country, 13 are available

for commercial ship repair activities. While dry docks at CSL, Cochin and HSL, Visakhapatnam can accommodate ships of maximum size of one lakh DWT and 57,000 DWT respectively, other dry dock can accommodate ships upto 10,000 DWT range. In addition, ship repair facilities have been set up at Madras Port by a private entrepreneur with two floating dry docks of 14,000 tonnes lifting capacity (TLC) and 2,400 tonnes lifting capacity respectively which can cater to ships of 40,000 DWT and 8,000 DWT respectively. In addition Western India Shipyard Ltd., is setting up ship repair facilities at Mormugao on the West Coast. A floating dry dock of 20,000 TLC has been installed which caters to ships upto 60,000 DWT. A graving dock with a capacity to repair ships upto 2,500 DWT is also under construction.

A primier national institution, namely, National Ship Design and Research Centre (NSDRC), Visakhapatnam, an autonomous body under the administrative control of the Ministry of Surface Transport, has been set up with a view to provide national technological infrastructure to assist Indian ship-building and shipping industries. It has the following objectives: (i) to assist shipping and ship-building industry with consultancy, research, maritime information and computer services; (ii) to strive for the elevation of standard of Indian maritime sector so as to keep it at par with international standards; (iii) to save foreign exchange hitherto being spent by the industries for the procurement of designs from abroad; and (iv) to offer services to the industry in matters of improving efficiency and productivity.

Ministry of Surface Transport provides grant-in-aid to the entrepreneurs who take up indigenous development of ancillaries for ship-building. The grant-in-aid available can be to the extent of 70 per cent of the total development cost. For availing grant-in-aid, the private entrepreneurs are required to apply to the public sector shipyard who, in turn, would sponsor the proposal for consideration of the Ship Ancillary Development Committee under the Ministry.

Hindustan Shipyard Limited at Visakhapatnam was set up in 1941 in the private sector Scindia Steam Navigation Company Limied. Because of difficulties faced by the owners, the Government was requested to take over the shipyard and accordingly a new company viz., Hindustan Shipyard Limited was incorporated in 1952. In 1962, the shipyard became a cent per cent public sector enterprise. Thereafter in 1971, ship repair facilities were added besides various development programmes for augmenting installed capacity of the yard. An off-shore platforms yard for construction of well-platform for ONGC was set up in 1985. The present capacity of the yard is two platforms per year. The shipyard has plans to increase the capacity to three well-platforms during the Eighth Plan period. With the completion of Stage II Modernisation and Expansion Programme, the installed capacity of shipyard was increased to the equivalent of 3.5 pioneer class vessles by 1989-90. The shipyard has produced and delivered 107 vessels of different sizes and specification viz., dumb barges, bulk carries, product carriers, passenger-cum-cargo vessels and high technology drill ships besides petrol supply-cum-support vessels in addition to off-shore well-ahead-platforms. The shipyard has successfully completed and commissioned 11 off-shore platforms in Bombay High and Godowns basin for ONGC. The 11 platforms consist of 22 structures viz., jackets and 11 decks.

Hooghly Dock and Port Engineers Limited, Calcutta (HDPE) came into existence on 30 June 1984, as a new Government public sector undertaking with a view to securing better utilisation of available infrastructure thereof, to modernise and increase the capacity for ship-building and ship repairing so as to reduce the import of ships, vessels and crafts. The company comprises of two working units in Howrah district of West Bengal-one at Salkia and another at Nizirgunge. The unit located at Salkia Works constructs various types of ships, passenger and other vessels craft, dredgers, tugs, floating dry docks, fishing trawlrs, off-shore platform supply-cum-support vessels for *Department of Lighthouses and Lightships, etc. This unit has an outfit at Kidderpore Dock Complex of Calcutta port for repairs of various types of ocean-going vessels and dredgers. The second unit Nizirgunge Works is engaged in the construction of fishing trawlers, fire floats, barges, mooring launchers, grab hopper dredters etc., and repairs of different types of vessels besides general fabrication and machining jobs.

Cochin Shipyard, set up with Japanese collaboration, is designed to have a dock for building ships upt 86,000 DWT and a repair dock to accommodate ships upto 1,00,000 DWT. The shipyard has so far built and delivered five bulk carriers of 75,000 DWT each and two crude oil tankers of 86,000 DWT each. The construction of one more oil tanker of 86,000 DWT will commence in the near future. The second tanker in this series was launched on 29 February 1992 and delivered to SCI on 29 October 1992 in a record time of eight months only. The Order Book Position of CSL has improved in so far as it has received order for construction of three tugs for Indian ports.

The Government has approved a capital restructuring plan for the ailing Cochin Shipyard Limited. The restructuring involves conversion of loans amounting to Rs. 119.14 crore into seven per cent non-cumulative preference shares and coversion of accumulated interest at normal rate amounting to Rs.

136.35 crore into interest free loans. In addition, after considering various ways and means of revival of Indian shipyards, orders on a package of reliefs to shipyards have been issued by the Government in September 1993. As a result of various measures, Cochin Shipyard, *which has been able to improve its operational performance to generate a cash margin and reduce the accounting loss, thereby eliminating the need for cash-credit facility which it had been availing of till 1990-91 against Government guarantee. As such, the yard has become a viable unit.

India has got about 14,500 km of navlgable waterways which comprises of rivers, canals, backwaters, creeks, etc. At present, however a length of 3,700 km of major rivers is navigable by mechanised crafts but the length actually utilised is only about 2,000 km. As regards canals, out of 4,300 km of navigation canals, only 900 km is suitable for navigation by mechanised crafts. About 160 lakh tonnes of cargo is being moved by Inland Water Transport Inland Water Transport (IWT) is a fuel efficient and environment friendly mode. It is also known for higher employment generation potential. IWT operations are currently restricted to a few stretches in the Ganga-Bhagirathi, Hooghly rivers, the Brahmaputra, the Borak river, the rivers in Goa, the backwaters, in Kerala and in the deltaic regions of the Godavari-Krishna rivers. Besides, the organised operations by mechanised vessels, country boats of various capacities also operate in various rivers and canals.

The Inland Waterways Authority of India was set up on 27 October 1986 as a statutory body corporate under the Inland Waterways Authority of India Act, 1985. The Authority is entrusted with the responsibility of development, maintenance and regulation of national waterways and also to advise the Central and the state governments on matter relating to development of IWT.

Considering the need to develop Inland Waterways and Inland Water Transport to play its rightful role in the transport network of the country, the Government had identified 10 important waterways for consideration to declared them as National Waterways. The Ganga between Allahabad and Haldia (1,620 km) on 27 October 1986, the Sadiya-Dhubri stretch of the river Brahmaputra (891 km) on 26 October 1988 and the Kollam-Kottapuram stretch of West Coast Canal (168 km) along with Champakara Canal (14 km) in Kerala with effect from 1 February 1993 have so far been declared as National Waterways and the same are being developed for navigation by Inland Waterways Authority of India. It is also proposed to consider the declaration of some more waterways like the river Godavari, Sunderbans, waterways in Goa and the river Barak (subject to techno-economic viability) during Eighth Five Year Plan.

The Central Inland Water Transport Corporation (CIWTC) with its head-quarters at Calcutta was set up as a public undertaking in May 1967. The CIWT is mainly engaged in transportation of goods by Inland Waterways in the Ganga-Bhagirathi-Hooghly, Sunderbans and the Brahmaputra rivers. They are operating regular cargo services between Calcutta and Pandu (near Guwahati), between Calcutta and Karimaganj (Assam), Calcutta-Bangladesh, and between Haldia and Patna. The Corporation is also having a shipyard called Rajabagan Dockyard in Calcutta which is engaged in the construction and repair of inland vessels and harbour crafts. A deep-sea ship repair division with units at Calcutta and Port Blair is also functioning under CIWTC.

In the wake of the economic reforms the government has allowed private participation in facilities including building operation and maintenance of container terminals, setting up of storage and warehouse facilities;

pilot services, dredging operation and maintenance of port craft and other equipment. Two dry docks at Calcutta have been privatised. Leasing out of two berths is under consideration of the government. Also, under consideration are proposals for privatisation at other ports. Ports and highways, besides power, constitute core areas where private investment is invited to overcome capacity shortages. Major orts have identified a large portfolio of projects amounting to US $ 2 billion where private sector involvement is feasible. In addition, governments of the States with a coastline have identified such projects worth US $ 1 billion.

Since infrastructure services are central to growth, the government is keen on raising private investment in the sector substantially. The Prime Minister, Mr. Deve Gowda told a gathering of international business leaders at Destination India conference recently: "We realise the critical importance of infrastructural development to sustain economic growth. Government considers it a high priority area for investment by foreign and multinational companies. We have already initiated policy measures and programmes to attract both domestic an foreign investment in these areas. Tax holidays and other fiscal incentives are being offered for the infrastructure projects. We have gained some experience in the past couple of years with these sectors and we are aware of the need to further simplify procedures and ensure greater transparency. We are ready to examine any suggestions to improve the system".

Shipping, shipbuilding and inland water transport are other areas in charge of the Ministry of Surface Transport where growth has fuelled expansion in the last fifty years of freedom. Liberalisation measures have been taken to facilitate the growth of the shipping industry as well. A working group on shipping constituted by the Planning Commission has recommended the acquisition of an additional 3.7 million GRT at an investment of Rs. 15,000 crore during the ninth plan period to increase the total available GRT in excess of nine million. Linked to the shipping industry is the Ship-building and repair industry. In the past 50 years, four major and three medium size shipyards have been established in the public sector, there was none before.

The Hindustan Shipyard Ltd. at Vishakhapatnam and the Cochin Shipyard can construct vessels up to a maximum size of 45,000 dwt and 86,000 dwt respectively. There are about no fewer than 35 small shipyards in the private sector. The shipping industry has been declicensed and is open to private sector irrespective of the size of the ship except for the construction of war ships. Mechanised sailing vessels upto 10,000 dwt including fishing trawlers and ship ancillaries have been allowed automatic approval for foreign collaboration up to 51 per cent equity capital.

For years ship repairing facilities in the country have been far too limited. Ships have to be repaired outside the country resulting in foreign exchange outgo. The situation will change verysoon. Ports have been advised by the government to make available land and water front areas for private entrepreneurs who may be interested in setting up ship repair facilities.

In land water transport, also a responsibility of the Ministry, is a pollution free and inexpensive mode of transport and the Ministry puts a lot of emphasis on its development. Subsidy up to 20 per cent of the cost is given to private transporters in this sector. Government vessels are given to private operators for carriage of goods via inland waterways.

There are three national waterways in operation: Allahabad Haldia (the Ganga Hugly) river system; Sadiya Dubri (on the Brhamaputra system) and Kollam-Kottapuram (Kerala) Proposals have been finalised to declare Cheralta to Rajamundri on the Godavari river in Andhra Pradesh and Zuari and Mandovi rivers and Cumberjue canal in Goa and the international route between Sagar and the Bangaladesh border in Sunderbans as national waterways.

In sum, an enabling framework for private investment in the key infrastructure sector of surface transport is being made operative. This is done under the economic reforms which are currently being effected. Infrastructure development is recognized as the linchpin of Indian prosperity. Not far into the next century, deficiencies like port capacities stretching beyond their limits and road networks under tremendous pressure will be left behind, taking the development process of the last 50 years to a new credo.

Overseas shipping has an extremely important role to play in India's international trade. The country has the largest merchant shipping fleet among developing countries and ranks 17th in the world in shipping tonnage. As on 31 August 1995, the operative tonnage consisted of 460 vessels totalling to 6.84 million GRT.

Thee were 71 shipping companies in the country in operation as on 31 March 1995 including the Shipping Corporation of India, a public sector undertaking. Of these, 39 are engaged exclusively in coastal trade, 22 in overseas trade and the remaining 10 in both coastal and overseas trade. Shipping corporation of India, which is biggest shipping line of the country, had a merchant fleet of 124 vessles of 31 lakh GRT as on 31 March 1995 and operated on almost all maritime routes. Shipping Corporation of India tonnage accounts for about 49 per cent of the total India tonnage. Major private sector shipping companies which own one lakh or more GRT are: (i) Great Eastern Shipping Company Limited (5.97 lakh GRT); (ii) Eassar Shipping Limited (4.54 lakh GRT); (iii) Chowgle Steamships Limited (2.02 lakh GRT); (iv) South India Shipping Corporation Limited (2.76 lakh GRT); (v) India Steamship Company Limited (1.52 lakh GRT); (vi) Surrendra Overseas Limited (1.56 lakh GRT); (vii) Century Shipping (1.61 lakh GRT); and (viii) Varun Shipping Company Limited (1.27 lakh GRT).

National Shipping Board is a permanent statutory body established in 1959 under the Merchant Shipping Act, 1958 to advise the government on shipping matters. Ship Acquisition Licensing Committee deals with ship acquisition proposals received from shipping companies. Inter-ministerial high level committees look into problems of the shipping companies. Indian National Shipowners Association seeks to promote the interest of national shipping and other allied industries.

India's National Ship Classification Society was formed in March 1975 under the Companies Act, 1956. Its activities are: (i) to provide a faithful and accurate classification and record of mercantile shipping classed with Indian Register of Shipping (IRS); (ii) to establish and administer standards for the construction and periodical survey of ships and other maritime structure; (iii) to approve design of, to survey and to issue reports on land based installations, machinery, materials, and apparatus of all kinds; and (iv) to aid and develop marine technology in India through research and development work. Government has authorised the IRS to assign international load lines and carry out Cargo Ship Safety Construction Surveys of India Flag Ships. In order to maintain acceptable standards and provide worldwise coverage for its services, IRS has entered into agreements of mutual cooperation with all major international classification societies by virtue of which ships can also be classed dually with IRS as well as corresponding society with arrangements for survey all over the world. These agreements also enable IRS to get technical backup whenever required for its varied services from different sources.

There are three training establishments for the merchant navy officers. TS Chankya at Bombay imparts pre-sea training to navigation cadets. Lal Bahadur Shastri College of Advanced Maritime Studies and Research, Bombay conducts post-sea Instrumental Courses in Navigation and Engineering. Marine Engineering Research Institutes at Bombay and Calcutta impart training to the marine engineering cadets.

Coastal Shipping is an energy efficient and comparatively cheaper mode of transport if the carriage of bulk traffic over long hauls is involved and also particularly when origin and destination of traffic stream is located along the coast. India has along coastline of 5,560 km. Coastal shipping can play an important role in integrated transport network of the country particularly when inland modes are strained. the coastal tonnage which was 3.12 lakh GRT on 1 April 1985 (beginning of Seventh Plan) was increased to 6.93 lakh GRT on 31 March 1995.

An Inter-Ministerial Working Group set up by the Government to study the simplification of customs procedure, implementation of infrastructural facilities, financial aspects, etc., has also recently made certain recommendations for the development of coastal shipping in the country. The acceptance of these recommendations is under consideration of the Government.

At the time of Independence, there were only 17 lighthouses in India. Since then, Aids to Navigation have increased in number and variety. Government looks after general navigational aids while states, port trusts and other agenices are responsible for local aids. However, under the Lighthouse Act, 1927, the Government exercises general control over all aids through Department of Lighthouses and Lightships, which in turn maintains various navigational aids along the coast of India besides launchers and HF/VHF/radio telephone sets. At present, there are 163 lighthouses, one light vessel, twenty radio beacons, four Dacca Navigator Chain Stations, six LORAN-C stations, eleven reacons and ten lighted buoys. The Department of Lighthouses is maintaining three lauches, one mechanised lighted boad and two large ocean going vessels, M.V. Sagardeep and M.V. Paradeep for attending light stations at various places including off-shore islands. The Department is also maintining 39 Very High Frequency/Radio Telephone sets for maintaining communication with lighthouses situated in remote and isolated places.

— India has a road network covering 2.7 million kilometers which makes it the third largest road network in the world. However, this network is not adequate for speedly and efficient transportation. Half of this is made up of unsurfaced roads. The National Highways which are artirial routes have currently a network of 34,298 km. Although they carry nearly 40 per cent of the goods and passenger traffic, the national highway network constitutes less than 2 per cent of the total road network.

— Road transport is the dominant form of transport for people and goods in India. Over 80 per cent of passengers and over 60 per cent of freight move by roads. It is estimated that by the year 2000 road traffic will account for 87 and 65 per cent of passenger and goods traffic, respectively. The quality and capacity of national highway have to be enhanced consistent with the traffic expansion and overall economic growth of the country. Traffic movement on the highways is suffering from frequent stopovers and congestion as almost 15 per cent of national highways and 75 per cent of state highways are single lane roads. The problem is further compunded by inadequate road pavement thickness, poor riding quality, existence of a number of railway level crossings that need replacement, weak and distressed bridges/culverts, congested city sections, lack of wayside amenties and inadequate road safety measures. The deficiencies in the road network have contributed to safety hazards, besides entailing higher transportation cost. These highways will, therefore, require major augmentation of capacity as well as structural upgradation. About 20 per cent of national highways need widening from single to double lanes and about 50 per cent of two lane roads have to be strengthened. 30 per cent of existing two lane roads need to be four laned apart from developing expressways on selected corridors. The maintenance of roads is no less important than their expansion and the vast network of roads built over the years needs to be preserved.

— The magnitude of the task on hand and the volume of funds required for this purpose are clearly beyond the capacity of the public sector. In the past, roads have generally been financed from budgetary sources and constructed by the Public Works Departments. As the budgetary allocation is not adequate to meet the challenges states above, the National Highways Act has been amended to enable the levy of a toll on selected improved sections of National Highways.

— The amendment of the Natioal Highways Act to allow the private sector to construct and charge a fee or toll will permit the private sector to participate in construction, maintenance and operation of roads on Build, Operate and Transfer (BOT) basis. Several reforms/measures taken by the Government to attract private sector participation in Highways Development are summurised and encompass land acquisition, environmental clearance, simplification of procedures, tolling of 4-lanes, by-passes and bridges, equity participation in the highway sector and sharing of force majeure risks.

— After the amendment of National Highways Act in 1995 to allow private sector particiapation, steps have been taken to initiate national highway projects through private sector participation. Two projects of bypasses (Thane-Bhiwandi in Maharashtra and Udaipur in Rajasthan) and one project or Road Over Bridge (at Chalthan in Gujarat) involving an investment of Rs. 42 crore have been awarded on BOT basis.

— The provisions relating to foreign investment in the road sector have been considerably liberalised. Automatic approval will be accorded for foreign equity participation upto 74 per cent in the construction of roads and bridges. In addition to this, automatic approval would be given for majority foreign equity upto 51 per cent in support services to land transport, like operation of highways bridges, toll roads and vehicles.

— External assistance is being obtained for the improvement of National Highways through international agencies such as the World Bank, Asian Development Bank and Overseas Economic Cooperation of Japan. The Government of India has activated the National Highways Authority, which is an autonomous body created through an Act of Parliament and has been entrusted with eh Asian Development Bank Project costing about Rs. 800 crores in 5 states viz., Haryana, Rajasthan, Bihar, West Bengal and Andhra Pradesh.

— The State Road Transport Undertakings operate a fleetk of overk one lakh buses employing 8.3 lakh workers. The undertainds, with a few exceptions, face serious financial constraints due to various factors such as the social commitment to operate even on uneconomic routes, absense of cost-based fare structures, overmanning, poor management and widespread inefficiencies.

— Indian vessels carried about 29 per cent of the total sea-borne cargo during 1994-95. The share of Indian vessels in 1994-95 in Petroleum Oil and Lubricants (POL) was 54 per cent, in bulk carriers 17 per cent, and in liner traffic 9 per cent. Long—term targets for Indian shares in bulk carriers and liner traffic are 50 and 40 per cent, respectively. The fleet strength at the end of October, 1996 was 481 vessels of 7.02 million Gross Registered Tonnage (GRT), against 468 vessels of 6.9 million GRT in October, 1995. Overseas trade during 1994-95 was 147 million tonnes against 137 million tonnes during 1993-94.

— The Shipping Corporation of India (SCI) showed a better financial performance during 1995-95 compared to 1994-95. It has earned a record net profit after tax of Rs. 323 crore in 1995-96 registering an increase of 61 per cent over 1994-95. SCI's gross internal resources rose to Rs. 554 crore in 1995-96 as against Rs. 395 crore in 1994-95. Its gross tonnages as on October 31, 1996 was 3.11 million GRT (about 45 per cent of the total Indian fleet).

— There are two major public sector ship building yards, Hindustan Shipyards Limited, and Cochin Shipyards Limited. Due to various reasons i.e. high construction cost, heavy interest burden on borrowing, low order book position, excessive manpower etc. these yards had been incurring losses. However, as a result of revival measures initiated by the Government in September, 1993 the two yards have shown an improved performance. Cochin Shipyard Limited has earned a net profit of Rs. 11.16 crores during the previous year. Hindustan Shipyards incurred a net loss of Rs. 118 crores in 1995-96.

— The International Safety Management (ISM) code, was adopted by the International Maritime Organisation (IMO) in November, 1993. This code is to come into force in 1998 for passenger ships and tankers and by 2000 for other vessels. The shipping companies are required to provide special training to on shore staff and crew on board in order to implement the Code. The Directorate General of Shipping has constituted a Sub-Committee which is in dialogue with the shipping comanies to implement the Code well before its due date.

* In order to promote the development of Indian shipping, a new shipping policy was initiated in 1990-91 and several policy reforms have since been made in conformity with the liberalisation o the Indian economy.

Inda has one of the largest road networks in the world. The country's total road length was 20,65,209 km in 1991-92. Seventh Plan laid emphasis on a coordinated and balanced development of road network in the country under (i) primary road system covering state highways; (ii) secondary and feeder road system covering state highways and major district roads; and (iii) rural roads including village roads and other district roads.

Substantial outlays were proposed for road development in the rural and tribal areas. In the first three Five Year Plans and three Annual Plans, Rs.1,121.58 crore was spent on road development. During Fourth, Fifth, one Annual Plan and Sixth Plan, Rs. 5,160.09 crore was spent on this. Outlay for road development under the Seventh Plan for Central sector was Rs. 1,019.75 crore, for state sector Rs. 3,666.98 crore and for union territories Rs. 513.31 crore. During the Seventh Plan, Rs. 6,179.75 crore was spent on *Central sector roads. For state sector roads, an amount of Rs. 1,303.25 crore was spent during 1990-91. For the Eighth Five Year plan, an outlay of Rs. 2,600 crore and Rs. 10,610 crore has been approved for Central sector roads and state sector roads repectively. During 1992-94 of the Eighth five Year Plan, an amount of Rs. 1,070 crore has been spent on Central sector roads and expenditure on the state sector aggregates to Rs. 3,709 crore approximately.

Government is responsible for national highway system. In 1947 approximately 2,500 km of missing roads links and thousand of culverts and bridges which did not exist, were required to be constructed to have an integrated and continuous network. There was an increase in missing road links with addition of new roads to the national highways system in later years. upto 31 March 1994, road links including diversions cosntructed totalled 4,624 km, widening and strengthening single lane section to double lane carriage was done in 24,574 km, widening to four-lane completed in 442 km, strengthening of weak two-lane pavement has been done in 12,365 km. In addition 507 major bridges and 2,856 minor bridges were also completed. Present natioal highway system includes a total road length of

34,058 km. An expenditure of Rs. 1,481.70 crore during the Seventh Plan and Rs. 860.50 crore during 1990-92 had been incurred on development of national highways. During Eighth Five Year Plan, an outlay of Rs. 2,460 crore has been allocated for development of national highways. During 1992-93 and 1993-94 a sum of Rs. 1,028 crore has been spent on development of national highways. Though the national highways constitute only two per cent of the total road length, they carry nearly 40 per cent of road traffic. There are altogether nine on-going external loans for the improvement of national highways. Out of these, one (US dollar 306 million) is from World Bank. Three *(total jap Yen 36,915 million approximate equivalent US dollar 369 million) are from Overseas Economics Cooperation Fund (OECF), Japan. the World Bank loan includes six NH sub-projects in the states of Punjab, Haryana, Orissa, Maharashtra, Madhya Pradesh and West Bengal and one state highway project for reconstruction of bridges in Orissa. Three subprojects in the states of Punjab, Haryana and Orissa are in progress and action for inviting tenders for the remaining three sub-projecs is under process. The first ADB loan (US dollar 188 million) provides for development of national highways in three states namely, Andhra Pradesh, Haryana and Uttar Pradesh and four state roads in three states namely, Andhra Pradesh, Karnataka and Tamil Nadu. The second ADB loan (US dollar 250 million) provides for improvement of national highways in Karnataka, Kerala, Rajasthan and of state roads in Andhra Pradesh, Orissa, Uttar Pradesh and West Bengal. The works under both these loans are in various stages of progress. The third ADB loan (US dollar 245 million) is for development of national highways in the states of Andhra Pradesh, Haryana, Rajasthan, Bihar and West Bengal. The procurement process is in progress for these sub-projects. The project for improvement of Mathura-

Agra Section of National Highway No. 2 in Uttar Pradesh in under OECF loan (Jap Yen 4827 million).

State highways and district rural roads are the responsibility of state governments and are maintained by various agencies in states and union territories. Roads are being developed in rural areas under Minimum Needs Programme (MNP). The objective of it being to link all viallges with a population of 1,500 with all-weather roads. Government also assists in development of certain selected roads in states.

Raised in May 1960 for development of roads of strategic importance in northern and north eastern border areas, Border Roads Organisation (BRO) has now spread its activities throughout the country and is presently working in states of Rajasthan, Jammu & Kashmir, Himachal Pradesh, Maharashtra, Tamil Nadu, Andhra Pradesh, Uttar Pradesh, Sikkim, Assam, Meghalaya, Nagaland, Tripura, Manipur, Mizoram, Arunachal Pradesh, Bihar and Andaman and Nicobar Islands. It has so for constructed over 24,000 km of roads and is also presently maintaining them. BRO has now diversified into construction of airfields, buildings and permanent bridges involving high degree of technical expertise, with special emphasis on mechanisation and quality control. With proven efficiency, credibility, professionalism and overall cost effectiveness, many other governmental agencies are coming forward in a big way for entrusting works to BRO and specially in those remote areas where no one else is prepared to work. The BRO is building technical institutions, schools and hospitals in far-flung places for the upliftment of the people of those regions. It has been occasionally taking up civil engineering works on behalf of other agenices in difficult areas.

Table: Road Length in India

(Km)

	Surfaced	Unsurfaced	Total
ALL INDIA	10,43,365	10,21,844	20,65,209
States			
Andhra Pradesh	81,449	71,747	1,52,896
Arunachal Pradesh	2496	5,204	7,520
Assam	10,841	58,072	68,913
Bihar	33,980	53,713	87,693
Goa	4,567	2,986	7,553
Gujarat	73,354	19,153	92,507
Haryana	26,498	3,263	29,761
Himachal Pradesh	6,971	17,859	24,830
Jammu and Kahsmir	8,325	6,104	14,429
Karnataka	86,158	50,241	1,36,399
Kerala	32,637	1,04,706	1,37,343
Madhya Pradesh	80,354	56,846	1,37,200
Maharashtra	1,47,760	98,018	2,45,778
Manipur	2,741	4,024	6,765
Meghalaya	2,931	4,901	7,832
Mizoram	1,268	2,440	3,708
Nagaland	6,842	1,963	8,805
Orissa	57,983	1,73,396	2,31,379
Punjab	47,568	8,649	56,217
Rajasthan	60,211	62,423	1,22,634
Sikkim	1,842	73	1,915
Tamil Nadu	1,18,637	67,899	1,86,536
Tripura	4,448	8,560	13,008
Uttar Pradesh	95,520	1,26,982	2,22,502
West Bengal	28,690	30,404	59,094
Union Territories			
Andaman and Nicobar Islands	807	45	852
Chandigarh	1,766	–	1,766
Dadra and Nagar Haveli	331	16	347
Daman and Diu	–	–	–
Delhi	14,952	6,846	21,798
Lakshadweep	N.A.	N.A.	N.A.
Pondicherry	1,739	1,509	3,248

Note : Data given above is as on 31 March 1992.

Railways in recent years has been spurred to augment internal generation of resources through economy in working expenses and enhancing its earnings. The share of its internally generated resources has risen from a mere 25 per cent during the Fifth Plan to 58 per cent during the Eighth Plan. Railways is an important infrastructure sector and a provider of vital non-traded service which has a bearing on the overall competitiveness of the economy. It is, therefore, necessary that a distinction between the network of railway lines, and the railway rolling stock which uses this network to provide transport services is maintained. The high capital intensity and long gestation lags act as disincentives to investment in line networks. This is not, however, applicable to railway service, which can be viable and competitive. Conventional market borrowing is, therefore, restricted to funding rolling stock which is essential to sustain railway services. This has resulted in raising its liabilities on account of market borrowings through the Indian Railway Finance Corporation (IRFC). The lease charges being payable to IRFC as per budget estimates have already exceeded Rs. 1650 crore during 1996-97 and constitutes about 10 per cent of the ordinary working expenses. The resource requirements of Railways are huge and therefore cannot be adequately met through internal generation of resources and conventional market borrowings alone. This calls for greater innovations in management and in funding of assets and services provided by the Railways. A start has been made by allowing private sector participation in selected Railway projects/activities. These include Build-Own-Lease-Transfer (BOLT) and Own-Your-Wagon (OYW) Schemes. These initiatives can inject limited amount of competition in selected areas, and also ease the strain on railway ways increased from Rs. 20101 crore in 1994-95 to Rs. 22418 crore in 1995-96, representing a growth of 11.5 per cent. In 1995-96, the total working expenses (including appropriations to the Depreciation Reserve Fund and Pension Fund) were Rs. 18525 crore as against Rs. 16590 crore in the previous year. The working expenses thus showed an increase of 11.7 per cent. Consequently, the net traffic receipts of Railways have shown an increase from Rs. 3511 crore in 1994-95 to Rs. 3893 crore in 1995-96. The net railway revenue comprising the net traffic receipts and net micellaneous receipts, amounted to Rs. 4135 crore in 1995-96. The ratio of net revenue to capital-at-charge and investment from capital fund, works out to 15.2 per cent in 1995-96 as compared to 13.7 per cent in 1993-94 and 15.3 per cent in 1994-95. The ordinary working expenses, forming a major part of the total working expenses, registered a higher increase of 13.2 per cent in 1995-96 on account of interim relief, increased PLB cost, and hike in energy charges etc. After making payment of Rs. 1264 crore as dividend to general revenues, the excess amounted to Rs. 2871 crore, which partly contributed to the investment requirements of the Railways.

In 1995-96 Railways contributed Rs. 2246 crore to the general exchequer, consisting of payment of dividend of Rs. 1264 crore and net accretion of Rs. 982 crore to Railway funds kept with the general exchequer. Railways dues of Rs. 895 crore remained outstanding against certain State Electricity Boards and power houses as on 31st March, 1996. The inability to settle outstanding financial dues with Railways, bestowed on the recepient of railway services, financial accomodation without payment of interest. Railways transaction with RBI also closed with a net deposit of Rs. 908 crore in 1995-96.

The railway budget for 1996-97 envisages a surplus of Rs. 1916 crore, after providing for payment of dividend to general revenues in full. The fare and freight rate increases in the railway budget for 1996-97 consisted of the following. Freight rates of all commodities increased by 10 per cent excepting certain essential commodities. Minimum distance for charge raised from 75 kms to 100 kms; no increase in second class fares; upper class and AC 3 tier/chair car fares raised by 10 per cent; fares of Rajdhani, August Kranti and Shatabdi Express trains also increased by 10 per cent; sleeper class fares increased by 5 per cent for distance beyond 200 kms; parcel and luggage rates rationalised by replacing the existing GPA, CP1 and CP2 by new general parcel scale (GPS), concessional parcel scale (CPS) and modified luggage/motor car scales; and no increase in first and second class monthly season ticket and quarterly season ticket. They are expected to fetch an additional revenue of Rs. 927 crore. The plan outlay for railways for 1996-97, the terminal year of the Eighth Five Year Plan, has been budgeted at Rs. 8280 crore, including budgetary support of Rs. 1419 crore. Market borrowings, BOLT and OYW schemes are expected to fetch an additonal Rs. 2750 crore. The rest of the plan outlay of Rs. 4111 crore is to come from internal resources. In the plan, priority has been accorded to rolling stock, track renewals, safety works and electrificatioin.

As a carrier of 12 million passengers and over one milion tonnes of freight everyday, the Indian Railways have played a vital role in the socio-economic development of the country. However, not every effort to improve its performance has been successful, feels the author. The Indian Railways travel in one day a distance that is three and a half times the distance between the earth and the moon. In other words, the Indian Railways traverse in less than seven hours a distance that a satellite takes six days to cover. But as the world's single largest railway system under single management, which carries 12 million passengers and over one milion tonnes of freight everyday, these statistics do not come as a surprise.

At the time of Independence the first task was to integrate all 42 different lines owned by Rajas and Maharajas and British companies into one system, to give shape to the Indian Railways. Even more important was to make up as fast as possible for the manpower and other losses suffered on account of the partition on the country. A major consequence of this was that the rail link with Assam and the North-East was virtualy cut off and had to be restored at top-most speed. Once that was achieved, attention was turned to improving passenger amenities, building indigenous manufrastructure and modernizing the system.

Among the first step in that direction was to replace wooden coaches with steel-cum-aluminimum coaches which were nore durable and sturdy, were better suited to higher speed, and were less prone to catch fire. But a more significant decision was to introduce diesel engines which ran faster than the steam engines. Not everyone was happy when the first high speed diesel engine was imported from Canada but looking back it could be described as an important landmark in pushing the speed of the Indian Railways.

The country having firmly embarked on the path of planning with its accent on building a more or less self-reliant economy, almost all import by the Indian Railways was generally accompanied by agreement to transfer technology. Before long, the country was meeting several needs of the Railways indigenously with the setting up of big facilities like the Integral Coach Factory at Perambur (Chennai), Diesel Locomotive Workshop at Varanasi and Chittaranjan Locomotive Works. The Indian railways had embarked on the path of self-reliance in the early years of the young nation.

The manufacture of diesel and electric locomotives within the country was a signal that the days of the steam locomotives were going to end. It was only in the 1970s that a decision was taken not to manufacture any steam locomotives in the country. Economic considerations and the competition from the diesel and electric locomotives led to the decision to end the magnificent era of steam locos. It was a sad news for the lovers of those "black beauties" which, however, could neither match the speed nor the capacity and performance of the diesel and electric locomotives. Ecological considerations, though not in vogue then, would have also been cited as a reason for saying good-bye to the steam engine.

Incidentally, the steam locos will not disappear totally from the map of the Indian Railways. The "toy" trains of Darjeling and Ooty will continue their run into the next century. Another narrow gauge train, on the Kalka-Shimla route, however, was "converted" to diesel some time back.

The Indian Railways consist of and extensive network spread over 62,915 km. comprising Broad Gauge (40,609 km.), Metre Gauge (18,501 km.) and Narrow Gauge (3,794 km.). Electrified networks with 12,306 km. account for 19.6 per cent of the total route kilometerage. The thrust areas identified for the Eighth Plan period included replacement and renewal of overaged assets, augmentation of terminal and rolling stock capacities and gauge conversion and electrification. Indian Railways completed gauge conversion of 1,351 km. in 1992-93, 1,619 km. in 1993-94, 1,805 km. in 1994-95 and have set a target of 1,000 km. for 1995-96.

During 1995-9, the revenue earning freight traffic moved by the Railways was 390.7 million tonnes. This was 7 per cent higher than the performance in 1994-95.

The freight traffic carried during April-November 1996-97 at 260.7 million tonnes, increased by 6.3 per cent over April-November, 1995. The growth has mainly been in coal, pig iron and finished steel from steel plants, cement, foodgrains, iron ore for export and other goods, etc. However, there is a decline in fertilizers and POL both of which showed negative growth rates. The slow down in industrial production and economic activity in general in the current financial year has also, to some extent affected freight demand fron the railways in like manner. Moreover, for items such as cement, fertilizers and petroleum and petroleum products (POL), considerations of operational flexibility and continuity of arrangements already made have necessitated an increased dependence on road transport and also on pipelines in the case of petroleum.

The existing modal shares between rail and road do not conform to optimal shares as judged by the criterion of least economic cost. The Railways are trying to attract freight traffic in view of being a more energy efficient and environment friendly mode of surface transport through the Container Corporation of India (CONCOR) and various other marketing schemes.

The Railways employ about 16 lakh workers, the largest number for any undertaking in the country. A comprehensive plan for human resource development is required to upgrade skills, retrain workers and achieve higher productivity. While staff productivity in terms of the number of traffic units per employee, asset productivity in terms of net tonne kilometre per wagon day, wagon turn-around time, loco-utilisation, etc. have improved over the year, there is still scope for further improvement.

The budetary support to the Railways has declined sharply from 75 per cent of the Railway's Plan outlay in the Fifth Plan to 42 per cent of the outlay in the Seventh Plan and further to 19 per cent during the Eighth Plan. This has forced the railways to repriortise ongoing projects of line expansion, renewals, gauge conversion and electrification of key routes and has adversely affected procurement of rolling stock.

The Railways have so far met the challenge by relying less on budgetary support and more on internal generation of resources which, in future, may have limitations with increased outlay on account of the Pay Commission recommendations and growing lease rentals, ertc. Alternative sources of funding based on market borrowings are also being looked at although the servicing costs would be higher. Private sector participation through schemes like Build-Own-Lease-Transfer (BOLT) and Own-Your-Wagon-Scheme (OYWS) are also being explored. However, only limited success has been achieved in these areas till now.

For some time now, there has been considerable concern within Rail Bhawan over the resource crunch to finance the annual Plans. The Chairman of the Railway Board, Mr. C.L. Kaw, has been on record as saying that while most of the money may come from market borrowings, it was not a financially prudent way because of high market interest rates. But his concern may have something to do with the Railways' efforts, so far unsuccessfull, to receive a substantially higher budgetary support from the Government. The Railways say that the Government must pay more if all the social obligations imposed on the railway network are to be carried out.

Yet, there is something to be said in support of the railways demand for more money from the general Budget. If market borrowings continue, Indian railways may soon be engulfed in a debt trap. In 1997—98, for instance, about a third of the annual Plan of Rs. 8300 crore will have to be financed by market borrowings. Of the Rs. 3050 crore thus expected to be raised, the bulk—Rs. 2150 crore—will come from the sale of bonds and the rest, about Rs. 900 crore, from schemes like BOLT and Own Your Wagon which involve the private sector. It may also not wise to depend too much on raising money through the Indian Railway Finance Corporation which had trouble raising Rs. 1850 crore and meeting debt and interest payments last year.

The finance crunch in one manner is a peculiar problem of the Indian Railways imposed by the Government which is very keen to spread the railway network in the backward and far—flung areas. This would contribute not only to the development of these areas but also help in removing the sense of isolation among the people there.

The aim is laudable and immensely desirable. It is not good for a country of India's size and diversity to allow a sense of isolation grow among the population living in the border areas of the country. But the stark fact is that the financial health of the railways and, more importantly, the poor traffic that these far flung areas would generate, will nonly add to the problems of the Railways if the network expansion plans are concentrated in the areas of low return. There is perhaps a case for ordering a cost—benefit analysis which will help the Railways arrive at a rational pricing strategy. But it would be worthwhile only if this analysis is to be accepted and implemented.

with egalitarian considerations coming to dominate in the country, the first Janata Government had decided that Indian Railways should have only two classes, first and second. But to make the journey for the long distance traveller at least reasonably comfortable, cushioned seats were introduced in the second class coaches.

Soon, it was also decided that non-air-conditioned first class coaches will also go and their manufacture was stopped. The new second air-conditioned class came to replace the non-AC first class. The old type of first class coaches carried a maximum of 16 passengers in a compartment that resembled a drawing room with long sofa sets along the walls. It was a luxurious way of travelling, if one did not mind the heat and the dust of summers.

The new ACII generally carries 46 passengers. Obviously, the rise in passenger traffic was forcing the Indian railways to increase capacity. An attempt was made to popularize double-decker coaches. The idea could not catch on as the double-decker coaches were not considered safe enough in Indian conditions.

The Indian Railways, however, succeeded in their attempts to run faster trains, running at speeds of more than 100 km per hour. The first attempt in this direction was the introduction of Rajdhani Express between New Delhi and Howrah capable of running at 130 km per hour. The train proved to be an instant hit with the passengers and demand for similar trains on other trunk routes began to be made forcefully.

Though its implementation took an inordinately long time for reasons not seen initially, a landmark event in the history of post-Independence Indian Railways was the decision to build an underground railway system: the Calcutta Metro. Indian Railways has at least developed an expertise to execute such a project anywhere in India or abroad.

However, the country's priorities continued to be start more surface and long-distance trains like the Rajdhani Express and the next in the Rajdhani series was introduced on the New Delhi-Bombay route. Today

Rajdhani trains link Delhi and almost all State capitals, except those in the North-East. Jaipur and Ahemdabad are also not on the rajdhani map but will be included soon when the Delhi-Ahmedabad route is converted to broad gauge. It may be added here that for safety reasons the Rajdhani trains are not run at their maximum permissible speed.

A faster train, the Shatabdi series, has also been introduced from Delhi in recent years and has proved to be very popular with tourists and inter-city travellers. The travelling schedule of the Rajdhani trains enables the trveller to spend the night on the train and reach his or her destination next morning well in time for a full day business. On the other hand, the Passengers travelling by Shatabdi, which is capable of a speed of 160 km per hour, can even return to Delhi in the evening. The all air-conditioned Shatabdi trains is said to be providing a competition to the airlines flying from Delhi to destinations like Agra, Jaipur, Chandigarh and Bhopal. Of course, like the Rajdhani trains, the Shatabdi trains also do not run at their maximum permissible speed.

It is possible to introduce a still faster train or accelerate the speed of the existing trains with the induction of the state-of-the-art 6000 horse power three-phase AC electric locamotives, imported from Switzerland. But the present track, signalling and other conditions will not allow faster trains. For the time being the advantage of the new locomotives would be in boosting the hauling capacity of both the passenger and goods train. For instance, the new imported engine can haul 26 coaches or even more, against 18 or 19 in the present trains.

It is not that only faster passenger trains are envisaged. There is an equal interest in upgrading the technology and with it the hauling capacity of the more efficient wagons are also being introduced to increase the capacity of the goods trains. After all, the goods trains are the real bread winners of the Indian Railways.

Though there is no hurry to allow trains to run at speeds well in excess of 160 km per hour, some preparations seem to have already been made to plunge India into the realm of really fast trains with the recent decision to import from Germany 21 high speed passenger coaches which can be used in trains of 300 km per hour speed. The agreement to import them includes transfer of technology.

The electrification of tracks, which so far has covered 20.8 per cent of route kilometres, will also be helpful in introducing still faster trains for both passenger and goods traffic.

But it is not possible to introduce really fast trains without improving tracks and the signalling system to bring them to specified standards. A "Bullet" like train would also require a dedicated track, exclusively for such a train. It is doubtful if the present shape of Indian economy would allow such a luxury. The effort at the moment is to improve tracks and upgrade their maintenance to make them safer and comfortable for the present generation of high-speed trains. The welding of tracks will eliminate the common hazard of saboteurs removing fishplates. About 70 per cent of welding job has far been completed.

There has been an interesting by-product in this exercise. Ecologists must be quite pleased to see the wooden sleepers being replaced with concrete ones thus drastically cutting the need for consumption of wood. The amount of saving of wood can be judged from the fact that in the last 10 years or so, about 65 million concrete sleepers have been manufactured to meet the requirement and still a lot of wooden sleepers have to be replaced. It is estimated that the task would completed only towards the end of the century.

One of the travails of journey on the Indian Railways ususally begins at the very initial stage the booking of ticket for the journey. The introduction of computerized reservation, beginning with Delhi in mid-1980s, has made that task comparatively less cumbersome. But the introduction of computerisation has been bigger boon in the field of freight traffic. Today, for instance, it is possible in Delhi to trace the progress of a goods wagon almost at the drop of an eyelid; before computerisation the process would have taken several days.

The job of modernisation and speeding up the railways would not be complete without introducing a unigauge system in the country. But it is a big task, involving huge expenditure. Of the 62,800-km of route length in the Indian Railways, metre gauge accounts for 24,000 km and narrow gauge account of another 4,000 km.

The areas not served by the broad gauge often complained that their economic advancement suffered because of this Goods and passengers travelling long distances across the country required transhipment for want of a single gauge link. But in the early 1990s, the Government decided that the country has no option but to adopt a policy of unigauge. The alarming decline in freight traffic—lost to road transport—could have also forced the decision.

— Development of rail network in backward areas.
— New line from Udhampur to Baramulla and Kumarghat—Agartala, Lumding—Silchar, Harmuti —Itanagar and Bridge at Bogibeel on Brahmputra.

— Rs. 400 crore for new lines as against Rs. 220 crore in the current year.

— More than Rs. 300 crore for rail infrastructure development in North—East.

— More than Rs. 100 crore for expansion of railway system in Jammu and Kashmir.

— Originating loading of 390 MT during 1995—96. Target of 410 MT of freight loading during 1996—97.

— Computerised reservation provided at 271 locations upto 1995–96, likely to be made available at more than 300 locations by March, 1997.

— Computer reservation facility is available at Srinagar, Port Blair, Panaji, Shillong, Agartala, Imphal and Gangtok etc. which are not connected by rail. It is being made operational at Aizawl, Itanagar and Kohima.

— To provide universal facility of return and onward reservation, software is already operational at New Delhi and Secunderabad PRS. It is to be extended to Mumbai, Calcutta and Chennai.

— Satellite based telephone service on many long distance trains. This facility already introduced on Mumbai—Delhi Rajdhani Express trains during next year.

— AC 3 tier coaches operating on all Rajdhani Express trains and 51 pairs of other Mail/Express trains.

— Unreserved Second Class coaches attached ot many trains during the current year.

Catering will be provided from 01.04.97 in Hazrat Nizamuddin—Trivandrum, Hazrat Nizamuddin—Bangalore and Hazrat Nizamuddin—Jammu Tawi Express. Changes will be included in the fare itself as in other Rajdhani Expresses.

Finance

Since 1924-25 railway finances remain separated from general revenues. They have their own funds and accounts and the Railway Budget is presented separately to Parliament. However, the railways contribute to the general revenue a dividend on the capital invested. Quantum of contribution is reviewed periodically by a Parliamentary Convention Committee.

Over the years Indian Railways have made concerted efforts to achieve self-sufficiency in production of rolling stock in the country. Locomotives are build in Chittaranjan Locomotive Works (CLW), Chittaranjan, Dieseal Locomotive Works (DLW), Varanasi and BHEL, Bhopal, a public sector company which has developede capability to manufacture electric locomotives for the Indian Railways. In 1993-94, CLW manufactured 140 broad gauge electric locomotives, DLW produced 138 broad gauge diesel locomotives (including 13 locos for public sector units) and 14 metre guge diesel locos. Diesel Component Works (DCW) has been set up by the railways at Patiala for manufacturing and repairs of components of diesel locos and sub-assemblies. The project has attained the rated capacity for manufacture of components for diesel engines, its repairs and rebuilding of diesel locomotives. Bu!k of passenger coaches are manufactured in Integral Coach Factory (ICF), Perambur, Madras and Rail Coach Factory, Kapurthala. Integral Coach Factory (ICF), manufactured 1,038 fully furnished coaches and the new Rail Coach Factory (RCF) set up at Kapurthala produced 1,025 coaches in 1993-94. In addition to ICF and RCF, three are two more units in public sector, viz., M/s. Jessops, Calcutta and Bharat Earth Movers Limited (BEML), Bangalore, who also manufacture coaches and electrical multiple units. A wheel and axel plant has been set up at Bangalore to cut down imports in this field. The plant performed excellently during 1993-94 and helped the railways to save valuable foreign exchange.

Railways production units are striving to develop new products for the Indian Railways. AC3-Tier coach has been manufactured by RCF which would make AC travel cheaper and comfortable. Further, production of 5000 HP electric locomotives and full efficient diesel locomotive have also commenced at chittaranjan Locomoive Works and Diesel Locomotive Works respectively. Diesel multiple units for suburban non-electrified routes and mainline electric multiple units for electrified sections have been manufactured by Integral Coach Factory, Madras.

Passenges originating had risen from 12,840 lakh in 1950-51 to 37,080 lakh in 1993-94 and passenger kilometre from 66.52 billion in 1950-51 to 296.2 billion in 1993-94. Despite constraint of resources, the railways have been able to cope with increasing demand of passenger traffic. Railways are the premier mode of passenger transport both for long distance and suburban traffic. During 1993-94, Indian Railways introduced 135 new trains, extended the run of 49 trains and increased the frequency of 10 trains in non-suburban sector. Similarly, in suburban sector, railways introduced 88 new trains and extended the run of 154 trains.

Freight Traffic

Rapid progress in industrial and agricultural sectors has generated higher level of demand for rail transport, particularly in core sectors like coal, iron and steel, ores, petroleum products and essential commodities such as foodgrains, fertilizers, cement, sugar, salt, edible oils, etc. Revenue freight traffic increased from 732 lakh tonnes in 1950-51 to 3,587 lakh tonnes in 1993-94. Transport effort measured in terms of net tonne kilometres (NTKm) increased from 38 billion in 1950-51 to 252.4 billion in 1993-94. Some of the measures taken for improvement are: (i) line capacity augmentation on certain critical sectors and modernisation of signalling system; (ii) measures such as unit train operation for bulk commodities like coal; (iii) increase in roller-bearing equipped wagons; (iv) increase in trailing loads to 4,500 tonnes; (v) operation 'UNI-GAUGE' on Indian Railways; (vi) strengthening the track structure by providing heavier and stronger rails and concrete sleepers; and (vii) production of prototype electric locomotive of 5000 HP for freight operation by Chittaranjan Locomotive Works.

Operational Efficiency

The railway Budget, presented by the Railway Minister, Mr. Ram Vilas Paswan in the Lok Sabha, took care not to increase the fare structure for the second class and suburban travellers whose reactions can be instant if not violent. Mr. Paswan made it clear that the largest public sector employer was willing to share the burden of meeting some of the development and social goals of the Government.

Thus came a clear commitment to extend the railway network in the backward regions of the country. A railway line to Kashmir, some capitals of the North eastern States and some hill region of UP is going to be a reality in the near future. Mr. Paswan also announced that while all 56,000 casual labourers would be absorbed, he would also terminate the move to engage the private sector in carrying out certain services like clearing operations so that the jobs reverted back to the employees of the Indian Railways.

As in the previous year, the upper class passengers (AC and first class) were asked to bear a 10 per cent hike in fares while the second class sleeper travellers were asked to pay only 5 poer cent extra. The night travel cost is clearly rising every year, though few would crib about it if it is accompanied by better services.

Some economists, however, have not been impressed with the decision to spare the second class traveller because it makes little sense to concentrate on higher classes alone for resource mobilisation. About 1.20 crore people travel by second class, but they account for only about 10 per cent of passenger traffic. It need not be emphasised thay even today the majority of Indians either do not travel at all or board a train very rarely.

A big hike that has already alarmed the industry was projected infreight charges: 12 per cent against 10 per cent last year. A basket of 15 items, deemed essential commodities, was exempted from this hike, though it is doubtful if these commodities would eventually manage to hold the price line.

The official estimate in Rail Bhawan is that the 12 per cent increase in freight traffic would contribute no more tan a 0.127 per cent rise in the wholesale price index. Industry is worried because it has been introduced at a time of industrial slowdown and rising inflation.

Mr. Paswan's efforts at "selective" adjustments in the fare and freight structure will yield him a revenue of Rs. 1800 crore which is almost double the amount last year. This would please rail Bhawan, though not necessarily for long if the hike in freight rates results in further loss of goods traffic to the road transport sector.

The share of the railways in the country's total freight traffic has declined drastically to 42 per cent from nearly 90 per cent in 1950—51. If the railways hope to capture at least 50 per cent of the freight traffic in the next two years or so, any further upward revision may not be wise, though it is hard to see how it can be avoided. Besides, the 12 per cent hike in freight has come in the wake of 10 per cent hike announced just seven months ago when Mr. Paswan presented his first budget.

It is a argued that the periodic steep rise in freight and passenger fares could be avoided, or minimised, if the railways improved their efficiency and functioned purely as a commercial propositon. This may not be such an easy task in Indian conditions where, for instance, the demand for more trains goes on mounting even when in other countries the number of trains is being brought down. There has been a steadyu deterioration in the operating ratio of the Indian railways which is an indicator of how the revenues are used to meet operating expenses.

Possibly because introducing new trains has now become so common, the budget did not have a long list of new trains, except a modest number of five "golden jubilee" and seven other trains. Frequency of 10 trains was also increased. Of the 17 new lines announced, the Planning Commission has given clearances to 12. But a generous number of surveys—37—for new lines would be taken up in 1997—98, apart from five for gauge conversion and three for doubling.

The budget might have included many more new schemes if only the size of its Plan had been kept at Rs. 11,000 crore, as demanded by the Railways, and not pegged at Rs. 8300 crore. The budgetary support at Rs. 1831 crore works out to 22 per cent when the railways had pressed for a hefty 40 per cent support.

The budget has set a target of carrying the highest ever freight trafic of 430 million tonnes in 1997—98, projecting the figure on the success of meeting the previous year's target of 410 MT. However, it is to be remembered that much of the freight carried in the previous year was low revenue yielding traffic as a result of which the financial target was missed by Rs. 325 crore. This was made up partly because the passenger traffic earnings went up by Rs. 130 crore. The Railways also carried more coal and ffodgrain, though the latter is low income yielding traffic.

The activities of Civil Aviation are broadly divided into three areas; operational, infrastructural and regulatory-cum-developmental. On the operational side, Indian Airlines Ltd. and private airlines (scheduled and non-scheduled) provide domestic air services. Air India Ltd. provides international air services. Indian Airlines Ltd. Also provides air services to neighbouring countries. Pawan Hans Helicopters Ltd. provides helicopter support services primarily to the petroleum sector. Infrastructural facilities are provide by the Airports Authority of India (AAI). The two authorities viz. International Airports Authority (NAA) were merged on April 1, 1995 to form a single authority viz. Airports Authority of India (AAI) as a result of enactment of Airport Authority of India Act, 1994. The regulatory and developmental functions are lookded after by the Ministry of Civil Aviation and the Directorate General of Civil Aviation.

With the repealing of the Air Corporation Act, 1953, on March 1, 1994, the monopoly of Indian Airlines, Air India and Vayudoot over scheduled air transport serivices came to an end. Seven private operators, who were hitherto operation as air texis, have been granted the status of scheduled airlines. In addition, 21 air taxi operators have been given the permit for charter/non-schedule air transport services. A new policy for private investment in civil aviation has been announced allowing for 40 per cent foreign equity in domestic airlines.

Domestic air services are operating in a competitive

environment and this has effectively been in existence since April, 1993. By September, 1996, 34 aircrafts in the 120 plus category belonging to the private airlines were in operation. The natural consequence of creating a competitive environment in this sector was that, by March 1996, 41.1 per cent of the domestic air transport was being catered to by private air services. The number of passengers carried by private operators has increased from 15,000 in 1990 to 4.1 lakh in 1992, 29.2 lakh in 1993, 36 lakh in 1994 and 48.9 lakh during 1995. The ushering in of competition in domestic services has two major implications for Indian Airlines. First, it had to share the market on its profitable trunk routes with private operators. Second, it had to contend with the loss of critically skilled personnel to private operators who offered much higher emoluments. This affected its ability to optimally deploy its existing aircraft capacity. India Airlines has since geared itself towards coping with the challenges brought forth by competition.

Several measures which have been taken by the public carriers mainly centered on making the organisation adopt a market oriented approach to decision making and to considerably improve the quality of its product. It has improved its passenger facilities both on board and on the ground, on time performance, flight safety measures and has also increased employee participation to provide better services.

For Indian Airlines Ltd, the year 1995-96 has been considerably better than the last few years. The Company made an operating profit of Rs. 156.51 crore in 1995-96 as against Rs. 36.24 crore in 1994-95 i.e. an increase of 332 per cent. The Company has laid stress on passenger facilitation by increasing the seat pitch on the Boeing-737. It has also increased the number of seats in the Executive class of A-320. Other measures include improvement of flight service, adoption of convenient time schedules and agreements with Global CRS companies to enable passengers to have access to flight schedules globally. These measures taken by the Company have started yielding positive results, and the seat load factor increased to 73.4 per cent in 1995-96 as against 69.7 per cent in 1994-95.

Indian Airlines laid stress on cargo promotion in association with M/s. GATI and its earnings from cargo have increased from Rs. 89.7 crores in 1994-95 to Rs. 112.7 crore in 1995-96. The company also provided the ground handling services to various foreign and domestic carriers. As a result, the company's profitability increased and the net loss came down from Rs. 188.7 crore in 1994-95 to Rs. 110 crore in 1995-96. The Company carreid 7.7 million passengers and performed 722.8 Revenue Tonne Kilometers in 1995-96.

Indian Airlines still incurred losses due to the heavy incidence of depreciation, interest and financing charges associated with its A-320 fleet. It has also had to contend with increases in overhead costs, increases in exchange rates, etc. During 1995-96, the company increased its domestic fares effective from 1.10 1995 on an average by 20 per cent and dollar fares with effect from 1, January 1996. But this was not sufficient to meet the increasing costs of operations.

The price of ATF was revised from 3rd July, 1996 and the annual impact of this has been estimated to be Rs. 60 crore in 1996-97. Consequently the company has increased its domestic fares effective from 22nd September, 1996 and proposes to increase dollar fares effective from 1st March, 1997 to offset some of its losses. Constant efforts are being made to monitor the uneconomical routes and to improve its market share by aggressive marketing strategies.

Air India Ltd. incurred a net loss of Rs. 271.8 crore in 1995-96 as against profit of Rs. 40.8 in 1994-95. According to provisional estimates the company also incurred a net loss of Rs. 195 crore during April-September, 1996. While the total operating revenue of the company increasd by 14.6 per cent from Rs. 2980 crore in 1994-95 to Rs. 3,426.5 crore in 1995-96, the total operating expenditure of the company increased by 24.9 per cent from Rs. 2,920 crore in 1994-95 to Rs. 3,647.5 crore in 1995-96. The resumption of losses was due to factors such as flights and disruption of flight schedules; the incidence of depreciation and interest on account of acquistion of four Boeing 747-400 aircraft; increase in expenditure by 24.9 per cent due to insurance, fuel and oil, landing lease, rental and hire charges; increases in allowances payable to the employees and payment of additional perquistes as per the Memorandum of Understanding reached with the Unions, associations, guilds; and the drop in its yield. Air India's overall load factor of 62 per cent is also low compared to other international airlines. Air India's share of international traffic originating from India came down from 42 per cent in 1981 to 35 per cent in 1991 and 20.4 per cent in 1994. However, in 1995 Air India's market share had improved marginally to 22 per cent.

In addition four B-747-400 aircraft which were acquired recently, Air India acquired two more B-747-400 aircraft in December 1996. To provide for growth in the short-term, Air India wet-leased a few aircraft. Five new stations were added in 1995 i.e. Manchester, Amsterdam, Tel-Aviv, Entebee and Perth. With the acquisition of two new aircraft, new destinations like Chicago and Zurich are being introduced. Air India has formulated a four pronged revitalisation strategy comprising the following: (i) growth in fleet, capacity, passenger carriage and market share, (iii) increase in efficiency and greater productivity, and (iv) development of human resources. There has been an improvement in on time performance of Air India which is over 85 per cent in 1994-95. While profits have declined, most of the physical parameters have improved in 1995-96 as compared to 1994-95.

Pawan Hans Helicopters Limited (PHL) basically provides helicopter support services to the petroleum sector i.e. ONGC and Oil India Limited and connects remote and inaccessible areas. It also provides air support services to several customers which include the Governments of Punjab, Madhya Pradesh and Arunachal Pradesh, Lakshdweep Administration, GAIL, BSF, and the Revenue Department. The total revenue flying hours during 1995-96 were 18,582, as compared to 18,458 during 1994-95. The revenue earnings and net profits during 1995-96 were Rs. 156.68 crore and Rs. 37.26 crore respectively, compared to Rs. 134.25 crore and Rs. 39.97 crore respectively in 1994-95. The flying hours during April-September, 1996 were 10470 and revenue and net profit were Rs. 87.72 and Rs. 26.50 crore respectively.

The International Airports Division (IAD) of Airports Authority of India (AAI) manages, operates and develops five internaional airports at Mumbai, Calcutta, Delhi, Chennai and Thiruvanthapuram. IAD earned a net profit of Rs. 113.59 crore in 1995-96 as compared to a net profit of Rs. 97.7 crore during 1994-95. During 1995-96, expenditure grew by 35 per cent whereas revenue increased by 27 per cent. Passenger and Cargo traffic at 256.4 lakh and 561582 tonnes during 1995-96 were higher by 12 per cent and 14.2 per cent respectively than in 1994-95. IAD has declared a divided of Rs. 22.72 crore (20 per cent of post tax profit) for 1995-96 as against Rs. 15.28 crore (25 per cent of paid up capital as on 31.3.1195) for 1994-95.

A number of projects like modernisation of air traffic

services at Mumbai and Delhi airports, installation of Airport Surveillance Radar/Monopulse Secondary Surveillance Radar at Ahmedabad, Guwahati, Hyderabad and Thiruvananthapuram, development of 12 model airports for upgradation of facilities and improvement in the quality of the services at the airports have been taken up. Although investments in airports of the North Eastern region are not economical, a large number of operations have been taken up there. Sixty per cent of investment on projects which have the prior approval of NEC is borne by the North Eastern Council. Development work in other areas like Jammu & Kashmir, Lakshadweep, Himachal Pradesh, Andaman & Nicobar are also under way.

The Civil Aviation Sector has two functional divsions–operational and infrastructural. On the operational side, Indian Airlines, Vayudoot and private air taxis provide domestic air services and Air India provides international air services. Pawan Hans provides helicopter services ONGC in its shore operations and to inaccessible areas and difficult terrains. Indian Airlines operations also extend to the neighbouring countries, South East Asia and Middle East. Vayudoot Limited is in the process of being merged with Indian Airlines. Its network which linkds the remote places in the North Eastern Region is being taken over by the newly created Short Haul Operations Department of Indian Airlines. India has been a member of International Civil Aviation Organisation (ICAO). India got elected to the council of ICAO in the triennial elections held in September 1992 at Montreal by a record margin of votes.

The Department of Civil Aviation is responsible for the formulation of national policies and programmes for developmnt and regulation of civil aviation and for devising and implementing schemes for orderly growth and expansion of civil air transport. Its functions also extend to overseeing the provision of airport facilities, air traffic services and carriage of passengers and goods by air. The Department is also administratively responsible for the Commission of Railway Safety, a statutory body set up under the Railway Act.

Policy Initiatives

In a major policy change, the Government has ended the monopoly of Indian Airlines and Air India on the scheduled operations by repealing the Air Corporation Act, 1953. The Government has also converted Indian Airlines and Air India into public limited companies to enable these airlines to tap the capital market to meet their growth requirements and also to give them greater autonomy in order to face the challenges of stiff competition. There are at present six private scheduled airlines operating on the domestic network rendering the passengers a wider choice of flights. Apart from this, 15 air taxi operators are providing non-scheduled air services. The existing policy on air taxi services provide for a route dispersal plan to ensure operation of a minimum number of services in the north eastern region, Andaman and Nicobar Islands, Lakshadweep and Jammu and Kashmir.

In order to help the Indian exporters and make their exports more competitive, the Government had introduced in April 1990 an 'open sky policy' for cargo. Under this policy any foreign airlines or association of exporters can bring freighters to the country for upliftment of cargo. The Government have also permitted market forces to determine cargo tariff, with IATA rates as the floor rates.

The charter flights bringing foreign tourists in the country are now allowed to operate to certain domestic airports cleared for tourist charter operations in addition to the international airports. The minimum payment to the Indian tour operator by the foreign charter operator is 350 US dollars per person for a seven days package for the period from 1 October to 31 March and 300 US dollars for the period from 1 April to 30 September. However for tourist from SAARC countries, the amount to be remitted is 50 per cent of the aforesaid amount.

Air taxi services can be operated as non-scheduled flights both on chartered and non-chartered basis to 93 airports in the country open to civil operations. The seating capacity of aircraft used for air taxi operations is so regulated as to ensure an orderly growth of air transport services in the country. The air taxi operators are free to charge any fare in their own commercial judgement. The procedure for import of aircraft for air taxi services has been simplified by dispensing with the requirement of licences for import of aircraft, components, etc.

Directorate General of Civil Aviation (DGCA) is the regulatory organisation for enforcing civilian regulations, air safety and airworthiness standards. It is responsible for (i) regulation of air transport services to/from/within India; (ii) formulation and implementation of standards of airworthiness applicable to all civil aircraft registered in India; (iii) certification of aircraft operators and licensing of air crew, engineers and airports; (iv) investigation of air accidents and incidents; and (v) rendering advice on matters relating to air transportation and processing of aviation legislation. DGCA also coordinates all regulatory functions with the International Civil Aviation Organisation (ICAO).

Bureau of Civil Aviation Security (BCAS) is a nodal body on all civil aviation security matters. It is responsible for the formulation of the National Civil Aviation Security programme and its application. It sets the guidelines/standards of the security measures and monitors their enforcement at the airporst through periodical/surprise inspections and conduct of dummy checks and also imparts training in aviation security on a regular basis. It has four regional offices at Bombay, Delhi, Calcutta and Madras, which have a bomb detection and disposal squads.

The Airports Authority of India formed on 1 April 1995 by merging the International Airports Authority of India and National Airports Authority, is responsible for providing safe, efficient air traffic services and aeronautical communication services for effective control of air traffic in the Indian air space.

The Authority manages 92 civil airports and 28 civil air terminals at defence airfields in the country. It controls and manages the entire Indian air spce extending even beyond the territorial limits of the country, as accepted by the International Civil Aviation Organisation (ICAO). The Authority comprises of a National Airports Division and an International Airports Division. Air Traffic Control (ATC) Services, Communication Services and Radio Navigational aids are provided by the National Airports Division at all the airports including the five internationals airports viz.,Delhi, Calcutta, Madras, Bombay and Thiruvananthapuram. It has a Civil Aviation Training College at Allahabad which imparts training to various operational cadres like communication, ATC/radar controllers. The College is being modernised under a UNDP plan and will emerge as an important training establishment in the South-East Asia conforming to ICAO standards. It also has a Fire Service Training School at Narayanpur near Calcutta for imparting training and conducting refresher courses in fire fighting and rescue services.

The International Airports Division of the Authority

is responsible for providing services and facilities for efficient operation of air transport at the five international airports of the country. The Division is also responsible for the planning, construction, maintenance of terminal buildings, airfield pavements, visual ground aids, passengers and cargo handling, airport fire services etc., at the international airports. It has established an Institute of Aviation Management and the Fire Training Centre at New Delhi to impart training in aviation management and fire fighting/rescue services.

India has bilateral air services agreements with 74 countries. Air India Limited is the major international carrier of the country. It operates services to USA, Canada, Europe, the Russian Confederation, the Gulf/ Middle East, East Asia, Far East, Africa, Australia. Air India owns a fleet of 26 air craft consisting of nine B747-200, two B747-300, four B747-400, three A300-B4 and eight A310-300 aircraft. Air India has also plans to augment its fleet through the induction of three A310-300 aircraft in 1995-96 and two additional B747-400 aircraft in 1996-97. During 1993-94, Air India carried 19,77,668 passengers as against 21,81,000 in 1992-93. The drop in carriage of passengers has been due to flight engineers strike and changes in scheduled deployment due to induction of Boeing 747-400 aircraft and training of pilots.

Indian Airlines is the major domestic air carrier of the country. It also provides services to 11 countries viz., Pakistan, Maldives, Nepal, Sri Lanka, Malaysia, Bangladesh, Thailand, Singapore, UAE, Oman and Kuwait. Its operations cover 66 destinations including 14 abroad. The Airlines owns a fleet of 10 Airbus A300, 30 Airbus A320 and 18 Boeing B737 (excluding 2 Boeing 737 set aside for disposal) and 2F-27 (leased out). Presently six private scheduled airlines and 15 air taxi operators are supplementing the air transport services provided by Indian Airlines on the domestic sectors.

Pawan Hans Limited has been providing helicopter support services to the petroleum sector including ONGC, Oil India Ltd., and Enron Oil and Gas, USA at Bombay. Apart from this, it also provides services to certain state government and public sector undertakings. The company presently has an operational fleet of 20 Dauphin, one Bell 206L4, two Robinson R 44 helicopters, as also two leased MI 172 helicopters. Out of these, 11 Dauphins and two MI 172 helicopter are presently deployed with ONGC for their offishore oil exploration work. One Dauphin each is operating with NTPC, Government of Punjab, Lakshadweep Administration and Enron Oil and Gas, USA at Bombay. One Robinson helicopter is leased to Oil India Limited. One bell 206L4 and one Robinson R 44 are being used for business charters for which there is a growing demand. In addition, the company has undertaken operational and maintenance contracts of helicopters belonging to Government of Madhya Pradesh, Gas Authority of India, Border Security Force and a private party. It achieved total flying task of 19,270 hours during 1994-95 as compared to 18,812 hours in the previous year. The average monthly deployment of helicopters has also improved.

Indira Gandhi Rashtriya Uran Akademi located at Fursastganj (UP) is an autonomous body established to provide an opportunity to commercial pilots to achieve higher standards in flying and ground training. The Akademi is equipped with modern and sophisticated trainer aircraft, flight simulators, computer based training system (CBT) and excellent audiovisual training aids. Commercial Pilots Licence courses with multi-engine endorsement and instrument rating are conducted on a regular basis. The Akademi has trained 248 fixed wing pilots and 20 rotory wing pilots till now. Besides there are 35 flying clubs/institutes which impart ab initio training and 11 gliding clubs/wings in the country.

Research and Development

Research and Development Directorate of DGCA is responsible for; (i) type certification of civil aircraft, engines, propellors and equipment: (ii) approval of modifications and repair schemes of civil aircraft; (iii) development testing of indigenous aircraft materials, parts and equipment; (iv) scientific laboratory investigation work on failed aircraft/power plant; sructural parts and components; (v) design and development of gliders, light trainer aircraft, glider launching winches; (vi) quality control monitoring and testing of fuel samples, etc; and (vii) economics of aircraft operation and performance evaluation.

With our large pool of skilled technical manpower, relatively low manpower costs and extensive manufacturing base, we should be in a position to have a much larger share of aerospace market from the West, says the author. Aviation in India strarted witha special flight by the grand old man of Indian aviation Mr. J.R.D. Tata and since then, aviation has never looked back though this vital means of transport has not been without its periods of glory and setbacks.

Standing as it does now at the threshold of the 21st century, India can boast of new planes like the spanking new 747—400s, but it has to accept the blot of unfortunate crash of the Saudia plane and Kazakh Airlines aircraft, which is a pointer towards what needs to be done.

Aviation is one of the most significant technological advances of our time. Apart from its strategic importance, it has a major role in economic development.

Our country has been fortunate in having started aeronautics related activities as early as the 1940s when Hindustan Aircraft Ltd., forerunner of today's Hindustan Aeronautics Ltd. was established in Bangalore. Over the years, a number of academic and R&D institutions have also been set up which have created an extensive range of skills and capabilities. The strong domestic base contributes to the capacity of our aerospace industry to generate significant economic activity.

India's industry is reaching out of forge new partnerships as our economy is opening up. This applies to the aerospace industry as well. With all our experience and skills, India's share is only 0.1 per cent in the world aerospace market which is valued at Us $ 300 billion per annum.

Prospects

With out large pool of skilled technical manpower, relatively low manpower costs and extensive manufacturing base, we should be in a position to have a much largest share of the market from the West. The strengths of our academic and R&D institutions and the extensive capacity of our industry in both the public and private sectos have to be put together to meet our nation's requirements as also to develop an international presence.

By the year 2010, it is projected that passenger traffic will more than double, Aisa-Pacific being the fastest growing region. Airport infrastructure requirements upto the year 2010 are expected to be of the order of US $ 350 billion. Large investments will also be required in air traffic management, communication, navigation and surveillance systems and upgrading of other systems at airports.

Within the country, over the next 10 to 15 years, a

number of new aircraft may have to be inducted for a variety of uses. Airport systems will have to be upgraded and manpower will hve to be trained on a large scale.

We have had notable success in a number of areas such as making training and combat aircraft, as also space vehicles and satellites. New knowledge and skills have been acquired in the curse of design and development of launch vehicles, the Light Combat Aircraft and the Advanced Light Helicopter. Using these skills, we can provide internationally competitive products and services.

To our friends from other countries we can say that there are ample oportunities for cooperation in the growing Indian economy and in the aviation sector. India would welcome mutually beneficial partnership in which we share knowledge, skills and resources. The cooperation can be in a manner in which the strengths of two sides are drawn on and commercial benefits shared equitably.

During the year 1995-96 the domestic air transport operations in the country witnessed appreciable growth in traffic as the total traffic carried by Indian Airlines and private operators reached the 12.8 million mark. Seven private operators were granted status of scheduled operators and 18 companies are holding air taxi operator's permit.

Better Performance

During the said period scheduled airlines operated 67,908 flights carrying 49,71,064 passengers and air taxi operators have operated 8,609 flights carrying 1,16,153 passengers. Tourist charter flights had brought in 84,811 tourists by 844 flights during the year.

Air India introduced four new destinations during 1995-96–Manchester, Amsterdam, Entebbe and Tel Aviv.

Also the airline operated 182 flights from different points in India carrying 18,513 Haj pilgrims.

Indian Airlines improved its operating profits form Rs. 36.24 crore in 1994-95 to Rs. 114.35 crore in 1995-96.

Pawan Hans Limited increased its net profit to Rs. 51.58 crore during the last year. The company started helicopter services to Arunachal Pradesh in the North-east in December thereby meeting a long standing demand for airlinks from the State. It has also finalised the purchase of two Bell helicopters and part of its fleet expansion programme.

Alliance Air (Airline Allied Services Ltd. a wholly owned subsidiary of Indian Airlines) started its airline operations from 15 April' 96 after the transfer of one Boeing 737 aircraft from Indian Airlines.

The second aircraft was transferred by Indian Airlines on 25 April, followed by two more planes in July and August this year. The route network was further expanded when Alliance Air took over services of the fifth and sixth planes in the first week of September. It has taken all its senior personnel from Indian Airlines adding upto 183 employees.

The on-time performance of Indian Airlines has significantly improved with the passenger load factor going up from 68 per cent in 1994 to 72.3 per cent in 1995. The Average number of passengers carried by Indian Airlines has also increased by about 5 per cent during 1995.

Special marketing efforts have been initiated, which include setting up of special counters, Computer Based Automatic Information System, KERB squads to inform passengers of delays and cancellations, introduction of J class in all A 320s and improvement in inflight service and improved safety. The airline also added Kaula

Lumpur and Yangon (Rangoon) to its international network. The year ended with Indian Airlines getting the best airline award against the stronger contenders in the private sector.

Last year saw the process of stablisation and substantial presence of the private airline operators in the domestic transport industry.

Twenty-four aircraft were sanctioned to the private airlines, including 13 Boeing aircarft. The total seats carried by both Indian Airlines and private operators add up to 50,000 seats a day.

While Indian Airlines has a capacity of 28,000 seats, the private operators have 21,000. The total passengers carried per day has been around 36,000 representing an overall load factor of 73.6 per cent. Private operators carry 40 per cent of the traffic with their fleet. The domestic airline traffic has increased dramatically from 7.5 million in 1990 to about 12 million by 1995.

As far as international airlines are concerned, more than 2 million additional seats have been offered to international passengers and Air India entered into unique code sharing agreements with four airlines.

Air India has seen a great deal of transition and consolidation. The main thrust areas of the airlines were expansion of routs, introduction of new destinations, better product, more productive utilisation of resources and improvement of image. After a gap of a decade or so, Air India expanded its fleet by inducting four B747-400 aircraft, orders were placed for two more and were delivered in November this year.

New destinations like Perth, Johannesburg, Durban, Manchester and Amsterdam were opened, as have Madrid, Entebbe and Tel Aviv. More international operations were introduced from Chennai, Thiruvananthapuram and Bangalore and the number of direct point services increased.

An ambitious programme of fleet renewal is being taken up to achieve growth of operation. Though Air India's profits had dwindled this year because of increased interest and depreciation burden due to acquisition of new aircraft and increase in cost of operations, the health of the airline is improving.

Determination and dedication to regain its lost place of pride amongst the international carriers is making the airlines forge ahead. The passenger load factor has increased from 59 per cent to 68 per cent. The number of passengers carried showed an upward trend too.

Several measures have been taken by India to upgrade its product and services. These include introduction and use of Malayalam language for the Gulf sector, upgraded inflight services in long-haul sectors and setting up of special counters and multiple check-in facility at Delhi and Bombay airports. Airport lounges at major centres like Hong Kong, Bangkok, New York and London have been upgraded.

Air India has entered into code sharing arrangement with Scandinavian Air Services, United Airlines, Finnair and Kuwait Airways. It has also entered into joint venture agreements with Gulf Air, Malaysian Airways and Air Mauritius.

In 1995 the profits of Air India declined considerably due to reduction in overally yield, increade in expenditure and hiring of aircraft, higher material consumption and outside repairs due to aging fleet, world-wide increase in insurance rates and increased depreciation and interest due to acquisition of new aircraft.

The process of acquiring the Medium Capacity Long Range aircraft is in an advanced stage. The year ended with the hope that Air India will expand its network dramatically, once it inducts new aircraft by phasing out the aging aircraft.

Another major development was the merger of National Airports Authority of India and International Airports Authority of India into a single entity called Airports Authority of India to give a unified direction. During the year 1995, tremendous work has been done in the construction of terminal buildings, providing navigational aids and installation of sophisticated radars at Thiruvananthapuram and Hyderabad. Special thrust has been given to the North-eastern region, Jammu & Kashmir and smaller airfields in Uttar Pradesh.

New Terminal buildings have been completed at Jaipur, Lucknow, Vadodara and Calicut airports. Sophisticated communication facilities were provided at many airports—Agartala, Belgaum, Jorhat, Tezpur, Tirupati, Jammu, Varanasi, Bangalore and Calicut. Over Rs. 440 crore are planned to be spent in the coming year for the development of airport infrastructure.

Lucknow and Jaipur model airports have already been inagurated and work on the other ten airports is in an advanced stage of completion. Work has also been undertaken for construction of new airports at Kargil in Jammu & Kashmir, Taru in Meghalaya, Lengpuri in Mizoram and Androth in Lakshdweep.

A big boost was given to private investment in airport construct with a cabinet clearance on the proposal for Calicutt airport. A memorandum of understanding was signed between the Government of Karnataka and private consortium for constuction of an international airport in Balgalore in December last year. It is hoped that all 12 model airports would be ready by the end of the financial year 1996-97, Providing better and safe services to the discerning traveller.

Pawan Hans Limited has completed 10 years ofits service to the nation. The organisation has earned a profit of Rs. 40 crore during 1994-96. The company has started helicopter services in Arunachal Pradesh from December, 1995 by deploying on Dauphin helicopter having a capacity for 8 passengers. Next year, it will substitute Dauphin helicopter by a large 25 seater helicopter.

The company is planning expansion of its fleet to meet the demand of ONGC and other customers. It is purchasing 2 Bell 206 L4 helicopters to meet requirements of Customs Department and 2MI-172 helicopters to meet ONGC requirements. The company proposes to add upto 10 more helicopters to its existing fleet by March '97.

Proper dissemination of requisite information in a disaggregate and easy-to-understand manner is an effective means to plug many leakages in the delivery system. In fact, such information concerning development works at grass roots level should be made available without any favour or fear, it need be, against small payment for photocopies, etc. so that action may be taken against the erring persons concerned. This leads to the issue of decentralization and dissemination of information on development and welfare activities programmewise and villagewise, including the financial inputs, implementing authority, method, sources of funds and information and so on. Broadly, the areas to be covered for dissemination of information includes, inter alia, subjects asigned to the local bodies as well as basic minimum services in an easy to understand language and through accessible media, modern and\or traditional. Since the programme and schemes differ from place to place, the relevant information requires to be area-specific. In short, the right type of information to be made available and accessible to the people is desired in a disaggregate and comprehensible manner. Hence the whole process should be people-based and people-oriented. It should not be that unnecessary and unwanted information gets piled up. The need-based open house information system is a powerful tool in the hands of the people which will go a long way to achieve greater transparency, accountability and resultant efficiency in functioning at all levels—Central, State and sub-State—down to the village level.

It should be mandatory on the part of the government to release such information at all levels not only sectorwise but also workwise and villagewise. Kerala has reportedly brought out some 600 booklets on plan schemes in local language for dissemination among the Panchayats. On a very limited scale, the Maharashtra-based voluntary organization like the Foundation for Research in Community Health (FRCH) does so in Marathi and even Dr. Chitra Naik's voluntary organization has also attempted in this direction. Thus, in this great endeavour, besides the government and Panchayati Raj, the voluntary organizations, and committed social workers like Anna Hazare play a predominant role in carrying out such widespread awareness campaign and bringing out transparency in activities.

In this context, resource mapping may be a useful exercise for total resources available at various levels which will provide a broad spectrum of the resource deployment. It would not be impossible to bring out such information on a massive scale in this hi-info-tech age.

The delivery channel, open house information system, Panchayati Raj and such organizations are only means to achieve the absolute end of poverty. This calls for the strengthening of productivity potential of the economy and creating space for involving the poor in the development process through decentralization ensuring participatory democracy with proper institution and organization and empowerment of the deprived ones. Most of the present poverty allocation programmes are relief oriented rather than development oriented to achieve a sustainable growth with egalitarian bias. But the alleviation approach will never be able to root out poverty within a reasonable time-frame even with a higher growth.

It is common knowledge that even a good organization can be badly run. Ultimately, it may be emphasized that an individual can, make or mar the system. Here the character counts. And charity begins at home. How prophetic, today, are the words of Dr. S. Radhakrishnan uttered on 14 August 1947, "A free India will be judged by the way it will serve the interests of the common man in the matter of food, clothing, shelter and the social activities.... Unless we destroy corruption in high places, love of power, profiteering and black-marketing, we will not be able to raise the standards of efficiency in administration as well as in production and distribution of the necessary goods of life."

Even on the eve of the recent Republic Day, President Shankar Dayal Sharma emphasized, "I feel convinced that India's need today is for a profound moral and ethical rejuvenation.... Simultaneously, there must be a forthright and outright rejection of casteism and communalism with its sinister nexus with corruption and criminality.... Our approach will have to be value-based and people-centred."

In a developing country like ours, the new economic policy aiming at more market-oriented liberalization, privatization, and globalization does not, as the experience of other countries in a similar situation suggests, appear to be very friendly to the backward areas and the weaker sections of the society. It is something like a five-star hotel, open to all without any distinction of caste, creed, colour or status. But actually who can avail of it? Thus, without adequate infrastructure facilities and purchasing power, the poor often get marginalised in the process of development and the spatial and income disparities get widened. It is also implicitly agreed that the reform process would hurt the poor most and, therefore, there is need for a 'human face' approach which would make the process less painful. Hence, this calls for an effective State intervention with poverty alleviation and other welfare measures.

Funds

Keeping in view the above fact, even the Ninth Plan (1997–2002) approach paper is reported to have envisaged an outlay of Rs. 60,000 crore for rural development which is double the amount allocated for the purpose in the Eighth Plan. So far so good. But mere more allocation of resources will not solve the problem. In fact, there is a dearth of a scientifically co-ordinated approach to rural development, management, organization and involvement of the people in the development process. So the most important question is: How will this amount be spent and how far their benefits will percolate down to the grass roots level? Our past experience so far has not been so encouraging. Even after five decades of Independence, one-third of our people (310 million) live below the poverty line. They do not have sufficient food to meet the calorie requirement of their bodies. Out of a rupee spent by the government, it is borne out, hardly 10 to 15 paise reach to the poor at the end, the remaining paise absorbed by the administration and leaked out to vested interest. If such is the state of affairs, out of Rs. 60,000 crore envisaged for rural development, only Rs. 6,000 to 9,000 crore is likely to be spent during the five years, erosion in the inductory value due to inflation apart.

In the absence of a sound delivery system, the financial allocations are not often fully fructified and their benefits do not reach out unto the last poor in the expected way. Investments sans proper organization go awry. So far the delivery organisation has been one of the weakest links in our planning process. However, there is a silver lining to the dark clouds. The recently re-incarnated Panchayati Raj institutions (PRIs) can delivery the goods, provided they are empowered with adequate funds, authority, accountability and requisite information on village-level workers concerned and programmes for development and welfare. Today the poor illiterate villagers do not know fully the details of development works carried out in their villages. They do not get information on the money spent on such works and the copies of bills, vouchers and the muster roll of the workers in respect of construction of schools, health centres, community halls, roads, wells, houses, etc. to verify the facts. Sometimes the works reported to have been completed are only on paper. In a sense, information is power. The suppression of information from the people, breeds embezzlement, misappropriation and corruption. Over the years, enormous amounts have been spent in the name of village uplift and welfare of the poor and crores of rupees have been misappropriated. Taken together the amount involved in such decentralized corruption can total up to a huge scam of the meanest type looting the poor. Today even mute animals are not spared as in the reported 'fodder-scam.'

Communication

With the number of telephones in India aggregating to a

mere 5.8 million to service a population of over 850 million people, telecommunications is an industry of tremendous growth potential. It is also one of the most profitable business areas in India today with the pay back on a line being only two years.

The new Ministry of Communication has drawn up a very ambitious 26 point program for this Industry. Some of the highlights are that private participation has been invited for building and operation of telecom networks in 'growth centres and satellite towns'.

In the new Industrial Policy, telecom equipment was delicenced and thrown open to foreign investment. Several joint ventures came up- GPI and K.K. Birla, Ericcson with their long term collaborators the Jiwarajkars, AT&T with Tata Telecom, Fujitsu with the Punjab State Electronic Production and Development Corporation and Alcatel with B.K. Modi. Of these companies gearing up to meet the indigenous requirements, the last two are near ready to commence production of equipment to meet the specifications set out by the Department of Telecommunications.

The Ministry of Communication has in October this year allowed eight private companies to establish cellular telephone systems in the four metropolitan cities kof Delhi, Bombay, Calcutta and Madras. In each of the four metros, the two private companies would operate the system along with their two foreign partners. Tenders are expected to be floated soon inviting private manufacturers to set up value-added celluler telephone systems in other secondary cities in the country. Mobile telephones will be made available against foreign exchange payment. Video conferencing, Email, Radio Paging and other value added services and manufacturing of ten thousand line exchanges, will be available to joint/private sector without licensing (capacity) regulation.

Until now only terminal equipment and PABX manufacturing was permitted in private sector subject to lecensing.

New Import Export Policy

A new Import-Export Policy was announced on 1st April, 1992. The policy statement eliminated a number of import categories, exceptions and exemptions, special lists, open lists etc. The new 5 year exim policy makes trade "free" subject to a small negative list. Even the short negative list which prohibits import of certain items is likely to be curtailed further during the year.

The Finance Minister, Dr. Manmohan Singh, while inaugurating the International Asia Pacific Conference on private sector has stated that "bureaucratic controls would be fully dismantled, quantitative import restrictions phased out and customs tariff reduced to international levels to make the private sector vibrant."

Collaboration by non-Small Scale Industrial units for items reserved for the SSI sector is allowed subject to the condition that the firms concerned would undertake to export at least 75% of its output. Applications for 100% EOUs are cleared by the SIA and those for 100% Export Processing Zone (EPZ) units are cleared by the Development Commissioner of the particular EPZ, subject to the guidelines aplicable to such units.

Export obligations are no longer imposed in other cases of collaboration. Instead, the export offers made by the applicants are taken note of as being in the nature of a gentlemen's agreement, and are not linked to legal or bank guarantees. Their fulfilment is a matter of trust, and not compulsion.

The Government has liberalised the guidelines for * automatic approval in 30 days for all cases involving an equity of upto US $ two million.

The Government has initiated steps to deregulate the domestic civil aviation industry and bring an end to the public sector monopoly in domestic civil aviation. The Ministry of Civil Aviation has proposed to withdraw the three major constraints on private taxi operators namely:

- Restriction on level of fare.
- Route restriction.
- Flight time restriction.

The ministry has given support to the 'open sky policy' for air taxi licenses in India. Selling Indian airlines or Air India is however not on the immediate agenda.

Liberalisation and 'open sky policy' has opened the vast domestic market to new scheduled airlines in India. There are 22 registered private airlines of which a few are already operational. The most notable being East West Airlines which has already acquired 3% of the total domestic market, that was till now monopolised by Indian Airlines.

The ministry of Civil Aviation and Tourism has recently invited foreign capital and technology for 'collaborative partnership' for an "integrated development of the Indian aviation industry".

'Liberalisation window to opportunities was the theme of the 41st annual convention of the Travel Agents' Association of Inida, held at Hydrabad recently.

Many interesting facts emerged during the convention. Partial convertibility has made visiting India and even shopping an inexpensive proposition. For example, there is a charactered flight every day from Uzbekistan carrying 240 passengers stopping at New Delhi for a day of shopping!

In a radical departure form the Industrial Policy of

1956, the Union Government has announced that it will allow 100% foreign equity participation for setting up of power plants in India. It has also permitted substantial modification in the Electricity (Supply) Act 1948 to hasten the private sector's participation in the ailing power sector.

These two decisions have been taken by the cabinet and the bill containing the amendments in the Electricity (Supply) Act and the 100% foreign equity participation proposals will be tabled soon before the Parliament.

The 100% foreign equity participation proposals allows free repatriation of profits and other incentives. Besides, it will facilitate foreign parties to set up power plants without time delays, which are solely responsible for the cost escalation in the power projects.

Proposals from foreign investors for new power units are expected to be cleared through a high powered committee. The domestic private company's proposals will be cleared through a single window to minimise bureaucratic and other delays. The Government is likely to invite various foreign consortia including non-resident Indians (NRI's), particularly those in Japan and the UK to come forward.

Since the 1960's, the two public sector companies, Oil & Natural Gas Commission (ONGC) and Oil India Limited have held a monopoly over oil exploration in India. ONGC is seeking a change of its status to an autonomous corporation with the freedom to raise its resources directly from markets in India and overseas. It is prepared to enter into new projects such as country wide gas grid in collaboration with the private sector. It is understood that 73 drilling and exploratory blocks have been offered to international oil companies through international tendering. The Government has invited offers for joint ventures to develop designated medium-sized as also small sized oil and gas fields offering a range of incentives. Companies may singly or as a consortium bid by the 31st December 1992. Major tax concessions are made both for Indian and foreign companies engaged in oil exploitation. Income Tax will be levied at a flat rate of 50% without surcharge as against 65% now applicable to foreign companies in other businesses.

The Government has accorded status of importance to the Bombay High oil producing belt in the Arabian Sea and initiated highly sophisticated defence procedures for safeguarding the rigs from aggression.

Potential estimates claim that India should produce 70 metric tonnes of crude per annum by 1999 and will be considered a major economic power of the next century.

The rate of tax applicable to foreign companies continue to be 65%. Surcharge is not levied in the case of non-resident assessees.

Section 80 HHC of Income Tax Act 1961 provides for 100% exemption from income tax if the entire business income is generated from exports. The deductions available to an assessee involved in exports in now to be calculated on a new formula. The formula makes a distinction between a manufacturer exporter and a trading exporter. The actual deduction is calculated taking into consideration the FOB value of the exports as against the turnover and profits/gains of the business.

Under the provisions of Section 80-0, 50% of technical services fees, royalties etc derived under an approved agreement are deductible from income. This concession which was available to Indian corporate bodies has now been extended to non corporate bodies. This concession has been granted with the prupose of encouraging professionals such as architects, accountants etc to earn foreign exchange for the country. Further clarifications are expected from the Government on how this scheme would be applied to professionals as prior approval of agreements may be very difficult to administer.

Some immediate effects of the changes outlined above can be seen from the following events:

— As early as April 1992, a 1243% increase in foreign investment has been registered in India since the announcement of the liberalised industrial policy in July 1991.

— Foreign Collaborations in India recently approved by the Indian Government include companies like General Motors, General Electric, Coca Cola, Suzuki, Leasaffre (French), GERB (German), Buhler (Swiss), IBM, BMW, Ford etc. In the communication sector, AT&T, Siemens, France and British Telecom have shown keen interest in bidding for setting up cellular phone networks in India.

— 100 senior Japanese business executives spent a week in India in February 1992 and Nomura Securities Company has established a presence in Delhi. The opening of a trading office of a securities house in known to be a major jumping off point for further investment in India.

— 200 foreign participants attended the Euromoney conference in Delhi on "Business, Finance and Investment in India" in the last week of March, 1992.

New Horizons

In the recent few months, with the Bombay Stock Market Scandal in which banks and financial institutions stand to lose upto Rs. 30 billion, inflation running upto 13% on occasions and other regional and national political problems, the feeling has been that the Government is now in the danger of letting opportunities slip away. The Government did announce de-licensing of the electronic industry, liberalisation which would permit foreign financial institutions to invest in India and permission to open branch offices by foreign companies in the last few months to counter the allegations that there has been a slow down in the economic reform process. Although there may be some truth in this allegation the process of liberalisation has certainly not stopped. The Government has given an assurance that it will endeavour to proceed with the intended further liberalisation as promised.

On the whole, along with devaluation of the rupee in June 1991, the new trade policy and the further reforms promised includding full convertibility of the rupee, if the new Industrial Policy and its effect does turn out to what it promises to be, new horizons will open. This should lead to faster growth of industries in India. Indian industries would be open and accessible to the world. The opening up of new areas such as air transportation and power generation for private sector participation will result in opportunities for contractors and financial institutions to bid for project and asset work. The feeling in India is that a clear signal has been sent to industrialists, both local and foreing, that the government really means business. The radical nature of the industrial policy has met and continues to meet some resistance from the bureaucratic machinery which it seeks to dismantle. Its fine print still requires further clarifications. But more important than the fine print is the inescapable fact the political power has finally recognised that it is time for a new order to emerge. For some, their efforts may have fallen short of expectations, but the Government has acted, at last.

This update has been prepared by Thakker & Thakker Solicitors & Advocates, Bombay, for the AIJA 1992 conference in Bombay on "Emerging Investment Opportunities in India". The Update is necessarily of general nature and seeks to provide information only on some of the major changes announced by the Government and cannot be regarded as legal advice.

Status of the Indian Telecom Network

India today operates one of the largest telecom networks in Asia comprising

— Over 20 172 telephone exchanges;

— About 118 400 route kms of coaxial terrestrial UHF/microwave radio relay systems up to 140 Mbit/s apart from analogue systems;

— 23 300 kilometres of optical fibre systems comprising of systems up to 565Mb/s;

— 50 per cent of Transmission network is digitalised.

About 7 700 cities and towns are connected to the National Subscriber Dialling (NSD) network and the Department of Telecommunications (DOT) plans to extend the facility to all automatic exchanges by 1997.

Fully automatic International Subscriber Diallilng (ISD) service is available to 237 countries through two international earth stations and submarine cable systems. Trunk manual service is also available to all countries.

To meet the low speed data communication needs of Business/industrial units in Remote and far flung areas, a Business. Message Network (RABMN) with a hub-station near Delhi, having a capacity of 1000 subscribers has been commissioned. About 456 Very Small Aperture Terminals (VSAT) are deployed in this network for providing data service at maximum speeds up to 9.6kbits.

A dedicated Packet Switched Public Data Network

(PSPDN), with international access for computer communication services is available in the country with speeds up to 2Mbit/s.

For providing international connectivity, a Gateway Packet Switching System (GPSS), is available which offers the capability of sophisticated telecommunication networking terminals and computers internationally.

INSAT satellite systems are being used to provide over 4126 two-way speech circuits through 165 earth stations across the length and breadth of the country. In 1975, the government of India took a decision to have its system for meeting domestic communication needs of the country and approved the scheme in 1977 for the multi purpose Indian National Satellite System (INSAT).

The INSAT-I series of satellites, comprising four satellites were launched in 1982, 1983, 1988 and 1990 respectively. INSAT-II series of the satellites comprising four satellites in orbit and one ground spare, are being manufactured indigenously. Under this series, INSAT-IIA was launched in July 1992 and INSAT-IIB Satellite was launched in July 1993.

The present space segment comprises of * INSAT IIA and IIB Satellites in orbit. The ground segment of INSAT-ID & INSAT-IIA, IIB comprises of 82 fixed Satellite earth stations. In addition to the above, 29 satellite earth stations have been commissioned as captive networks to meet the telecommunication needs of Government undertakings.

Besides above fixed satellite earth stations the ground segment also comprises 23 mobile terminals including three Flyaway Terminals. These terminals are capable of being transported to different parts of the country by road/air to restore the telecommunication services as well as to meet an urgent telecommunication

Profile

Capital	–	New Delhi
Area	–	3,287,560 sq km
Population	–	915 million (1995)
Urban Population	–	27% (1994)
Population Growth	–	1.9% (1994)
GDP	–	USS 231,870 million
GDP, per Capita	–	USS 257 (1993)
Currency	–	Ruppee
TelephoneDensity		
Rural	–	0.25%
Overall	–	1.07% (1995)
Waiting list for Telephone Lines	–	2,496,850 (1993)
Cellular Subscribers	–	-
Facsimile Machines	–	50,0000 (1994)
Telex Subscribers	–	49,063 (1993)
International Outgoing Traffic (million mins)	–	614.2 (1994)
Network Digitization		
Switching	–	53.9% (1994)
Transmission	–	29.8% (1994)

need from any part of the country. There are also nine special routes/networks.

About 185000 villages out of 604 734 villages are provided with telecommunications facililties;

There were 2.5 telephones per 1000 population in the rural areas at the end of march 1995, as against the figure of 107 in the country as a whole. These figures are expected to become 3.00 and 15.00 respectively by the year 1997 as per the modest government investment. Private sector participation, which is expected shortly, will raise telephone density considerably.

The total equipped capacity of the Indian local network is 12 million with over 10 million main lines. There has been a rise of 25 per cent in telephone traffic in 1991-1992 and 35 per cent in 1992-1993 as compared to the previous year.

The pending demand however is 215 million and is growing at over 20 per cent per annum. In the past the registered demand has grown at a rate of 10 to 13 per cent per annum while the supply remained between 9 to 10.5 per cent. As a consequence the waiting list has grown. Over the last two years, we have stepped up the growth rate to 15 per cent per annum to see a slight dip in the demand.

The Indian Telecommuinications network provides nearly 400 000 Long Distance Switching Circuits with 94 per cent digitization.

A number of state-of-the-art switching technologies have been inducted in Indian network, ie FETEX 150, EWSD, AXE 10, No.5 ESS, OCB 283, System X, NEAX 61E and the indigenous CDoT.

Enhancement of capacity and digitalization of the transmission network is being carried out with optical fibre, digital microwaves and satellite.

A great emphasis is being laid on R&D of sophisticated digital switching and transmission equipment to meet india's urban and rural needs. The Centre for Development of Telematics (C-DoT) has successfully designed a family of digital-SPC switching systems from small to large main automatic exchanges.

Technology for several transmission products such as 10 channel UHF-600 MHz, 2/8 and 8/34 Digital mux, Satellite Based Rural Telegraph Network (SBRTN) Single Channel VHF and 2/8 Mbit/s OLTE has also been indigenously developed by CDoT and technology successfully transferred to a large number of local manufacturers. CDoT technology has also been offered to other countries as well.

Value added services are being indigenously developed exchanges through introduction of better signalling features such as Common Channel Signalling No. 7 and through ISDN.

The ultimate goal of R&D units is however to lead to the development of an Intergrated Services Digital Network (ISDN) and eventually to Broadband ISDN (B-ISDN) through Synchronous Digital Hierachy (SDH). Digital Access Cross Connect System (DACCS), Asynchronous Transport Module (ATM) etc.

There is a Telecommunications Engineering Centre (TEC) for issuing of specifications, type approvals, interface approvals and evaluation of new telecom products and for standardisation.

Over the years, the Department of Telecom, have built up extensive training facilities starting at the apex with Advanced Level Telecommunications Training Centre, near Delhi, set up with the systems and support of the UNDP and ITU.

The Telecommunications Training Centre at Jabalpur and 11 Regional and 25 State and District Level Training Centres also provides extensive training facilities. India has been extending assistance to Asia and Pacific countries too in meeting their training needs in the high tech areas of telecommunications.

Through DOT's consultancy group known as Telecommunication Consultancy India Limited (TCIL), India has been offering a wide spectrum of consultancy services in the international arena.

These include technical and management support, training, inspection, rehabilitation, modernization of existing systems, techno-economic studies in the core sectors of engineering and design studies, besides construction management and electronic data processing etc.

The consultancy services, include feasibility studies, network design studies, software support, installation, testing and commissioning of switching systems and transmission systems, operation and maintenance of networks.

TCIL has executed various contracts abroad and has been operating in about 28 countries.

The Indian Telegraph (Amendment) Bill, 1995

The National Telecom Policy 1994, has inter-alia laid emphasis on achieving the universal service, bringing the quality of Telecom service to world standard, provision of the widest permissible range of services to meet the customer's demand at reasonable price and participation of the companies registered in India in the area of basic telecom services as also making arrangements for protection and promotion of consumers' interest and ensuring fair competition. The Department of Telecomomunications feel that to achieve these objectives, there is need to separate regulatory functions from service providing functions which will be in keeping with the prevailing general trend in the world. It has, therefore, proposed to set up an independent Telecom Regulatory Authority to be called 'Telecom Regulatory Authority of India' which, to begin with, will be non-statutory in character but will have well defined functions and responsibilities and powers to play the role of a watch-dog body for the Telecom sector in an effective manner.

The Indian Telegraph Act, 1885 regulates the functioning of Telecommunications services in the country. Under Section 4 of the Indian Telegraph Act, 1885, the Central Government has the exclusive right of establishing, maintaining and working telegraphs and under the first provision of this section, it may grant a licence on such conditions and in consideration of such payment as it thinks fit to any persons to establish, maintain or work a telegraph within any part of the country. Under Section 4(2) of the Act, the Central Government may by notification in the Official Gazette delegate to the Telegraph Authority all or any of its powers under the first proviso to subsection (1). Section 3(6) of the Indian Telegraph Act, 1885 describes Director General (Posts and Telegraphs) as the Telegraph Authority and includes any officer empowered by him to perform all or any of the functions of the Telegraph Authority under the Act. Presently, the Secretary, Department of Telecommunications who has been notified as the Director General Telecommunications in his capacity as a Telegraph Authority exercises regulatory powers and performs regulatory functions as delegated by the Central Government under the Indian Telegraph Act, 1885. In order to vest the powers of the Telegraph Authority with the proposed Regulatory Authority in respect of certain assigned functional areas. It has become necessary to amend Section 3(6) of the Indian Telegraph Act, 1885 by including "any statutory or non-statutory authority".

The secretary, Department of Telecommunications stated in evidence that at present all the regulatory authority under the Indian Telegraph Act is exercised by the Secretary, Department of Telecommunications. This power of the telegraph authority can be further delegated by him to another officer of the Government. It cannot be delegated to a statutory or a non-statutory authority as such. So, the basic purpose of the proposed amendment of Section3(6) of the Indian Telegraph Act, 1885 is to delegate certain regulatory powers of the Telegraph authority to the proposed Telecom Regulatory Authority.

The Secretary, Department of Telecommunications further clarified that the reasons for not coming up with a comprehensive Bill to setup a statutory with independent powers at this stage, are that the Government would like to watch the working of such an authority for a year or two and learn from such an experience. After getting the feed-back from the Chairman and Members of the authority and various interest groups viz, operators and subscribers etc., it would frame a comprehensive law to make it a statutory authority. Then the authority will derive its powers directly from an Act of Parliament.

The witness further told the Committee that "the need for amendment is based not only on Government perceptions of the local market but also arises from the international experience that wherever there has been a situation of more than one player in the market scene, a need has been felt for an independent umpire. The current trend in the telecommunication sector the world-over is to distance policy making functions, operational functions and regulatory functions from each other and to entrust regulatory functions to an independent Regulatory Authority for regulating Telecom services".

The Secretary, Department of Telecommunications informed the Committee that in due course the proposed authority would be independent and autonomous; it would operate outside the Government, at arm's length from the Government so that it could inspire the confidence of various operators as well as the subscribers. He further added that for this purposes the intention of the Government is to ensure that it is manned by people of eminence and independent views. Therefore, the Cabinet has decided that it would be chaired by a retired or a serving Chief Justice of a High Court or a retired or a serving Judge of the Supreme Court and it will have two members who should have worked in the State Government or the Central Government in a position not lower than the position of an additional Secretary to Government of India for a period of three years. These Members would enjoy the status of Secretary to Govt. of India. It was further stated that the tenure of the Chairman and the Members would be secure and protected. Their removal will require the same safeguards as are available to Judges of the Supreme Court. Similarly their emoluments and other terms and conditions of service would not be changed to their disadvantage. The Secretary Department of Telecommunications stated that the apparent idea was to send across a strong signal that there would be an authority who would act independently, impartially, in an objective manner to protect the interests of the operators as also of the subscribers.

Clarifying the position further in reply to a query by the Committee, the Secretary, Deptt. of Telecommunications stated that soon after the amendment of law, two things would follow. Firsts that Department of Telecommunications would set up this authority by means of a Resolution of the Government. Secondly the Department would issue a notification that the authority set up under that Resolution is vested with the powers of the Director-General of Telecommunications under Section 4 of the Indian Telegraph Act in respect of certain matters. Once that is done, the authority would be clothed with the powers of Telegraph Authority in relation to its are a of work. However, it would still be a creature of the executive arm of the Government. Later after an year or so it will come before the Parliament with a comprehensive Bill.

In reply to a query regarding the impact of Telecom Regulatory Authority after its inception on working of Telecom Network in the country, the Ministry informed that it was excepted that the Telecom Regulatory Authority would have healthy impact on the working of telecom services in the country, since it will act as a watch dog for telecom sector, ensure level playing field as also monitor quality of services and protect and promote the consumer interest.

Asked whether after setting up the Authority, it would be possible for Government to set aside any decision of the proposed Authority, the Secretary Deptt. of telecoommunications replied in negative. He further added that the intention was that there would be not right of appeal to the executive wing of the Government. The orders issued by the proposed Telecom Regulatory Authority can only be challenged before the High Court or the Supreme Court.

In the light of the Government view known to the Committee, the Committee agree with the amendment of Section 3(6) of Indian Telegraph Act, 1885 for inclusion of any statutory or non-statutory authority within the definition of Telegraph Authority and support the Bill. The Committee hope that steps will be taken to set up a statutory Authority.

Science & Technology Development

The investment in Research and Development. (R & D) has increased from a paltry Rs. 20 crore in the First Five Year Plan. Presently there are 214 universities, 400 national laboratories and 1300 in-house R & D centres in the industrial sector. Several Science & Technology departments have been set up in the areas of environment, non-conventional energy resources, bio-technology, ocean development, industrial research, space, atomic energy, defence, health, agriculture and electronics.

Identification and promotion of priority areas in R & D is done by Science an Engineering Research Council (SERC) set up under the Department of Science & Technology (DST). DST supports 12 autonomous research insitutions as well, for furthering research work in several discipline. Technology Information, Forecasting and Assessment Council (TIFAC) has been set up for generating technology forecasting and technology assessment documents and enabling a technology information system that is interactive and nationally accessible.

Industrial research in several diverse fields of scientific activity is being undertaken through a network of 40 laboratories and 81 field stations set up by the Council for Scientific and Industrial Research (CSIR). In the field of bio-technology, more than 24 specialised R & D centres have been developed for pursuing state-of-the-art research. Identical efforts for promoting new avenues of research are being undertaken in the field of ocean development as well.

The Union Budget for 1996-97 has taken various measures to promote R & D facilities. A matching one time grant has been awarded to CSIR and the Indian Council of Agricultural Research (ICAR) for modernisation of laboratories and institutes. The Technology Development and Application Fund created in 1995-96 has been proposed to be strengthened by Rs. 30 crore. A Five Year Tax Holiday under Section 80-IA of the Income Tax Act has been allowed to companies exclusively create for participation in R & D activities. The existing procedure for awarding weighted deduction under Section 35(2AA) of the Income Tax Act on sums paid for scientific research to a National Laboratory or a University or an IIT has been amended, by deleting the condition of approval by an outside body. In order to encourage R & D efforts, goods developed and patented in India and concurrently in specified countries have been exempted from levy of excise duty for a period of 3 years. The exemption procedure for customs duty on import of equipment and consumables for R & D institutions has been rationalised as well.

Private Sector Partcipation

The Value added service sector has been open to the private sector since 1992. In respect of value added services, except radio paging and mobile telephony services, companies registered in India are permitted to operate under licence on non exclusive basis. In the area of Radio paging and Cellular Mobile Telephone Services, however, a policy of selection is being followed in the granting of licences through a system of tendering.

A tender for operation of radio paging services in 27 cities was earlier invited and 14 companies have been granted operating licences. For other areas of the country comprising 19 territorial telecom circles, tenders have been invited, and licensing is being progressively done. Commercial service has been started in 22 cities by one or more operators to over 48,000 subscribers and in the rest of the five cities the service will start very soon.

Eight companies have been selected for the franchises of cellular mobile service in the four metro cities namely Bombay, Delhi, Calcutta and Madras. In respect of rest of the country, a tender had been invited. The evaluation of 33 bids for the 20 telecommunications circles, is expected to be completed shortly. Service has commenced in Calcutta and Delhi in September 1995.

With a view to supplement the efforts of Department of Telecommunications in providing telecommunication services to the people, 81 bids received for grant of licence for operation of basic services in 20 telecom Circles are now under evaluation.

The government has decided to create an autonomous Telecom Regulatory body called the Telecom Regulatory Authority of India (TRAI). This will have well defined functions, responsibilities and powers to play the role of a watch-dog body for the telecommunications sector in an effective manner. The Authority will regulate its procedure for conduct of business with the approval of the government and will be expected to ensure transparency and accountability.

Profound changes are taking place in Telecommunication sector the world over and India is no exception. The Government of India has taken bold initiatives to liberalise and expand the telecom network in the country.

Some of the milestones in this direction are:

— 1984

Manufacture of Customer Premises Equipment delicensed.

— 1991

New Industrial Policy permitting private sector to manufacture all types of telecommunications equipment.

Other salient features are:

No industrial Licence is required;

Automatic approval of foreign equity investment up to 51 per cent in the case of manufacturing projects:

Automatic approval of foreign collaboration in the

case of telecommunications sector with technology fees up to Rs. 10 million net of taxes and/or royalty up to five per cent for domestic sales and/or eight per cent for exports.

The possibility for more than 51 per cent foreign equity and higher technology fees/royalty in manufacturing projects through special approvals;

All foreign investment proposals for telecommunications services require the specific approval to the Government of India.

1992

Value added services thrown open to private sector participation.

1994

New National Telecommunications Policy allowing private sector participation in basic services announced.

The National Telecommunications Policy announced by the Government would be instrumental in bringing about phenomenal expansion and improvement in the telecom sector.

The objectives of the Telecommunications Policy are:

— providing Telecommunications for all and Telecommunications within the reach of all;

— Universal Service Obligation at affordable and reasonable price;

— Providing telecommunications services of world standard;

— To ensure that India emerges as a major manufacturing base and major exporter of telecom equipment.

The targets laid down in the policy are as follows:

- — Telephones to be available on demand by 1997;
- — All vjillages to be provided with telecommunications services by 1997;
- — In urban areas a Public Calling Office (PCO) should be provided for every 500 persons by 1997;
- — Special emphasis on the quality of telecoommunications services provided to the customers will be given;
- — All value added services available internationally to be introduced in India, preferably by 1996.

The other important aspects of the policy are:

- — Private initiative would be used to supplement the departmental efforts to raise additional resources both through increased internal generation and adopting innovative means, like, leasing, deferred payments, build-operate-and-transfer, build-lease-and-transfer.
- — A suitable funding mechanism for indigenous R&D is proposed to be set up;
- — Pilot projects will be encouraged directly by the government in order to access new technologies, new systems in both basic as well as value added services.

With low telephone penetration rates, India represents one of the world's most attractive markets for telecommunications service providers and equipment manufacturers. Service sector opening of the basic telecom services to the private sector is the biggest opportunity for foreign direct investment. The growth potential in the basic telephone service in India is tremendous taking into consideration the low telephone density at present.

The challenge in rural telecommunications in India is indeed quite formidable. Out of the 604 734 villages in the country, only 185000 have telephone facility. Over 420,000 villages are still without a telephone facility.

Under the National Telecommunications Policy, one public telephone will be provided in each of the over half a million villages by 1997. Provisioning of a single telephone in each village, as per the telecom policy, may involve an investment of the order of S billion US Dollars. The sub-sector of value added services is already open for private investment. This sector in India represents one of the world's largest opportunities for supply of services and equipment.

The Indian Switching market, which is estimated to increase from about 2.5 million lines now to over 3.00 million lines in 1996-1997 represents-one of the largest market in the Asian region. The digital switching markets in India has witnessed a true metamorphosis since 1991 when the new Industrial Policy was announced by the Government.

A number of foreign companies attracted by DOT's liberalised procurement policies, have set up local production ventures in India. The opening up of the Import Policy in 1992 has opened this largest market to international competition.

The market for providing private networks is also growing very fast. Major international companies have already announced their plans for making an entry in this market.

The Radio Transmission Equipment market in India has undergone extensive changes in the post industrial liberallization period. With the diversification or production of transmission equipment which was earlier limited to the public sector companies, the present production base has expand with the setting up of the manufacturing facilities in the private sector.

With the opening up of Microwave Radio systems to competition, a number of multinational companies have entered the radio equipment market. The digital microwave radio equipment market has potential for large investments since most of the radio frequency spectrum in microwave is still available for deployment.

The investment opportunities in the optical fibre cable and equipment as well as infrastrucure equipment for value added services such as cellular and paging are immense. With the possibility of the entire long distance network being converted to optical fibre media, a number of international companies are getting their products validated at present. The investment opportunities in this area are extremely good.

Another area expected to sustain great demand in the coming decade is VSATs with voice transmission. The steady increase in the number of customers demanding high bit rate data transmission and separate corporate networks has given spur to VSAT development.

With increased availability, VSAT services are likely to get a big push and, therefore, the opportunities in this sector are excellent.

— The gross receipts of the Department of Post during the year 1995-96 were Rs. 1150 crore. Gross working expenses were Rs. 2472 crore and net working expenses Rs. 1810 crore. there was, therefore, a deficit of Rs. 660 crore. During the year 1996-97, as per budget estimates, the gross receipts are expected at Rs. 1350 crore and gross working expenses at Rs. 2616 crore. With net working expenses at Rs. 1962 crore the deficit is estimated at Rs. 612 crore for 1996-97. (BE).

— The Budget of Department of Post has been in deficit continuously over the years, and no dividend is being paid to the general revenue. Modernisation activities, through inductin of new technoloy, has been initiated on a modest scale during the current plan. Its further expansion and spread during the next plan, are likely to improve the service efficiency. A modernised postal system should also be able to provide new value added services to yield revenue. Low tariff on most of the postal services for many years, and inadiquate agency charges for agency functions, are the main factors for the deficit. However, a moderate increase in some of the services i.e., printed postcard from 60 paise to 100 paise and registration fee from Rs. 6.00 to Rs. 8.00 and introduction of cmpetition postcard at Rs. 2.00 each is expected to yield additional revenue to the tune of Rs. 76 crore in a full financial year. The degree of subsidy, as indicated in Table 2.11 ranges from about 1 per cent in respected of money orders to 92 per cent on postcard.

— The network owned and operated by the Department of Telecommunications (DOT) has been generating surpluses, which is utilised for further exapansion of the net work. Net receipts increased to Rs. 4951 crore in 1995-96 (RE) from Rs. 3936 crore in 1994-95 reflecting an increase of 25.8 per cent. Net receipts are estimated at Rs. 5213 crore in 1996-97 (BE). The dividend contribution to the general revenues increased to Rs. 279 crore in 1995-96 (RE) from Rs. 270 crore in 1994-95. The operating ratio, which is a percentage of net operating expenses (excluding the provision for redemption of bonds) to operating revenue earned (excluding registration fee) has come down to 48.7 in 1995-96 (RE) from 48.8 in 1994-95. The plan outlay for Telecommunication Services (including all PSUs) for the year 1996-97 (BE) is marginally higher at Rs. 9874 crore from Rs.

9830 crore in 1995-96 (RE). The entire outlay (except Rs. 5.00 crore pertaining to WMo etc. which is by way of budgetary support) is to be financed from the internal accruals and extra budgetary resources of the Telecommunication sector. Internal accruals amounting to Rs. 7491 crore account for 75.9 per cent of total resources against 79.6 per cent in 1995-96 (RE).

— Though the telecom network in India is fairly large in absolute terms, (in 1994 it was ranked fourteenth in the world) yet the tele density was 1.4 per cent in March, 1996. An advanced and efficient telecommunications system can enhance international competitiveness of the economy. The DOT has been increasing the quantum of resources deployed for the development of the telecom infrastructure, although the pattern of financing has undergoes a sea change. During the first plan DOT received budgetary support which accounted for around 79 per cent of the total resouces deployed it. In the Eighth Plan, 78.7 per cent is expected from internal accruals, 21 per cent from borrowings and other sources, and only 0.3 per cent from budgetary support. In the coming years, substantial investment would be required to upgrade and expand the existing telecom network. The aggregate resource requirements for the provision of basic and cellular mobile telecom services as estimated bny the Expert Group on Commercialisation of Infrastruture Projects is placed at Rs. 1,91,500 crore by 2006. Thee estimates are at todays prices and duty structure.

— Of late, DOT has primarily relied on internal accruals. However, to meet its targets of network expansion, DOT will have to look to a larger resource pool. It will have to devise a tariff structure which largely reflects the cost oriented approach, subject to country's social obligations and thrusts.

— A corporate structure for the DOT will enable it to leverage its substantial assets and raise adequate funds to meet all its investment needs. Corporate structure would make DOT into an autonomous entity owned by the Government. In the short and medium term, the government will remain the dominant operator and provider of telecom services in the countrty. However, with the advent of private operators, the present tariff regime should orient as quickly as possible towards a costbased structure. It is imperative to have the tariffs reviewed to allocate costs for various services and identify the need, if any, of subsidies.

— As per the revised estimates for 1995-96, the total expenditure on Broadcasting was Rs. 974 crore as against total receipts of Rs. 549 crore. This shows an increase of 19 per cent and 20.4 per cent in total expenditure and receipts, respectively. As a result, the ratio of total receipts to total expenditure improved from 55.8 per cent in 1994-95 to 56.4 per cent in 1995-96. The rising trend in commercial receipts in broadcasting activity over the past few years is indicative of efforts being made in this direction. Commercial receipts were Rs. 426 crore in 1993-94, Rs. 450 crore in 1994-95, and Rs. 540 crore in 1995-96 (RE). Further break up of commercial receipts brings to the fore the overwhelming contribution of Doordarshan towards revenue generation. The commercial receipts in case of Doordarshan were Rs. 363 crore in 1993-94, Rs. 384 crore in 1994-95 and Rs. 460 crore in 1995-96.

— The important place commanded by India in world trade in coffee, tea, leather and spices on a historical basis has continued in recent years as wll. In 1994, India accounted for 2.4 per cent, 13.6 per cent, 2.5 per cent and 9.1 per cent of world trade in coffee and coffee substitues, tea and mate, leather, and spices, respectively. Furthermore, there has been a significant progress in export diversification, and India has emerged as an important exporter of iron ore and concentrates, and pearis, precious and semi-precious stones. In 1994, India accounted for 6 per cent or world exports of iron ore and concentrates and 10.9 per cent of world exports of pearls, precious and semi precious stones (Source: 1994 United Nations International Trade Statistics Year Book, 1995).

— During 1950, India accounted for about 1.8 per cent (1.85 per cent of exports and 1.71 per cent of imports) of world trade. After gradually declining to 0.57 per cent by 1980, India's share improved marginally to 0.63 per cent by 1985. The reason for improvement in the share was that while world trade declined in the period 1980-85, India's trade continued to grow. However it came down again to 0.53 per cent by 1991. The first half of the nineties witnessed a sharp increase in India's exports and imports have grown in dollar terms annually by 12.4 per cent and 9.4 per cent, respectively. The corresponding growth rates of world trade was about 5.7 per cent. The secular decline in India's share in world trade has been arrested and reversed, and the years ahead are likely to see a continuation of this increasing trend.

— The trade policy components of the reform process undertaken since July 1991 have been motivated by a full recognition of the important role that trade can play in promoting growth. The utilisation of the expanded scope for specialising in areas of comparative advantage is manifest in the improved growth performance of the economy. Furthermore, while exports have vigorously responded to the removal of the anti-export bias of a protectionist environment, domestic industry appears to have been stimulated by the expended availability of imported inputs and capital goods as well as the challenge of competing in the international market place. The positive response of Indian industry to liberalisation is amply demonstrated by the capital goods sector. The tariff on capital goods was as high as 85 per cent in the pre-reforms period. This has been reduced to about 25 per cent covering about 80 per cent of capital goods in 1995-96. The capital goods industry which witnessed a negative growth of 12.8 per cent in 1991-92, registered an average growth of about 23 per cent during 1994-96.

— The terms of trade, which measure the terms of exchange between a unit of exports and a unit of imports, have been improving in the post-reform period. Two common ways of measuring the terms of trade are the net terms of trade (NTT) and the income terms of trade (ITT). A time series indicating all parameters of terms of trade (TOT) for India since 1969-70 with the base of 1978-79 = 100 Indicates that there have been wide fluctuations in the TOT. The NIT (1978-79=100), which is an index of export prices divided by an index of import prices, improved from 109.3 in 1990-91 to 152.4 in 1994-95. It is

— It may be mentioned that India s purchasing power of exports as reflected thorough ITT has been improving continuously since 1985- 86. The value index of exports at 484 stands much higher than that of imports at 351 and hence, in terms of value, india has gained.But in terms of volume, the index of exports has been much less at 384 in comparison to that of imports at 515. This means that the volume of imports is increassing faster, though India is getting a better price for her exports.

— Compared to the experience of other developing countries, the improvement in the terms of trade for India has been very impressive. The NTT (1990=100), as presented in the UN's International trade Statistics Year Book, 1995, is reproduced below:

— Developing economies, with exports dominated by primary products, lost out to developed econoies,. Relavtive abundance of supply of primary products as well as the superior bargaining strength of developed countries have often ben adduced as two major reasons for the deterioration in the terms of trace. Gains in the terms of trade for India in the comparable period perhaps reflects her diversified export base as well as the relatively low international prices of oil in the relevant period.

Economies	*1980*	*1985*	*1990*	*1991*	*1992*	*1993*	*1994*
Developed	90	91	100	100	102	104	104
Developing	125	109	100	98	99	100	96
India	65	92	100	91	114	NA	NA

India is committed to further liberalisation of its import regime, notwithstanding the dismantling of licensing controls over a wide area. At the same time, there arc concerns whether developed nations of the world are implementing in letter and spirit their part of the obligations under the Uruguay Round Agreements. Many contries are resorting to protectinist devices in the guise of environmental hazards and exploitation of labour such as child labour. The obligations of providing access to imports of developing countries, especially textiles and garments, are being circumvented under one pretext or the other, even under the back-loaded integration of Textiles and Clothing into the World Trading System. Such restrictions are designed to keep out cheaper imports.

By virtue of the radical shift from a highly-regulated to an outward-oriented economy, India has attracted immense interest abroad, at both Governmental and private investor levels. India is one of the largest emerging markets, second only to China's, and the country has been experiencing inflows of foreign portfolio and direct investments—thought not as large as in China and a few other countries—which were unthinkable in the world of even 1980s. Economic strength has become the principal determinant of a nation's standing in the international community, and even the most powerful country, the United States of America, looks for market opportunities all over, more especially in the dynamic Asia-Pacific region, as the best shield of security.

With the end of the Cold War, the East-West barriers have broken down. The rapid spread of liberalisation and globalisation is a historic development which has blurred both East-West and North-South divisions. Developing countries have been compelled to adapt themselves to conditions of global interdependence although in the process they run grave risks in the medium-term and rare not assured of international safety nets.

In the rapidly changing world environment, each developing country must certainly concentrate on building its inherent strength and developing areas of comparative advantage and forge alliances with neighbours and, where promising, enter regional blocs which offer greater opportunities of trade and other exchanges to enhance national arena, disadvantaged nations must make common cause and unite to advance their pressing needs more effectively than what has been witnessed over the last fifty years in the post-decolonisation era. This is the only way of securing a post-cold war order which is just and equitable.

India has a long way to go before it could emerge as a strong global player, as currently it occupies the 32nd place as a leading exporter of merchandise, well below several countries in East and South-East Asia. It has to make up for the time lost in its inward-looking route to development which left the cuntry far behind in the international league, despite building a strong industrial base and possessing highly technical manpower, the third largest in the world. Indian planning did not take sufficient note of the gathering pace of global intergration with the frowth of merchandise trade exceeding the growth of output in virtually every year of the post-war period.

In recent years, India has begun to look East, is now a full dialogue partner in ASEAN (the 7-member Association of South East Nations) and excepts to find a place in the Asia Pacific Economic Forum (APEC) by 1999. These should promote greater intra-Asian trade and investment flows even as India strives to gain an increasing share of exports into developed economies of the West such as the European Union and North America. Trade with Russia and Eastern Europe as well as Central Asian States holds prospects of considerable expansion over present levels and a more promising development is the initiative taken by 14 states of the Indian Ocean Rim for an economic cooperation grouping with a Charter expected to be signed in March 1997.

The bilateral and pluralistic approaches cannot, and

should not, in any way dilute India's firm commitment to multilaterialism which is the best safeguard against domination of the global economy by a few powerful nations. India's immediate responsibility is to solidify South Asian cooperation through SAPTA and ensure its early graduation to becomes SAFTA (South Asian Free Trade Area) to make it a region of good neighbourliness less prone to conflilcts than at present. With 16 per cent of the world's population, India's weight in the international .economy remains negligible, and the building up of internal strength with determination through higher saving, and investments and greater efficiency in the use of resources is a pre-requisite for the country to claim its due share in the global market-place.

Looking Ahead

The fifth decade of Independence has triggered investment interest in India as never before. Policymakers should now bring in a lot more clarity on their objectives.

The rules of international trade have changed. Witrh trade barriers getting dismantled by the day, there is need to infuse a very high degree of competitiveness. A major development is the evolution of regional trade groupings like the European Community (EC), the North American Free Trade Association (NAFTA), ASEAN, APEC etc.

Though the south Asian countries have formed the SAARC, progress achieved in free trade among these has been slow. Apart from mere trade flows, potential benefits in terms of the phasing out of poliltical animosities and more cohesive regional developments are immense.... The EC experience proves this. Over the last 50 years Britain, France and Germany, who have been bitter adversaries for centuries, have been bonded together on the strength of mutuality of economic interests. The SAARC union could grow to include

China, the Central Asian Republics and the Indian Ocean rim countries, including South Africa, and forge close links with ASEAN and APEC in course of time. The comparable levels of economic development of most of the countries in this region would help in co-ordinated growth.

There is a huge market for such equiptment: there are capabilities in these countries to produce entire range of such equipment–generators, turbines, boilers, transformers, switchgears, motors etc.

The Korean automobile manufacturers—Daewoo Motors and Hyundai—indicate plants for developing India as a major centre for their global operations. Like we did in regard to Maruti, in the assimilation of mass production technology, India should attempt absorption of the high productivity levels of the Koreans, Americans and others; combine this with the strength of the massive availability of skilled manpower to win global markets.

With the progress of economic reforms in many countries of the world and deregulation of financial markets, the importance of private capital flows into Asia has increased from US $ 76.8 billion in 1994 to US $ 98.0 billion in 1995, while net official flows increased marginally from US $ 5.6 billion to US $6.4 billlion during the same period. Similarly, while there were considerable official flows to Mexico and the transition countries in 1995 in support of their comprehensive adjustment programmes, net private capital flows to the developing countries increased from US $ 140.4 billion in 1994 to US $ 166.6 billion in 1995. India has has modest, but increasing, success in attracting a growing part of these private capital flows. Furthermore, much of these private capital inflows into India has been of the non-debt creating variety, and helped to boost the balance of payments as well as the availability of investible resources in the economy.

The international financial community is appreciative of India's economic performance in the last years, but concerns continue to be expressed about the high fiscal deficit, the slowing down of structural reforms, continued restrictions on consumer goods imports, and tariff levels considerably higher than in other countries. Also, references are often made to India's move towards capital account convertibility (with some observers advocating a cautions approach), high level of subsidies, inadequate disinvestment in the public sector, need for further relaxation of rules to attract foreign investment and the continued high stake of the government in the public sector banks. On the whole, the international community is very positive about India's effort to achieve a high rate of growth.

Participants in the India Development Forum (IDF) meeting in September 1996 acknowledged the strong performance of the Indian economy and appreciated the new Government's declaration to continue reform measures to strengthen the social programmes as set out in the Common Minimum Programme (CMP). Various delgates stressed the importance of (i) fiscal consolidation, (ii) sustaining programmes in the social sectors, (iii) infrastructrue, (iv) provety eradication, (v) reforms in agriculture, public sector, and financial sector, and (vi) strengthening of legislation against child labour. In support of India's economic development, the donor countries pledged official assistance in 1996-97 of US $ 6.7 billion. Inclusion of US $ 400 million in long-term finance, promised on a bilateral basis at market rates, will raise this total to above US $ 7 billion. About 33 per cent of the total could be in the form of grants and interest-free loans.

With effect from January 1, 1997, India subscribed to the Special Data Dissemination Standards (SDDS) of the

International Monetary Fund (IMF). by subscribing to the SDDS, India ha committed itself to streamilining the tatistical system of the country to produce most of the data categories with a much shorter time lag, improved quality and coverage by December 31, 1988.

By virtue of the radical shift from a highly-regulated to an outward-oriented economy, India has generated immense interest abroad, but it has a long way to go before emerging as a strong global player, opines the author. India's development strategy launched in the 1950s, soon after Independence, aimed mainly at strengthening the industrial base of the country, especially in basic goods and heavy machine-building, and adopted the import-substituation model to achieve self-reliance. Exports were not viewed as an integral part of overall economic development, and such imports as became unavoidable were financed by drawing down foreign exchange reserves that had accrued to India at the time of Independence, in the form of sterling balances held in its favour for goods and services provided by this country during the Second World War.

Export pessimism dominated the mood of the early planners as it was rightly assumed then that until India's manufactures began to be diversified, there was little possibility of exporting manufactures while primary products and traditional manufactured goods faced poor demand prospects in the world market. It was during the later half of the fifties, when the Second Five Year Plan was under way with its emphasis on heavy industry, largely in the public sector, that it began to be realised that India needed to export to be able to finance at least part of the maintenance and developmental imports.

The foreign exchange crisis that was looming by mid-1957 reinforced the importance of export growth as part of planned development. The pessimistic view about the potential for export earnings gave way to a more positive approach in the Third Plan (1961-66) with the introduction of export promotion measures without deflecting from the thrust of import subsitution and industrialisation. It was clear by mid-estimated the import content of the inward-looking path of development opted by India. Pressures on balance of pyaments had already brought into existence the Aid-India-Consortium comprising the World Bank and developed countries interested in providing assistance to India. Renewed emphasis on exports was laid in the Fourth Plan (1969-74) which envisaged porogressive elimination of dependence on foreign aid while the Fifth Plan (1974-79) identified certain sectors such as engineering goods, garments, leather manufacture and marine products for achieving increases in exports.

Thus, as agianst virtual stagnation in the 1950s, export performance improved to an average growth of 3 to 4 per cent in the 1960s, and was more impressive in 1970s with an average growth of 6.3 per cent in volume and 15.9 per cent in value terms.

But in the three decades, India's share in world exports had declined throughout from about 2 per cent in 1950 to 0.65 per cent in 1970 and dropped further to 0.42 per cent in 1980. This was the period when there was impressive growth in world trade and the opportunities were seize by many smaller Asian developing countries as well as the industrialising economies in Latin America to great advantage.

Paradoxically, even as india's export growth was being maintained or marginaly improved upon, her share of world exports was declining. Over the three decades ending the Seventies, the share of exports in Gross Domestic Product (GDP) ranged from 4 to 6 per cent In a continental economy of India's size, the role of external sector in the development process was under-played so much that it took a successions of droughts, oil price shocks and balance of payments difficulties in the first two and a half decades of planning before the country could begin to see import substitution and export promotion as two sides of the same coin. But heavy reliance on quantitative restrictions on trade through import and export controls and detailed industrial licensing kept India a closed economy.

The Primary issuance of securities has a long history in India. The Indian bond market, measured by the estimated value of bonds outstanding, is next only to the Japanese and the Korean bond market in Asia. By January 31, 1995, the outstanding value of the Indian securities market was estimated to have reached Rs.3000 billion, almost 3.5 times its size in 1986. The size is deceptive as, despite attractive yields, secondary market trading has remained poor with virtually no quotation even in respect of listed securities. The estimated outstanding amount accounts for about 42% of GDP, as at the end of January 1995. Partial deregulation of interest rates in the early nineties and increasing emphasis on monetary policy in stabilization are the first major steps towards the emergence of an active debt market, with government securities spearheading the process. With the issuance of government securities at market determined coupon rates and the use of innnovative products, it has become possible, for the first time, for other issuers to offer debt products priced off the yield on government securities.

The process of financial sector reforms initiated in 1991, is far from complete. The Growth of the Indian Capital Market since Independence has been phenomenal. The number of stock exchanges increased from 7 in 1947 to 23 in 1994. Likewise the number of listed companies on stock exchanges grew from 1125 in 1946 to 7811 at the end of 994. Similarly, the quantum of listed capital registered a growth of about 565 times from Rs.270 crore in 1946 to Rs.152,322 crore at the end of March, 1994.

The basic objective of financial sector reforms is to promote a diversified, efficient and competitive financial system by a policy shift from detailed regulation and controls to one based on market forces. Alongwith dismantling administrative regulation, the goal is establishment of a system of prudential regulation, supported by a mechanism for reporting, monitoring and supervision of the compliance.

Another major plank of reform is injection of new competition into a hitherto virtually government owned financial system. For the first time in many years, six new banking licences have been granted to the private sector all of which have been implemented. The new banks are permitted to have financial joint ventures with fgoreign baks, particularly for accessing modern systems and technology. There has been a mushrooming of Non-Banming Finance Companies (NBFCs), some of whom have already built up a large net-work. Several well known investment banks have established a presence in India. Since April 1993, nearly 300 Foreign Institutional Inestors (FIIs) have been registered with the regulatory authority and quite a few are active investors in the domestic capital market which has been opened up to foreign portfolio investment in a limited way. Several new mutual funds have been set up by the private sector including some by global fund managers. The most spectacular growth has been registered when we compare the share of market capitalization to gross domestic products (GDP) which was 12.9% in 1946, while in 1991-92 it was 57.2% and further increased to 68.8% during 1993-98.

Trade Policy

Side by side with the announcement of New Industrial Policy for Promoting Small Tiny and Village Enterprises, the Government have also announced major reforms in the Trade Policy. The main objective of the trade policy have been to progressively reduce the system of administrative controls and lilcences and to link import except in the case of essential items. The major reforms in the Trade Policy are given below:

Exports were in the past allowed replenishment to provide for essential inputs required for the manufacture of products exported. To allow flexibility to enable diversification of export products and also as an incentive for exports, the REP licenses so issued, were allowed to be freely sold. The entitlement for REP licenses also varied from item to item. In view of the flexibility of the REP Licenses Government realise that to treat it as licence is an misnomer, under the new policy the REP licences have been replaced by a new instrument named 'Eximscrips'. Eximscrips will be issued on the basis of FOB value of exports or Net FOreign Exchange (NFE) earnings from exports as indicated below. The main features of the new systems are:

The basic rate at which Eximscripts will be issued against exports will be 30% of FOB value. Exports to hard currency areas will be eligible for Eximscrips valid for hard currency imports while exports to rupee payment areas will be issued Eximscrips valid for imports from these areas only. However, as a measure of transition, exports to rupee payment areas may continue to avail of REP licences valid for hard currency imports at the rate prevailing prior to 4th July, 1991. This transition facility will be available only for exports effected upto 31st December 1991.

Products such as gems and jewellery, handcrafts, newspapers, journals and periodicals and cinematographic films, which enjoyed higher rated of REP will receive Eximscrips at the same rates as before.

The Basis rate of 30% is inadequate for exports of certain products such as value-added agricultural projects, electronics, bulk drugs and marine products, formulations and certain categories of advanced engineering goods. These products will be eligible for an additional Eximscrips entitlement of 10 percentage points, taking the total Eximscrips rate to 40% of FOB value.

For exports made on the basis of duty free imports obtained against Advance Licences, Eximscrips will be available at the general rate of 30% but this will be applied to the net foreign exchange earnings. On the same principle. Eximscrips at 30% of NFE will also be available for all EOU and EPZ units.

The 30% of NFE rate of Eximscrips is also applicable to service exports, including software exports which is a thrust area. The definition of services covered under this category is being ratinallized and extended to include other services such as services of architects, textile designers, artists, management consultants, lawyers etc. The benefit will be available to services exported by resident Indians for which remittances are made to India. The details are being notified separately.

Eximscrips issued to exporters will be tradeable and can be used to import any item in the limited permissible list (Appendix-3), the non-sensitive canalised list (Appendix-5A) and for all OGL, items for actual users (Appendix-6, List 8, Part I and List 10). Eximscrips earned by exporters on their own exports can also be used to import non-OGL capital goods other than those on the restricted list (Appendix-1A). All REP licences issued against exports prior to 4th July, 1991 will continue to be valid for the life of the licence and will have the same import entitlement as the new Eximscrips. Additional licences issued to export houses/trading houses, which were earlier valid for a more limited range of imports, will also be valid for the same range of imports as Eximscrips.

With the introduction of Eximscrips, the system of issuing supplementary licences of raw material, components and spares listed in Appendix-3 will be discontinued except for small scale industries and for manufacturers of specified life saving drugs and equipment. In future, all import requirements of these items (with the exceptions indicated above) will be made through Eximscrips, Similarly items in Appoendix-4 and Appendix-9, which were earlier importable against supplementary licences, will henceforth be importable only against Eximscrips. Import of items appearing in Appendix-2 Part B (list of Restricted Items) and Appendix-8 (List of Scientific and Measuring Instruments Restricted for Import) of the Import-Export Policy 1990-93 will continue to require licences. Such licences as well as licences required for small scale industries and manufactures of life saving drugs/equipment will be called Special Licences as these will be limited and include special cases.

As a measure of import compression and to strengthen the linkage between import capability and exports, two further changes have been made. The category of unlisted OGL has been abolished and these items have been shifted to Appendix-3. They are now importable only against Eximscrips (except for SSI and manufacturers of life saving drugs and equipment). In the case of units subject to the Phased Manufacturing

Programme (PMP), many of which benefit from concessional duty on their imports of OGL items, all such items will henceforth be importable only against Eximscrips.

Eximscrips will be issued only after export proceeds have been realised. The procedure for issue of Eximscrips has been streamlined and Government will ensure that Eximscrips are issued within 48 hours of the receipt of the application accompanied by single document, namely, the bank certificate for the realisation of export proceeds.

Advance Licences

The system of advance licences is designed to provide exporters with duty free access to the inputs they need to produce competitively for world markets. This is an important instrument of trade policy especially in our situation where tariff levels are still high. The Government has taken the following steps to strengthen the system of Advance Licences as an instrument of export promotion:

(i) The procedures for considering Advance Licence applications have been simplified to ensure that advance licences will be issued within 15 days of application in all cases where input-output norms have been fixed. Where norms have not been fixed, the licence will be issued within 45 days.

(ii) The number of documents accompanying an Advance licence application has been reduced from 9 to 3 where norms are prescribed and to 4 where they are not prescribed.

(iii) Ar present norms have been prescribed for 540 items. This will be increased to over 1000 items by 31st October, 1991 and more items will be covered thereafter.

(iv) Substantial Manufacturing Activity as a necessary condition under the Advance Licence Scheme will no longer be applicable for exports to the general currency area. However, the value addition norms will remain in force. A large number of exporters will benefit under this scheme.

(v) A new Scheme of Transferable Advance Licence has been introduced for GCA exports in selected thrust areas, namely textiles, leather goods and engineering industries. Under this scheme exporters can undertake exports based on duty paid inputs obtained from the market and subsequently obtain advance licences for replenishment of these inputs by duty free imports. These advance licences will be freely transferable. The coverage of the scheme will be extended on merits.

(vi) Advance licence will specify values in free foreign exchange both for the purpose of import and export. The currencies in which such values are denominated will be limited to those notified for this purpose by the RBI.

(vii) The Existing procedure for obtaining Bank Guarantee (BG) and Legal Undertaking (LUT) from different categories of exporters in being streamlined and liberalised as follows:

(a) Export/Trading/Star Trading House and Public Sector Undertakings will have the facility of obtaining advance licence against LUT only without any monetary limit.

(b) All manufacturing units having an annual turnover of at least Rs. 5 crores (including both domestic and exports turnover) during the previous 3 year would also be able to avail of the LUT facility up to a value limit of 50% of their annual production.

(c) A new unit without any production or export performance to its credit would also be allowed LUT facility provided it is promoted by an existing company with an annual production of Rs. 5 crores for more than three years. In such a case, both the new company and the promoting company would have to provide LUT.

(d) Bank guarantee and/or LUT obligation will be concurrent to the fulfilment of export obligation.

(viii) Exporters would be allowed to dispose of the materials imported against advance licences by way of replenishment without seeking prior permission of the licensing authority in cases where no MODVAT facility has been availed of on the domestic material used in exports.

(ix) Adjustment needed on account of fluctuation of prices of imported individual items would be permitted within the overall CIF value of advance licence.

(x) The power of revalidation which presently vests in the Licencing Committee at the Headquarters has been delegated to the Licensing Authorities.

(xi) In case where applications for an advance licence are turned down, the exporter will be permitted to convert to the Duty Drawback regime by the Collectors of Customs so that shipments made in advance can be imported on payment of duty subsequent claims of duty drawback.

(xii) Exporters can obtain advance release orders for domestic supply against advance licences under which the domestic supplier gets the benefit of deemed exports. Henceforth, release orders will be issued across the counter without requiring the name of the domestic supplier, which could be given later.

The adoption of these procedures would reduce discretionary controls and delays and afford much greater freedom to exporters in procuring essential duty free raw materials to maintain their competitiveness in the would market thereby promoting exports from the country.

The export Processing Zone scheme and the 100% EOU scheme were introduced to provide for duty-free enclaves, which would enable entrepreneurs to concentrate on production exclusively for export. However, with increasing liberalisation in the DTA, the duty advantages enjoyed by EPZs/EOUs have become less important. While the procedures of Customs Bonding are very onerous. The schemes have not therefore taken off as expected and they have also not attracted foreign investment aimed at tapping export markets to the extent that was expected. The working of these schemes has been reviewed and the following changes made:

(i) All EOUs/EPZ unit will be eligible for Eximscrips at the basic rate of 30% applied to net foreign exchange earning.

(ii) The duty applicable on DTA sales from EOUs/EPZ units is being reduced to 50% of the normal customs subject to the duty payable not being less than the excise duty on the same product. The extent of DTA sales allowed will be accordance with their entitlement. DTA sales will be permitted in the ratio of 25:75 in relation to export sales in case of units while use of indigenous raw material is more than 30% of production. In all other cases the ratio of permissible DTA sales to export sales will be 15:85. The procedures for clearing goods from the EOU/EPZ units for DTA sales are also being streamlined.

(iii) In order to encourage exporters to set up EOUs or

EPZ units the net foreign exchange earned by EOUs or EPZ units can be clubbed with the earnings of their parent/associated companies in the DTA for the purpose of according Export House. Trading House of Star Trading House status for the latter.

(iv) The IPRS scheme for supply of steel to exporters will also be extended to EOUs and EPZ units. The Development Commissioners are being empowered to issue "payment authorities" in lieu of JCCI & Es.

Under the New Industrial Policy, most industries do not require an industrial licence except for a defined list. With a view to bringing about comparable streamlining in the procedure for EOU/EPZ approvals, a systems of automatic approvals is being established for all proposals which fall within certain parameters. Capital goods imports will be allowed under the automatic approvals procedure if they are fully covered by foreign equity or if they do not exceed 50% of the value of plant and equipment subject to a ceiling of Rs 3 crores. All proposals within the automatic approval parameters will be cleared within two weeks. All other proposals will be submitted to the Board of Approvals for consideration and decisions including issue of licences will be taken within 45 days.

A large number of issues relating to the operation of EOUs/EPZ units required centralized clearance in the Ministries of Commerce and Industry. Powers are being delegated to the Development Commissioners so that these approvals can be given on a decentralised basis. The specific approval of the Development Commissioner would not be required in cases of broad banding by EPZ units, where value addition is being maintained. The unit concerned would need only to provide relevant information to the Development Commissioner.

The following specific concessions to EOUs/EPZ units have also been extended:

(i) Allowing entry of imported raw material on "Provisional Assessment" basis, to expedite customs clearance.

(ii) Permitting units under the EPZ and EOU schemes to supply/transfer finished goods among themselves.

(iii) Replacement of multiple bond by a single bond, for obtaining import clearance.

(iv) Increasing the list of items under the "Special Imprest Licence Scheme" on selective basis.

(vi) Clarifying that containers stuffed in EPZ and EOUs are not to be reinspected at other points, as long as seals are intact.

Government have also decided to allow private parties to establish bonded warehouses within EPZs for stocking and sale of duty free raw materials, components, consumables and spares to EPZ units and EOUs. This will cut down delay in obtaining supplies of duty free materials which are in constant and regular demand by exporters. The details of this scheme will be notified shortly.

Other steps announced in the new Trade Policy have been the simplification of procedures for import of capital goods, decanalisation of number of items which were previously canalised, permission to allow established exporters to open foreign currency accounts in approved banks, raise external credits, pay for export related imports from such accounts and credit export proceeds to such accounts, its decision to re-designate the office of the Chief Controller of Import and Exports as Directorate General of International Trade with the principal function being to promote of exports, and facilitation of imports to promote export trade.

The policy changes now being implemented imply substantial reduction in the extent of licensing and in the number of types of licences. Supplementary licences for import of items in Appendixes-3 (except for SSI and manufacturers of life saving drugs and equipment), 4 and 9 of the Import-Export Policy 1990-93 have been abolished. Additional licences which were issued as an incentive to Export Houses and Trading Houses will stand abolished with effect from 1st April, 1992 and the incentive will take the form of an additional Eximscrip entitlement.

To achieve optimal import containment in the context of the present Balance of Payments situation, several steps have been taken. One of these is the shift of many items which are on OGL to the limited permissible list.

With these changes, the policy for import of raw materials components and other inputs needed for production has been simplified. Most raw materials and other inputs (except for those on the Restricted List) can be freely imported either against Eximscrips or on OGL. Some raw materials continue to be canalised but in more of these cases requirements beyond those provided by the canalising agencies can be met through Eximscrips.It is the policy of the Government to move to a situation where imports of essential raw materials and components needed for industrial production are regulated through appropriate tariffs. However, in view of the Balance of Payments position which necessitates continued import containment, this cannot be done immediately. Many items must therefore remain on the limited permissible list, with imports permitted only against Eximscrips.

The medium term objective of the Government is to progressively eliminate licensing and quantitative restrictions on capital goods and raw materials/

components so that all these items can be placed on OGL save for a small carefully defined negative list. This shift is proposed to be achieved over a 3 to 5 year period. The Government will appoint a High Level Committee to work out the modalities of achieving this transition keeping in mind the Balance of Payments position and the need to rationalise the reduce tariffs progressively to provide Indian Industry with an appropriate environment to develop international competitiveness.

Industrial Policy and Trade Policy of the Government of India

Over the years the Government of India has been adopting various measures for the liberalisation of the Industrial Policy, for streamling the licensing and foreign collaboration procedures, for reducing the number of agencies which the prospective investors have to approach to get the necessary approvals, etc., with the objective of attracting more investment and technology transfer. On the 24th July, 1991 the Government tabled before Parliament the Statement on Industrial Policy, 1991, which was followed by the issuance of a Notification by the Department of the Industrial Development to implement the Policy Statement and a series of Press Notes to set out the changes in the existing system and procedure for obtaining industrial licenses and approval of proposals for foreign and for foreign testing of indigenous raw materials and products and indigenously developed technlogies.

The new Industrial Licensing Policy of the Government of India has exempted form the requirement of obtaining industrial licence all industries, except those reserved for the Public Sector (Schedule I to the the Notification), those in respect of which Idustrial Licensing is compulsory (Schedule II to the Notification) and those relating to the items reserved for exclusive manufacture in the small scale sector (Schedule III to the Notification).

The exemption from Industrial licensing is also subject to:

The proposed project (except in the case of a project relating to electronics, computer software, printing industry, industry located within an area designated as 'industrial area' by a State Government before the 25th July, 1991 or the small scale or the ancillary sector) being not located with 25 kilo meters form the periphery of the standard urban area limits of a city having a population of more than one million according to the 1991 census; and of the Central and the State environmental laws and regulations including local zoning and land use laws and regulations.

Units qualifying for exemption from industrial licensing in accordance with the foregoing conditions are required only to file a Memorandum in the prescribed form, before establishement of the project, with the Department of Industrial Development (Secretariat for Industrial Approvals) together with a crossed demand draft for rupees one thousand in favour of the Pay and Account Officer, Department of Industrial Development and another Memorandum in the prescribed form at the time of commencement of commercial production.

Small scale and ancillary units are required, as before, to be registered with the Director of Industries of the concerned State. Manufacturing units with an investment in plant and machinery up to Rs. 60 lakhs, ancillary units with an investment in plant and machinery up to Rs. 75 lakhs and units which are willing to undertake an export obligation to the extend of 30 per cent of their annual production by the third year with an investment up to Rs. 75 lakhs are eligible for small scale registration.

The new industrial policy of the Government of India has announced major liberalisation for attracting foreign investment in respect of a list of high priority industries (Annexure III to the Statement of Industrial Policy, 1991). Foreign equity investment up to 51 per cent will be allowed subject only to the condition that;

— The requirement of imported capital goods should be covered by the foreign equity;

— Remittance of dividends should be covered by earnings of the company from export of items in Annexure III to the Statement of Industrial Policy , 1991. The amount of dividend payment may be converted by export earnings of such items recorded in Years prior to the payment of dividend or in the year of payment of dividend. This will be monitored by the Reserve Bank of India. However, such balancing will not be required beyond a period of seven years from commencement of production.

In all such cases the Reserve Bank of India has been authorised to issue automatic approvals of foreign investment and also grant exemption from the operation of the relevant sections of the Foreign Exchange Regulations Act, 1973.

9

International Cooperation

Cooperation with International organisations

India attended the following important meetings:

(a) ASEAN-India Joint Cooperation Meeting (April 1998)

(b) Indo-Slovenian joint Committee Meeting (May 1998)

(c) 58th Session of the Executive Council of the World Tourism Organisation (WTO) June 1998)

(d) Ministrial. Conference of WTO June 1998)

(e) Executive Council Meeting of WTO (November-December 1998)

SAARC Matters

Various matters relating to SAARC Technical Committee on Tourism included SAARC Cooperation in training courses, joint tourism promotional brochures, concession in transportation within the SAARC region, exchange of information, exploring the possibility of joint venture investment, joint tour packages, SAARC travel guide, joint tourism promotional film, SAARC joint tourism participation in international tourism fairs, etc. were dealt with.

Bilateral Tourism Cooperation Agreements

During the year, Bilateral Tourism Cooperation

Agreements were signed with Greece (January 98) and Mongolia (December 1998). During the year, the Ministry of Tourism participated in several joint commission meetings, inter-ministerial meeting and bilateral civil aviation talks with several countries including CIS countries, Eastern European and other countries. Various matters relating to the possibility of cooperation in areas such as human resource development, setting up of joint ventures, exchange of information and technical know-how, etc. were discussed with other countries. Proposals for signing Tourism Cooperation agreements with other countries are also in the pipeline. Minister of State for Tourism led an official delegation comprising the officials of the Ministry of Tourism an representatives of Travel Trade Kyrgyzsthan from 3rd to 8th October, 1998 to explore the possibilities of in promotion of tourism between India Kyrgyzsthan.

Promotional visits

In order to promote tourism to India, the Ministry was represented at senior level at a number of major international meetings, workshops, conferences such as 11th Exhibition, Incentive and Business Travel Mart in Geneva, seminar on facilitation in the Asian Region held in Phuket (Thailand), ministerial conference of World Tourism Organisation and 68th ASTA World Travel Congress in USA.

International conference and convention

Ministry of Tourism, Government of India is an active member of a number of leading international tourism organisations such as World Tourism Organisation (WTO), Pacific Asia Travel Association (PATA), Indian Ocean Tourism Organisation (IOTO) and International Congress and Convention Association (ICCA), etc. It has been the Ministry's endeavour to bring international conferences and conventions to India to give a fillip to tourism by providing adequate exposure to the foreign visitors and policy makers attending these conferences. Annual General Meeting and Board of Directors Meeting of IOTO was held from October 4th to 8th, 1998 in New Delhi and it is proposed to host a number of other major international conferences in the following year for which action is already underway.

10

India Tourism Development Corporation LTD.

ITDC since its inception in 1966 has been the pioneer and prime mover of the progressive development and expansion of India's tourism infrastructure. Entirely on its own, ITDC has emerged as the largest and most successful hotel chain in India providing all touristic services i.e. Accommodation, Catering, Transport, Duty Free Shopping, Entertainment, Publicity etc. under a single window. It also offers consultancy services from concept to commissioning in the tourism field, both for private as well as public sector. While functioning on commercial lines, ITDC has also been committed to the social objectives, Government policies, development of backward areas, maintenance of regional balance, national integration, etc.

Mission

To provide leadership and promote quality tourism brand for India achieving high level of excellence profit in the field of Hotels, Tours & Travel, Duty Free Shops, Human Resource Development and Consultancy creating tourism infrastructure as well as forging partnership with State Governments for undertaking tour projects.

Board of directors

ITDC Board of Directors presently consists of four Directors comprising two Official and two Functional Directors. One of the government Directors also holds additional charge of the post of Chairman & Managing Director w.e.f. 1st October, 1997.

Organisational set-up

The organisational set-up at the Corporate level comprises three business groups viz, Hotels & Catering, Duty Free Trade and Ashok Travel & Tours. Besides, there are some support. Service department namely Personnel, F&A, Hotel Sales, HRD & Training, MMD, Project Engineering, P&P and Vigilance & Security. In addition, there are four Regional Offices at Delhi, Mumbai, Chennai and Calcutta.

Network of ITDC services

The present network of services comprises 26 Ashok Group of Hotels (including 2 Palace Hotels and 2 Beach Resorts), 6 joint Venture Hotels, 5 Restaurants (including 4 Airport Restaurants), 11 Ashok Travels & Transport Units, I Tourist Service Station, 29 Duty Free Shops at six airports, a Tax Free Shop and one Sound & Light Show. The Corporation also provides catering services at Western Court, Hyderabad House, Vigyan Bhavan and National Media Press Centre at Shastri Bhavan, New Delhi, besides managing a Forest Lodge, a Restaurant and two Sound & Light Shows on behalf of the Central Ministry of Tourism.

Capital structure

The Capital Structure for the last two years and as on 30th September, 1998 is as under:

(Rs. in Crores)

	As on 31.03.1997	As on 31.03.1998	1998-99 (up to Sept. 98)
Authorised Capital	75.00	75.00	75.00
Paid-up Capital	67.52	67.52	67.52
Reserves & Surplus	160.62	189.17	
Net Worth	220.76	246.90	
Capital Employed	205.18	230.15	

No fresh equity was provided by the Government during the year. At present there is no outstanding loan liability.

Pattern of shareholding

The authorised and paid-up capital of the Corporation stood at Rs. 75 crores and Rs. 67.52 crores respectively. The pattern of shareholding is indicated below:

Government 89.97%

General Public 10.00%

Employees 0.03%

Financial performance

The tourism scenario during 1997-98 has not been encouraging and conducive mainly due to general recession in the economy, drop in business and corporate traffic, economic shake up in the south Asian economies, heavy devaluation of currencies of Far-East countries making them economical for foreign tourists, increase in operating costs, etc. The performance of hospitality industry was, therefore, adversely affected in private as well as public sector.

While the turnover during 1997-98 decreased marginally by 0.85% to Rs. 313.20 crores compared to Rs.

315.90 crores in 1996-97, operating profit declined by 29.19% from Rs. 86.10 crores in 1996-97 to Rs. 60.97 crores and the net profit decreased by 22.22% from Rs. 55.80 crores in 1996 to Rs. 43.40 crores.

The tourism scenario during the current year is also reeling through depression for the same reasons. The performance of ITDC up to September 98 has been lower as compared to the corresponding period of last year.

Memorandum of understanding (MOU)

ITDC has become a MOU signing Company from the year 1993-94. Its actual performance for the year 1997-98 vis-a-vis budgeted targets was rated "Fair".

Status of Mini Ratna

Based on the eligibility performance criteria, ITDC has been given the status of Mini Ratna. This will enable the Corporation for greater financial and operational autonomy on fulfilment of laid down conditions.

Subsidiary companies

ITDC's investment in its six subsidiary companies remained unchanged at Rs. 7.20 crores as on 31st March, 1998. Company-wise details are given hereunder:

(Rs. in Crores)

MP Ashok Hotel Corporation Ltd.	0.82
Utkal Ashok Hotel Corporation Ltd.	4.69
Ranchi Ashok Bihar Hotel Corporation Ltd.	0.36
Assam Ashok Hotel Corporation Ltd.	0.51
Pondicherry Ashok Hotel Corporation Ltd.	0.31
Donyi Polo Ashok Hotel Corporation Ltd.	0.51

Implementation of plan schemes

The emphasis in the Annual Plan 1997-98 continued on renovation/upgradation of existing properties. As against the plan outlay of Rs. 30 crores for the year, the plan expenditure incurred was of the order of Rs. 16.28 crores, representing 54.27% utilisation.

The Annual Plan 1998-99 envisages an outlay of Rs. 70 crores. While major emphasis continues to be on extensive renovation/improvement of existing properties, it is proposed *inter-alia* to undertake construction of a new hotel at Chandigarh, a joint venture hotel at Anandpur Sahib, reconstruction of Lodhi Hotel, massive renovation of Ashok Hotel New Delhi and computerisation of various systems at Headquarters and in the units.

Golden Jubilee celebrations

In order to celebrate the 50th Year of Independence, various events / programmes like Golden jubilee Menu, illumination of hotel buildings, cultural / fun theme performances / parties were organised round the year in ITDC hotels. Special events like freedom run / walk, fireworks, hosting theme lunches to prominent freedom fighters, sports competitions, tree plantation, cultural programmes, special buffet, etc. were also organised.

Besides, the following special offers arrangements were also made:

— The room tariff of ITDC hotels (except Ashok Yatri Niwas, New Delhi) was inclusive of breakfast, lunch and dinner.

— Twenty meritorious students from New Delhi were offered facilities to swim for one year at Ashok Group of Hotels based on their rank / outstanding performance in their CBSE Examination, 1998. The main objective of this offer was to encourage swimming amongst children.

— Special arrangements were made at Ashok Yatri Niwas including complimentary stay for 900 students (boys and girls) from different States who participated in the Historic March of the Nation and in the Flag Hoisting Ceremony at Red Fort, New Delhi.

Marketing and hotel sales

As part of its overseas marketing strategy, ITDC participated in major Travel Marts and Fairs, such as, WTM, London; ITB, Berlin; EIBTM, Geneva; PATA, Singapore; TAAI and SATTE in Colombo for promotion of Ashok Group of Hotels and to generate business. ITDC also participated in domestic Travel Fairs such as India Tourism Expo held in New Delhi, Travel & Tourism Fair at Mumbai and 9.24 INITT, Delhi. Familiarisation Tours for Travel Agents, Travel Writers and Journalists from various countries were organised to acquaint them with ITDC properties and tourism infrastructure facilities.

To create greater awareness and facilities, On-line reservation world-wide, ITDC Internet was further activated and hyperlinked to PATANET, SABRE. Specialised agencies like RESNET was commissioned for further augmentation of hotel rooms through On-line.

As a step towards getting higher share in 9.26 the domestic segment, ITDC participated in major tourist events like Tourist Trade Fairs in Calcutta, Mumbai and Tourism Exhibition Week to promote special packages for the domestic market. A number of important national and international conferences were also negotiated and organised.

Production and publicity

During 1997-98, P&P Division continued 9.27 to

undertake consultancy assignments in print-production of tourist literature for various Tourism Departments. These include publicity consultancy provided to the State Governments of Orissa, Bihar and Rajasthan.

During the year, the Division undertook a number of important assignments from the Ministry of Tourism which include design and production of a Tableau for the Republic Day Parade 1998, a Table Calendar on the occasion of Golden Jubilee of India's Independence, publicity material for the India Tourism Week and organisation of a 4-day Festival of Classical Music and Dance. The Ministry has also nominated ITDC as a nodal agency for Photo Contest and Bauddha Mahotsav 1998.

For the first time, ITDC advertised on Shatabdi Train by taking seat covers on Delhi-Bhopal and Delhi-Jaipur Shatabdi Express. This has created awareness of Ashok Group of services amongst train travellers.

Some of the future plans include mounting of SEL Shows at Khajuraho, Tirupati, Jalliawalan Bagh (Amritsar), promotion of Millennium Maha Yatra Package, Khajuraho Temples Millennium Celebrations 1999-2000 and Celebrations of 350 years of Shahjahanabad.

Accommodation and catering

During the year under review, the Ashok Group of Hotels hosted several international and national conferences and seminars which include prestigious events like NAM Ministerial Conference, Australian Federation of Travel Agents Conference, International Bar Association Conference, Rotary International Conference, National Tourism Award Presentation Ceremony, etc.

On the occasion of India Tourism Week celebrations from 25th to 31st January, 1998, Ashok Group of Hotels all over the country organised a variety of Food Festivals covering different Indian cuisines. These Food Festivals received good response from the public at large. A 4-day Indian Classical Music and Dance Festival was also organised by the Ashok Theatre in Ashok Hotel, New Delhi in collaboration with the Ministry of Tourism.

With a view to promoting Ashok Group of Hotels and popularising Indian cuisine abroad, ITDC participated by deputing team of Chefs / Cooks to prepare authentic Indian cuisine in Food Festivals at Nicosia, Taipei (Taiwan), Sao Paulo (Brazil), Ankara (Turkey), Stockholm, Bonn and Frankfurt (Germany). All the festivals evoked good response from the public and the Indian Food was highly appreciated both by guests and organisers.

Also for popularising Indian cuisine in domestic market, various Food Festivals like Punjabi Food Festival - Masti Punjab Di - at Ashok Hotel; Holi Festival at Hotel Samart; Punjabi Food Festival at Lodhi Hotel; Tamil Nadu, Kerala, Karnataka and Andhra Pradesh Food-cum-Cultural Festivals at Kovalam Ashok Beach Resort; Dogri Pahari Food Festival at Hotel Jammu were organised.

Duty free trade

ITDC's duty free shops continued to be listed as one of the'Giants' in international duty free world and also amongst the leading operators by the duty free data-base and directory.

With a view to increasing duty free business, ITDC is constantly upgrading/ promoting duty free shops. The main shop at the departure of IGI Airport, Delhi was upgraded with personalised counters for Fragrances, Spirits and Tobacco products. The Confectionery and Toys section was also augmented. The latest ranges in

Fragrances were added to the assortment. These together with`gift with purchase scheme'added to the excitement in the shops.

Training programmes were held to update product knowledge to sharpen the 'sale and customer handling' skills of the personnel handling of duty free trade.

Ashok travel & tours

Ashok Travels & Tours continued to offer a comprehensive package of services covering national and international ticketing, hotel bookings, ground handling, tour packages and tailor-made itineraries to suit all budget tourists.

During the year, the Ashok Travels & Tours, in collaboration with Air-India and Indian Airlines launched the Magnum Millennium Packages called`Millenniurn Maha Yatra' to facilitate NRIs and Youth to discover their roots. This is a comprehensive offer, which includes rebated airfare on Air India and Indian Airlines as well as discounted hotel tariff at about 20 destinations in India. Special LTC packages offering concessional rates were also floated for employees of Govt. and Public Sector Undertakings.

Ashok Travels &Tours was appointed as a nodal agency to look after the smooth handling of Students / Youth Packages being launched by Ministry of Tourism, Government of India under the Youth Exchange Programme during the Golden jubilee Year of India's Independence. Further, a Buddhist Pilgrimage Pack Tour was formulated in order to facilitate the Buddhist Pilgrims who attended "Mahabodhi Conference" held in October 1998.

Consultancy / Corporate services

With a view to disseminate ITDC expertise and promote

tourism, the Corporation continued to offer the complete range of its consultancy services from concept to commissioning in tourism sector.

Presently, the following consultancy assignments are in hand:

— Technical Consultancy Services for setting up and operating a kitchen in Parliament Library Building under construction.
— Technical Consultancy Services for setting up a Joint Venture Hotel project at Anandpur Sahib, Punjab.

Human resource development

The Manpower Development Centre (MPDC) of the Corporation was awarded "ISO 9001 Certification" for designing and imparting training in hospitality industry. The Centre is the first and only organisation in the Indian Hospitality Industry to have earned this recognition.

Keeping in view the requirement and nature of the service-oriented Hotel Industry, the HRD activities of the Corporation are directed towards 'Customer Care and Satisfaction'. To ensure customer satisfaction, the primary Awards focus is on creation of a new conceptual frame work of Total Quality Management (TQM) awareness and implementation. Thus the HRD activities included awareness for bringing changes in the language, changes in values and behaviour as per present day requirement and to find ways to bring total quality in our product and service.

During the year under review, 542 training programmes were conducted covering 6053 employees. Besides, 43 .employees were nominated in India and 4 abroad to professional courses conducted by reputed organisations. Further, 6 programmes were conducted for outside agencies and 5 programmes were conducted for the sponsored defence personnel. As part of the ongoing training activities, 77 Management Trainees and 200 Apprentices were trained.

During the current year (till September 1998),177 training programmes have been conducted covering 4167 employees besides conducting 5 programmes for outside agencies covering 72 participants. In addition, 17 employees were nominated in India and 3 abroad for professional courses conducted by reputed organisations.

Manpower

The total number of employees in the Corporation increased from 7825 as on 31st March, 1997 to 7884 as on 31st March, 1998. Of these, 2133 belong to Scheduled Castes (SC), 177 belong to Scheduled Tribes (ST) and 409 to Other Backward Classes (OBCs). A total of 201 employees were recruited, of whom 53 belong to Scheduled Castes, 9 to Scheduled Tribes and 32 to OBCs. In addition, 477 employees were promoted, of whom 76 employees belong to Scheduled Castes, 7 to Scheduled Tribes and 4 to OBCs.

Awards

During the year, ITDC was conferred with the following Awards: Laxmi Vilas Palace Hotel, Udaipur was awarded the National Tourism Award for Excellence for the year 1996-97 under the category of "Heritage Grand". A special award was presented to Ashok Hotel, New Delhi in appreciation of its cooperation by the Ministry of Tourism.

Implementation of official language policy

During 1997-98, the Corporation made concerted efforts to give fillip to the use of Hindi in official work through motivating employees, imparting them training in Hindi Workshop and nominating them for various Hindi training programmes. A prize distribution function was organised and cash awards were given to the winners of Hindi competitions. The Ashok Hotel, New Delhi bagged the "ITDC Rajbhasha Shield" for doing maximum work in Hindi during 1997. The Corporation continued bilingual publication of its house journal "Biradri" and newsletter 'The Ashok News".

Conservation of energy

The Corporation continued to maintain its thrust on energy conservation during 1997-98. The efforts resulted in saving 1, 39,497 units of HSD, 52,231 Kg of LPG and 1, 71, 976 Kilolitres of water. The consumption of electricity was almost the same as last year. This was achieved by creating general awareness amongst the staff and without investing in any additional gadget or equipment.

Industrial relations

The overall industrial relations continued to be cordial and good. There was no loss of mandays during the year.

11

Welfare Measures and Vigilance

Scheduled castes/scheduled tribes cell

The Scheduled Castes / Scheduled Tribes Cell in the Ministry of Tourism including the Office of the Director General of Tourism continued to function under a liaison officer of the rank of Director (Administration). The Cell looked into the grievances on service matters of Scheduled Caste and Scheduled Tribe employees of the Ministry and its attached/ subordinate offices. Directions were also issued from time to time by the Cell to all the administrative authorities under its control so as to ensure that the orders on reservation of SCs / STs in posts / services are properly implemented.

Reservation of SC, ST and OBC candidates

All recruitments in the Ministry and its subordinate offices were being made as per the orders of reservation issued by the Government from time to time. Reservation rosters were maintained and adequate representation continued to be given to SC, ST and OBC candidates. Half-yearly returns on the subject as prescribed by the Ministry of Welfare were sent to them regularly.

Employment opportunities to handicapped persons

As per Government instructions, employment opportunities were extended to handicapped persons and a half-yearly return on the same was sent to the Ministry of Welfare.

Admissions to hotel management and foodcraft institutions

In the case of admissions to Hotel Management & Foodcraft Institutes under the National Council, 15% seats were reserved for Scheduled Caste candidates and 7.5 % for Scheduled Tribe candidates.

Vigilance

The Vigilance Section in the Ministry of Tourism continued to be headed by a Chief Vigilance Officer in the rank of Joint Secretary and assisted by an Under Secretary and a Confidential Assistant. With this staff, every possible effort was made to look into the complaints received in the Department and get them processed/investigated promptly. Wherever necessary, the cases were being referred to CBI / CVC. A Grievance Cell has also been set up in the Ministry which continued to look into the grievances.